The NEW Sitcom Career Book

The NEW Sitcom Career Book

A GUIDE TO THE LOUDER FASTER FUNNIER WORLD OF TV COMEDY

MARY LOU BELLI
PHIL RAMUNO

Maplewood Press/Los Angeles

Cover Design: Delapp Design
Interior Design: Delapp Design

The NEW Sitcom Career Book
First published in 2013 by
Maplewood Press, Los Angeles, CA.

The Sitcom Career Book
First published in 2004 by Back Stage Books,
An imprint of Watson-Guptill Publications
A division of VNU Business Media, Inc,
Senior Editor: Mark Glubke

Library of Congress Control Number: 2013942219

ISBN: 9780989342803

Manufactured in the United States of America

First Printing 2013.

To the casts and crews of the early sitcoms that I watched as a child. To Nat Hiken, who published scripts of Sergeant Bilko, which was the first book I ever bought. And mostly to my Dad, who unknowingly used perfect sitcom joke construction when he made me laugh.

–Phil Ramuno

For Richard Marion and Linda Mancuso, both gone too soon, richly valued and never forgotten.

–Mary Lou Belli

Table Of Contents

ACKNOWLEDGMENTS

We would like to thank the people who assistance helped make this book possible, especially:

Mark Glubke, Garry Hart, Steve McPherson, Marcy Ross, Kate Zentall, Steve Rosenthal, James Dunn, Howard Devine, Meredith Hightower, Ellen Waggoner, Steve Stark, Dinah Lenney, Karen Kondazian, Barry Van Dyke, Jana Sue Memel, Kyle Bryan Hall, Devon DeLapp, and Jeff Black.

We also wish to thanks the people who were instrumental in guiding the acquisition of our sitcom knowledge including:

Jay Sandrich, Will Mackenzie, Aaron Rubin, Jim Drake, Bob Broder, Michael Kagen, Sy Rosen, Jeff Harris, George Quenzel, Michael Lembeck, Scott Arnovitz, Nancylee Myatt, Linda Mansuco, Peter Engel, Kerry Holmwood, Robin Schwartz, D.L. Hughley, Lee Shallat Chemel, Michael Lessac, Andy Cadiff, Andrew D. Weyman, Rick Hawkins, Al Burton, Alan Rafkin, Bob Claver, James Burrows, Robert Greenblatt, David Janollari and, of course, Charlie Dougherty and Jackie Zebal.

FOREWORD

If you want to make a good living, spend weekends at home, and create something with a second family that has a possibility of being very funny, situation comedy is for you!

I went to work for 11 years on Stage 19 at Paramount Studios and had the most extraordinary time. This was my second family. My *Happy Days* family. Garry Marshall (the creator and executive producer) along with Eddie Milkus and Tom Miller were the Dads. The cast and Jerry Paris (the director) were the kids. We played softball all over the country. We toured Germany and Japan playing baseball with the American troops. We played charades at Jerry's house. We ate together. We bought our first homes around the same time. We all went to each other's weddings....and kept on asking Tom Bosley what the hell a debenture was.

I loved the camera people, the boom people, and the craft service person, Louie. I loved that crew. Without a crew, no one will record your voice or the picture. No one will write it or direct it. The Show couldn't exist. The cast and crew are two halves of a circle. You cannot bring your stardom or celebrity to the center of the stage. You have to leave that in your car. You are a team and you are going to create a story. You will make it as funny as you possibly can in four and one half days and shoot it on the other half of the fifth day. Then you start a new one on Monday.

It's all about timing and trusting your instinct. When I'm in the middle of the process, it is as if the joke is desperately trying to breathe...is screaming its way out of my mouth. I have no control. It needs to come and it needs to come NOW. If I go against that instinct, I'm boring. And if I listen to that instinct, hopefully I'm funny.

Comedy is instinctual, but the craft of comedy, for the most part, can be honed. I believe the discipline of sitcoms can be learned: the lines, the blocking, the not-eating-donuts during the day. I had to learn how *not* to put handles on the beginning of jokes-- not to say "oh, by the way," or "hey, did you know." I also had to learn not to embellish a joke by adding a word or two after the punch line.

I used every morsel of my training from the Yale School of Drama in every area during my career and certainly during *Happy Days*. I always saw sitcoms as a one-act play where opening night is every Friday. If the show is scheduled for 7:00, you don't start at 7:10. You don't amble in saying, "I'm ready now. I just got off the phone." You must do it with discipline. In structure comes freedom.

If you are going to an audition, there is no right or wrong. The Producers know exactly what they want, but most of the time they don't. If you go with your instinct...just go with your muse...you *can* change their mind. I say that because I did. The Fonz was based on someone that Garry Marshall grew up with in the Bronx. As written on the page, the Fonz was much larger, much more imposing, much more Italian than I was. I never researched this character but I lived in New York City and knew these people...Actually, I was scared of these people.

I just improvised. The person that read with me was standing. I made a decision that I was going to use the six lines that I had to make him sit down. That was my objective. He did. Now I was the only one standing in the room. Then I stayed in character, turned around, threw the script in the air and walked out of the room with my muse.

The bond formed on the soundstage of a situational comedy should be, can be, and must be as emotional, thoughtful, empathetic, and tension filled as your family at home. It does not work if any person on the set thinks he is more important than the group. You are an undulating, pulsating organism that *together* figures out one of the most difficult questions on the face of the earth: What is funny?

If you've ever thought about a career in situation comedy, this book is an unbeatable resource. This book gives you a detailed look at what goes on in front of, as well as behind, the camera.

HENRY WINKLER
Actor, Author, Director, Producer

PREFACE

The sitcom. We all know what that is. It's *Lucy*, or *Happy Days*, or *Mary Tyler Moore* or *Cosby* or *Friends*. But even though we were weaned on these familiar icons –- they come into our living rooms night after night – they're not as simple as they seem. And don't get me wrong – they're meant to look simple. Not in a derogatory way, but in an elegant way. It's the closest thing to a perfect one-act play, a comedy form that started with the Greeks and has endured for over 2,000 years.

These 22-minute confections are part of our lives. We either watch them religiously or we have them on in the background while we're reading the paper, eating dinner, feeding the dog, changing diapers. They're literally part of the cultural soundtrack of our lives. You'd think something so familiar and so ubiquitous would be easy, right? Wrong!

When all the elements come together the sitcom is magic. (Think of the candy factory episode of *I Love Lucy*.) But that kind of magic doesn't happen without inspired writing, brilliant performances, and pitch-perfect direction. And the goal isn't to get it right once in a while; we're supposed to do it week after week and year after year. Anyone who's ever worked on a sitcom, anyone who's ever watched, knows instantly when it's happening and when it's not. And it usually doesn't. For every success there are literally dozens that fail and are quickly forgotten.

In short, the sitcom is truly an art form. Oh sure, scholars and critics will argue that television is disposable pop culture, but no one can deny the power and artistry of the sitcom when it all comes together. Everything is carefully crafted. Writers spend hours – even days or weeks – crafting the story and the script, creating rich, textured characters. It's not simple the "jokes" that are pored over and refined, but it's from the depth of the characters that the right jokes will come.

Making comedy is not simple and it doesn't "just happen." Five days isn't much time to block, rehearse, hone, and ultimately shoot an entire episode. Everyone, from the Executive Producer to the caterer, has to know exactly what he or she is doing for an episode to come together. This obviously takes careful planning and preproduction, but once we all assemble on the stage for the actual shooting phase, a great deal of money is at stake and there's very little margin for error.

So how does it all work? Well, this clever book is the first of its kind to dissect and analyze the sitcom with wit, style, and, of course, humor. An enormous amount of skill goes into each aspect of a show and *The Sitcom Career Book* is a rare glimpse into the creative process. When it all comes together, everyone is in sync with everyone else. The entire organism – which can amount to as many as 150 people – all sees the same thing. And though many people try to reinvent the system or breathe new life into it, sometimes the tried-and-true is the best path.

There are so many facets to sitcom production: writing, casting, directing, acting, wardrobe and set design, camera and technical operations, editing, sound effects, music and scoring. When it all comes together the end result looks easy and effortless. Think of Fred Astaire dancing; every step and breath are meticulously choreographed, but it looks absolutely spontaneous.

There's nothing like the rush of production night, when you have the audience for the first time and everything clicks. Despite the ups and downs of the production week, on show night when you have the perfect audience and everything is "working," you will hear that honest-to-God, rolling, real laughter. It's the greatest sound in the world and proof that all the hard work of the week – the rewriting and careful blocking, the arguments about just the right prop or costume, the meticulous guest casting, even the perfect jokes – pays off.

And the greatest thing is that the audience won't think twice. They just laugh. It looks simple. It looks easy. And that's exactly what we want them to think.

This book, written lovingly with a first-hand perspective, chronicles all aspects of production. Devour it, savor it because, short of actually being there in person, this is the next best thing.

Read on. See how we do it...

ROBERT GREENBLATT
Former programmer of Showtime and Chairman of NBC

The NEW Sitcom Career Book

THE LOUDER FASTER FUNNIER WORLD OF TV COMEDY

INTRODUCTION

When we wrote THE SITCOM CAREER BOOK eight years ago, we were both first time authors. Maybe naively, we hoped that the knowledge we had gained by helping create situation comedies for television might help a few people wishing to do the same and inform others who like that type of entertainment. Since that time, we have been overwhelmed by the reception our book received. Rather than filling our garages or the publisher's shelves with leftover copies, the book has completely sold out!

We received many compliments from other professionals who we respect and from readers who took the time to thank us for a "fun and valuable" book. We are thrilled that THE SITCOM CAREER BOOK is used regularly as a text in universities across the country and provided to the casts of shows about to go into production. Some of you encouraged us to get this second edition out as quickly as possible.[1] So here it is! THE *NEW* SITCOM CAREER BOOK.

We told you sitcoms were an enduring form of television entertainment and that is still the case. Yes, there are times when other types of television programming flourish, but eventually the focus comes back to sitcoms. As Steve Zuckerman mentioned in our original introduction, there is even a parallel between sitcom and the ancient "Commedia dell' Arte." APPENDIX 2 has an updated list of all the sitcoms ever on American television. Besides being fun to go back and remember those from your childhood years, it is a great resource to look at the beginning style of sitcom and trace the resilient nature of what Robert Greenblatt, now head of NBC, called it in the Preface "the closest thing to a perfect one-act play, a comedy form that started with the Greeks and has endured for over 2,000 years."

Having samples of many of these pioneering sitcoms available on YouTube, network websites, and other on-line sources, gives you a chance to compare them with modern shows. It is fascinating to see the 1950 CBS show *The George Burns and Gracie Allen Show*, which exists today only because a film (kinescope) was made by shooting a TV screen when it aired live. Despite the obvious vaudevillian style of using a theater curtain to reveal the set and the actors taking bows as they enter to applause, there is a definite connection to modern sitcom. George Burns started each episode with some stand-up comedy. *Seinfeld* started each episode the same way with Jerry Seinfeld doing stand-up comedy before and usually during each episode of his sitcom created forty years later.

1 Especially instructors who need it for fall semesters and sitcoms that will premiere next season.

Yes, technology does change but the art of storytelling and the art of making an audience laugh is still the same. But you do need to learn the rules of how to do that and that's what this book will do.

One of our SITCOM RULES is, "Hold for Laughs." Since sitcoms are not always shot in front of a live audience. Who decides if it is really funny? And what do actors do who are used to immediate audience feedback? We will discuss those things and others in our new chapters. We will look at why shows are not able to have or often choose NOT to have that live audience. We want to celebrate the skill that goes into creating a single camera sitcom and the benefits that this choice reaps.

Many other things have changed in the eight years since the first edition of this book. Sitcoms are no longer filmed or taped. They are all now digitally captured. And, there are more venues besides television that classic American sitcoms are being exhibited. There is a new international market and an internet market. We will discuss these new methods and new markets. Many sitcom veterans still scramble to fill the available sitcom jobs at the major television networks[2]. We hope that this book will provide some key information for anyone who wants a career in sitcoms. The good news is, that these new markets have caused a major increase in a need for new people to fill these jobs. And no longer are these jobs available only in New York and Los Angeles.

This book has even helped us to get jobs. Co-author Phil Ramuno was interviewed for a job exporting American sitcom style in Moscow, Russia for Sony International. Jeff Lerner, the Sony executive, asked about his many credits in making sitcoms. Phil mentioned that he and Mary Lou Belli had also just written THE SITCOM CAREER BOOK. Jeff said "Wait a minute," left the room, quickly came back with a bag from a local bookstore, and then pulled out our book. Phil got the job. Since executives find our book helpful in their understanding of the sitcom style, we know that you will also.

There are more SITCOM INSIDER insights and some additional sitcom jobs included in our SITCOM CAREER PROFILE feature that will help you know what training and advice you need to get the job you want on a sitcom. Knowing each person's function on the sitcom stage will always help you to be better at being part of this team. We continue with our original choice to often describe the making of sitcoms through the performance requirements of the actor. If you are an actor who wishes to learn this very precise type of storytelling, there are many great lessons here. But if you wish to become a director, writer, script supervisor, camera operator, or any of the dozens of others functions including special effects supervisor, you can learn much from our book because getting laughs from an audience is everyone's goal.

We have added to our SITCOM RULES, SITCOM VOCABULARY, and the SITCOM VOCABULARY QUICK REVIEW. Creating a two or three act twenty minute play and then making a recording of that play in a week or even as quickly as one

2 With somewhat lower salaries given that the new markets have taken away many viewers.

or two days, requires a shorthand that allows everyone to move quickly through the creative process. Knowing this shorthand language makes producers and directors happy that you were able to do your job with a minimum of time needed without long explanations.

We owe much of our knowledge to our mentors. Sadly a few of them are no longer with us. Some were a big part of the beginning of sitcom on television like Mort Lachman (*All in the Family, Sanford, Kate & Allie*), Aaron Ruben (*The Phil Silvers Show, The Andy Griffith Show, Too Close for Comfort*), Alan Rafkin (*Mary Tyler Moore, Dick Van Dyke, Murphy Brown, M*A*S*H*)and John Rich (*Gomer Pyle, That Girl, All in the Family*) Others were part of the second generation of TV sitcom like Linda Day (*WKRP in Cincinnati, Married With Children Sabrina, the Teenage Witch*) and Ian Praiser (*Bosom Buddies, Taxi, ALF*). They passed their knowledge to us and we are now passing it to you, who will become the next generation to create great sitcom.

THE *NEW* SITCOM CAREER BOOK will continue to show you why working on a sitcom is now one of the best jobs, not just in Hollywood, but in many cities around the world. You get paid, have great satisfaction in creating art, and still get to laugh all day.

Chapter 1 GETTING THE JOB!

In this chapter:

How to prepare for an audition.
Accessing information on a show
Analyzing a sitcom script
How to learn by watching
Dos and Don'ts for auditioning
Why Ks and Ps are funny
How to make strong memorable choices
What to wear to an audition
How to get your script read
Advice for getting the job
Audition tips
How a director prepares
Career profile of a sitcom casting director

The audition is an actor's job interview. He or she shows up, resume in hand, at an appointed time to meet someone who has a job to offer. Similarities with job interviews in the real world end there. Getting a normal job is based on experience, job aptitude, education, salary requirements, and personality. NOT IN SITUATION COMEDIES!

GETTING THE JOB—ACTOR

In sitcoms, an actor has to audition, which determines two things: Are you right for the part? And are you FUNNY?[1]

> **SITCOM RULE**
> ***Comedy comes in three.*** *A pattern is created with the first two items. The audience is fooled when the third item is not the expected completion of the pattern.*

Being right for the part encompasses a lot of things. The most important begins and ends with how you look. Most people might think that means how beautiful. It is not that

1 You might wonder where your acting skill comes into play. We're going to assume you wouldn't even get to the audition if you can't act.

simple. A dynamite actress may audition for the "best friend" part. If she's prettier than the lead actress (whose name just might be the title of that new show), she can kiss that part goodbye!

Being funny is next. Rick Kushman of the *Sacramento Bee* describes *Friends* as "One of TV's most consistent comedies throughout the years, partly on the strength of funny and just-goofy-enough writing, but mostly because the cast is so special. They each have that precious gift of comic timing..."

It is no coincidence that many sitcoms have been developed for stand-up comedians. Hollywood descends on Montreal's and Aspen's annual comedy festivals in search of new talent. This may not be tapping the most experienced acting pool in Hollywood, but it usually guarantees the laughs. Bruce Hills, COO of Montreal's Just For Laughs Comedy Festival tells us:

> In the late 80s, network talent executives realized that the Just For Laughs Festival was one-stop shopping for them. Within a couple of days, they could see the best stand-ups from around the world, including the best unsigned talent from North America. Basically, we scout all year round and take the pulse of comedy around the world and present them with the best of the best. Over 70 deals have been cut here at the Festival, involving every major studio and network in the U.S.

British actor Adrian Lester (*Primary Colors*, The Royal National Theatre *Henry V*) told us about his first American sitcom:

> I think you can tell a lot about a culture by what makes its people laugh. I spent a while doing nothing but watching all the sitcoms I could get my hands on. I had to learn very quickly to put away the classical theatre muscle and work on my funny bone.

We do not mean to EVER minimize the art of acting. We have great respect for those who are gifted artists and practice their craft with intelligence, creativity and integrity. But good acting is not enough on situation comedies. "Dying," as the saying goes, "is easy. Comedy is hard." Okay, you are a talented actor. Can you act and BE FUNNY?

Al Martin of the New York Comedy Club talks about his club's connection to the comedy scene:

> We get great diverse audiences here from all over the country. It's the same people who watch TV so it's the perfect place for people to try out material. We get new acts, top acts who are rehearsing material for HBO or *The Tonight Show*, or comedians who want to test material before they go to a major venue. It's a great place to be seen.

BEFORE THE AUDITION

So how does that interviewer (casting director) know if you are "right for the part" *and* FUNNY? ...By your audition. Casting director Patricia Noland (*Married ...With Children*) explains what she likes about being a casting director: "My favorite part of my job is working with the actors. It is a real joy to nurture talent, and help to launch a new career or participate in moving an existing career to the next step." Nolan also cautions,

> I think one of the most common mistakes an actor makes (especially a novice one) is to confuse the audition in a casting director's office with that of an acting class. Although it is perfectly okay to ask a question or two if the material isn't clear to them, they need to come prepared to do the scene, and not expect us to coax it out of them, or even coach them for any length of time. Oftentimes, we see many, many people for each role, and time just doesn't permit us to do that preliminary work. I've had actors flat-out tell me "Well, I read it over once, and I didn't really get it, so since I knew I was coming in to see you, I thought I'd just wait and let you walk me through it." NO! After I see what an actor has prepared, I often do have comments or suggestions, but only in a tinkering kind of way - not in a let's-build-it-from-scratch way. Actors need to realize that our job is to see many people (cast a large net) and then narrow down the choices we think our producers will respond to the strongest. Of course, this is why many agents and managers would prefer to bypass this step altogether, and have their clients go "straight to producers." I've found overall, however, that the best producers auditions are the actors who have come in for me once, taken some small direction (be it a wardrobe suggestion or a small adjustment – "Let's try it again, and take about half the anger out"), and then have the confidence to really nail it in front of the director and producers.

An actor auditioning for a sitcom will often get only a few pages of the script. Known as **sides,** these pages are an actor's guide to the story and character. An actor will go in and read the sides (consisting of a part of a scene, an entire scene, or multiple scenes) with the casting director, reader, or an actor who has already been cast.

Sides come from one of the versions of the script...and there have been many. A sitcom script starts with a story premise that is developed into an outline. This process starts about 6 weeks before the show goes into full production.

Many scripts are completed before actors show up for the first episode of the season.[2] One writer or writing duo turns the outline into a first draft, often known as the pre-table draft. As writer Keith Josef Adkins (*Girlfriends*) remarks,

2 A full season is usually 22 episodes. First time show creators have lots of butt to kiss just to get an order of six.

"The first draft is written by one entity. It comes to the writer's room, and it's read aloud by everyone. Then we begin pitching on jokes, arcs, etc. in order to shape it for the table. The point of this is to make sure the script feels and sounds like the TONE of the show. With so many writers, each one is bringing their very specific flavor and personality to the show. Although this is encouraged and gives the show its juice, ultimately each script must feel as if it is birthed from one mother."

This birthing process delivers a **table draft**. This is the version of the script that actually gets read the first time the cast is assembled. It takes place around a table: hence the name. At any time from premise to table draft, revision notes and comments may be given on the content and structure by network, studio, and production company executives to the head writer. This writing position has evolved into a position of great power. The head writer is usually just referred to as **show runner**.

A clever and informative article entitled "15 Steps to No Fat" authored by Marsha Scarbrough appears in *Written By*. It describes the evolution of an "Everybody Loves Raymond" script entitled "No Fat" written by Ellen Sandler and Susan Van Allen. Phil Rosenthal is the show runner and Ray Romano is the star of that show. The first few steps involve the initial pitch and outline. Then Scarbrough writes:

> The two-pager defines the spine of the story in a condensed narrative. It's re-written once with Rosenthal's input before being distributed to all the writers and discussed in The Room...After this "two-pager" is refined, it is sent to the network, the studio, and Romano. At this point Rosenthal suggests that Sandler work with Susan Van Allen on the first draft of the script...Sandler and Van Allen collaborate by writing some scenes together line by line at the computer and some scenes individually, then trading and revising each other. After a first pass, they solicit input privately from some of the other staff writers and do a rewrite. That version goes to Rosenthal who writes notes and jokes in the margins and returns it to Sandler and Van Allen...Sandler and Van Allen rewrite incorporating Rosenthal's notes to create the "writer's first draft"...The writer's first draft goes to the table in The Room. After an hour or more of general discussion on the overall script, the staff starts with the teaser and goes through the script line by line. A writer's assistant types this version into a communal computer as it is being revised. This process may take the better part of two or three days in The Room but the result is a funnier, fast, more focused script...The script is sent to Romano, who can only be in The Room when he's not involved in rehearsals on stage. After reading this "table draft," Romano spends lunch hour in The Room giving his notes on the script page by page.

The casting director has received either some version of the script, a scene, or sometimes as little as a description of the character and basic idea of the scene. He or she sends this to Breakdown Services[3] which synthesizes the information about each character in a script. The casting director edits the character descriptions and adds details they want the actor or agent to know. What results is a **breakdown.** Gary Marsh of Breakdown Services describes these sheets as the "Cliffs Notes on the characters." Ideally, a breakdown is a description of the character and what makes that character tic. Often, it's merely a summation of how a character serves the plot. A breakdown is the tool by which agents submit their clients for a possible audition.

Most actors receive the Breakdown Services info sheet from their agent along with their sides. This gold mine reveals what the project is, when it's set to go, and where it's being done. More important, it is "the who" of the character. It is the tool that can give an actor insight into what the writers had in mind.

Sometimes the sides and info sheet are limited or sketchy. In this time of advanced information technology, it is assumed that the actor can access additional information. For example, nearly every current series on the air has a website. Go to it! An actor can figure out the style of the sitcom based on the writer's previous work[4], the network's demographic, and the time slot. Do an Internet search. For example, if you wanted more information on Fox's *Oliver Beene*, you'd find that Robert Wilonsky, of the *Miami New Times*, wrote:

> If quality alone guaranteed success in the TV biz, then *Oliver Beene* will live long eough to enter puberty, if not college. It's the sort of show that defines FOX, home to the dysfunctional-family comedy ever since the

CASTING CAREER TRACK

I was head of casting for Turner Television, an in-house production company for the WB Network. Before that, I was the Casting Director for various pilots and series, which included the Saturday morning teen lineup for NBC.

I began my training in Casting with John Levey at Warner Bros. Television. I started as his Assistant, and was later promoted to an Associate Casting position under his supervision. Together we worked on such shows as China Beach, Head of the Class, Growing Pains, Life Goes On, *and* The Adventures of Brisco County Jr., *among others. Later I also worked under such terrific Casting Directors as Marion Dougherty, Joel Thurm and April Webster before starting on my own projects.*

I got my first job when the producers of Married... With Children *were looking to cast a spinoff from their show during the final season. Their casting director, Vicki Rosenberg, was too busy to take on another project at that time, so I was hired to cast the spinoff (called* Radio Free Trumaine*) with her as a supervisor. Later, when one of the producers, Stacy Lipp, was hired to Executive Produce another pilot for Columbia TriStar, she asked me to be her Casting Director on that project. And so it began.*

Patricia Noland,
Casting Director *USA High, One World*

3 If you can tear yourself from this, see Breakdown Services at www.breakdownservices.com.

4 A writer's credits can often be found at Internet Movie Database. (www.imdb.com)

> Bundys moved into the neighborhood and started lowering property values. The show makes sense on the network that airs *The Bernie Mac Show* and *That '70s Show* (*Oliver Beene* is, in an a sense Fox's *That '60's Show*), and it's the perfect Sunday-night closer, a curveballer from the bullpen after a lineup of *King of the Hill*, *The Simpsons*, and *Malcolm in the Middle*.

Knowing this should help you understand the style of the show.

If a writer was known for an inventive show like *Modern Family*, this can clue you into the tone of the new material. If the network is targeting viewers 18 years to 45 years, like the WB Network, an actor can tailor his delivery for a younger crowd. For example, if an actress is playing seductress, the acting choices she makes for an audience of 8 year olds would be very different from those she would choose for an audience of 30 year olds. If a show is currently playing in an 8 o'clock time slot, it has closer scrutiny from a network's Standards and Practices[5] department because the average viewer may be younger than those watching a 9:30 show. If you are interviewing or auditioning for an established show, your own viewing habits and familiarity with the style of the show is invaluable. Watch sitcoms!

PREPARING FOR THE AUDITION-ANALYSIS

So how does an actor best prepare for that all-important chance of actually getting a job? ANALYZE THE MATERIAL, then REHEARSE THE SCENE. First, read a script for content. Understand every line of dialogue and stage direction. Then identify the jokes. This is sometimes harder than it seems. When we teach, we begin each class with the same exercise; we call it FIND THE JOKES. All the students are given the same sitcom scene and are asked to circle the jokes. We ask for a total. We poll for who finds the most. You'd be surprised at how widely the totals vary! An old rule of thumb holds that sitcoms contain three jokes per page.[6] When you study a page carefully looking at odd character traits and reactions, you will often find many opportunities for a laugh.

What exactly is a joke? A joke is the funny part of the scene. It may not be a classic type of joke that a comic might say in a stand-up act, but it is something that makes you smile or laugh[7]. Sometimes jokes are not easy to spot. As you read the later chapters in this book, you'll find out more about the structure and

---

5 This department regulates the material that can or cannot be aired on that network, i.e. nudity, profanity, violence, commercial references, etc. These departments are now more integrated with the production companies.

6 Sitcom dialogue is double-spaced and therefore covers about 30 seconds per page unlike dramatic scripts' approximate one-minute pages.

7 Not everyone would actually laugh out loud at most sitcom jokes, which is why sitcoms are performed in front of an audience of 200 people. Let's hear it for group dynamics!

types of jokes common in sitcoms.

Just to give you a head start, here are two clues to easily spot jokes: Responses that end with words with *K* sounds and speeches that have a pattern of three. The *K* sound jokes are more than words with the letter *K*. Any hard consonant that sound "foreign" to the audience's ear will make them laugh.[8] This creates "funny sounding" words. The letters *C*, *T* and *P* in a word will often make it funny. Sounds weird, but it's true.

Here's an example, from the episode "The Ring Cycle" written by Jon Sherman, from the series *Frasier*, created by David Angell, Peter Casey, David Lee. Frasier (Kelsey Grammer) spars with his father Martin (John Mahoney) after a celebration dinner.

MARTIN

(as he sits) I already said thank you for dinner. What am I supposed to do, get down on my knees and kowtow to your fancy-ass American Express card?

FRASIER

No, I was referring to the gift we have for them.

MARTIN

(clambering to his feet) Oh! Right, I forgot about that. Yeah, and thanks for dinner, Fraizh, it really was excellent. I didn't think I'd like beef cheeks.[9]

Here's another example from the episode "Pop Art," written by Susan Nirah Jaffe, from the series *One on One*, created by Eunetta T. Boone, another Paramount sitcom. This is the episode where Flex (Flex Alexander) meets Natalie (Melissa De Sousa) for the first time. Flex is unaware that Natalie is his daughter Breanna's (Kyla Pratt) art teacher. Flex is making fun of the art teacher he thinks he hasn't met yet. He begins saying she sounds like one of those...

NATALIE

Feminists?

FLEX

Worse. She calls herself a "womanist." That's French for ugly.

---

8 It is no coincidence that the German Colonel Wilhelm Klink (played by two time Emmy winner for Best Actor in a Comedy Series Werner Klemperer), on "Hogan's Heroes" received so many laughs. The same goes for Apu on "The Simpsons".

9

NATALIE

(GASPING) No! They're the worst. She's probably filling your daughter's head with outrageous ideas like equal rights and self-respect. I bet she doesn't even shave under her arms.

FLEX GASPS.

FLEX

She probably wears Birkenstocks.[10]

Jokes that have a pattern of three follow the sitcom rule that begins this chapter: **COMEDY COMES IN THREE**. These jokes are easy to spot because the two alike items in the list are separated by commas with an odd choice for that list coming after the word *and.* Or, it may be three separate lines that follow a pattern. We all subconsciously identify patterns when two similar items are mentioned. We are already thinking of the next item in this identified list. When the odd choice comes up, it surprises us. Surprise is the key to making someone laugh.

Here's an example from the same *Frasier* episode. This occurs at the moment when Niles (David Hyde Pierce) and Daphne (Jane Leeves) put rings on each other's fingers. The Officiant was played by Sam Johnson.

OFFICIANT

By the power vested in me by the state of Nevada, county of Washoe, and the all-new Lucky 7 Resort and Casino, I now pronounce you Husband and Wife. Good luck![11]

Notice the word *casino* also has a *K* sound. When the third item in the list ends with a hard consonant, it provides a natural emphasis.

Here's another example of a run of three from the episode "Take This Job And Love It," written by Susan Nirah Jaffe, from the series *One on One*, created by Eunetta T. Boone. Duane (Kelly Perine) is scolding Candy (Shondrella) for trying to find a date through the personal advertisements.

DUANE

...the personals. The last bastion of the lonely. I, too, was like you, Candy Cane. Looking for love in all the wrong places. Bars. The car wash. Idaho[12]

10 Paramount Pictures Corporation. All Rights Reserved.

11 From the episode "The Ring Cycle" written by Jon Sherman, from the series "Frasier," created by David Angell, Peter Casey, David Lee. Paramount Pictures Corporation, All Rights Reserved.

12 Paramount Pictures Corporation. All Rights Reserved.

Did you notice the "K" sounds in Candy Cane and car wash?

Sitcom Exercise

This exercise is to help you watch sitcoms with a keener eye and understanding of the genre. Record one entire episode of a sitcom. Play it back the first time. Simply watch as a normal TV viewer. See if you can write a once sentence blurb describing the plot of the episode. Next, make a note of the three funniest moments you remember in the episode. Turn the TV back on. Fast forward to one of these funny moments. Watch it three times in a row. See if you can figure out what made you laugh. Do this with the other two memorable funny moments. Do any of these jokes end with K sounds or lines that have a pattern of three?

PREPARING FOR THE AUDITION-REHEARSAL

After studying your sides or the script, the next step is to rehearse. This means saying the words ALOUD for one character, with a partner saying the lines for all the other characters. This partner is **cueing** the actor. Practice the scene in this manner repeatedly until you are entirely familiar with the scene. There is a great debate as to whether material should be memorized for an audition. That is up to the individual. The better an actor knows the scene, the freer and funnier he is in the audition. The point is to be comfortable and free of tension. An actor's tension is not funny.[13]

Whether or not you have memorized the material, we still recommend that you hold the script. Two reasons: under pressure, you just may forget the lines. With the script in your hands, you can find the line. Then there's the subliminal message. An audition is not a final performance...or at least that is what an actor wants the producer to think. By holding the script, you let the producer know, you are directable and there is even more to your performance to come.

However, here's the catch: even though you're holding a script, an audition REALLY IS a performance! And a strange performance it is! Great acting is re-acting. It's playing a scene moment to moment with another character who needs something or wants something. The problem with auditioning is that other character may or may not be present. If that casting director you are reading with is not emotionally present, reacting is difficult...but not impossible.

Some casting directors are good actors; they give a lot to the partner with whom they are reading. Casting director Robi Reed (*Girlfriends, Sister, Sister*) believes that a casting director's training should include acting and directing classes to prepare for the job. Even with the best training, though, some may fall short. When this happens, an actor can't react because *nothing is going on.*

---

13 Well, actually it can be! Comedian Richard Lewis has had a very successful career with his self-effacing humor about his personal neuroses. Richard's tension is funny. Richard co-starred with Jamie Lee Curtis in a short-lived, yet wonderful show *Anything But Love* created by Peter Noah.

CAREER TRACK

Don't be afraid to be funny. Try to find humor out of real life situations. Organic humor. Not one-liner humor. Find the story-teller in you. Listen to good stories, tell good stories. Always, always throw in a twist. People love the thrill of a surprise. Watch lots of sitcoms. Study them. Watch comedy shows, and study your favorite comedians. And furthermore, know why you're laughing at something. Be clear about what tickles your fancy, and run with it. And be damn confident. Nobody likes a passive funny man.

Keith Josef Adkins (Award winning playwright and TV Writer, *Girlfriends*)

What to do in this case? PRETEND. For example, suppose a parent (played by the actor) is being begged by a child (played by the casting director) to go to a party. Suppose no begging is really going on. The auditioning actor must then go through the same thought process AS IF he were being begged.

In our experience, the actors who get seriously considered for each role are the ones that come into an audition with strong choices of how to play that character. Marc Hirschfeld, who was the casting director of dozens of series from *Married...With Children* to *3rd Rock from the Sun* and now heads casting for NBC says, "I look for an actor who commits to the audition material. I want to hire an actor who makes strong, intelligent choices. I want to hire an actor who is prepared and has obviously put some thought and energy into the role."

Actress Diane Delano (*Northern Exposure The Lady Killers*) lives and works by the philosophy, "I am what I am, and that's all that I am." She advises actors, "Don't apologize and never compromise what you are to fulfill another person's view of what you should do." Delano's strong choices allows her to be creative and approach her craft with a deep personal integrity.

As directors, we have been asked our opinion about a specific actor after an audition and responded that he or she was "okay." Okay doesn't get the part. One producer once described to us why he had not cast an actor whom he had used many times before. This producer assured us that he was a big fan of that actor's work. He also said that actor was perfect for the part. So why didn't he cast him? "You know, at the audition, he didn't nail it!" he explained. If you intrigue the decision makers with a strong choice, you will be seriously considered for the part. If the strong choice does not intrigue, it might be considered odd or inappropriate. At least you tried.

Peter Engel (executive producer of *Last Comic Standing, Saved by the Bell, USA High, and City Guys,* and many other Saturday morning hits) has a theory about young actors. "When you hire young actors, how much experience can they have?" he asks. Peter who launched the careers of such actors as Mark-Paul Gosselaar (*Franklin and Bash, Raising the Bar, NYPD Blue*) expounds on his litmus test for actors. "The key is that some young people fill space, other take up space." He gives an example. "I was looking for kids who would captivate me with their personality. I was looking for that before they ever read."

Engel says making an impression is key. "First thing is make me interested in you-- then try and do something with the part that makes it you. Don't change the character but do something that is memorable, something that makes it better." He also cautions, "Don't make it worse, and don't re-write it. Take what's there and make it you. We only need one of each character."

PREPARING FOR THE AUDITION–COACHING

Some actors get coached. That translates into paying money to someone who knows sitcoms better than you do. There are three reasons to get coached. First, a coach allows you to rehearse exactly what you will be doing at the audition. Second, a coach may know more about the material than you do. Third, the coach can help you make better choices about the material.

Academy Award winning actress Louise Fletcher (*One Flew Over the Cuckoo's Nest*) shares that her coach "can take the fear and panic and replace those with confidence and ease. I can concentrate!!" She explains that her coach "knows how to focus on the material and relate it to my own strengths which I have forgotten I had (because the fear and panic are in full command when we meet). Meeting with her coach, for an hour before an audition, has been one the "great finds" in her career.

Why rehearse an audition? An actor who prepares by himself is only studying the material; he isn't actually practicing the scene. Sitcoms are predicated on timing and rhythm. Stage, film, and television actress Robin Bartlett (*Mad About You, The Powers That Be*) says about sitcoms, "Making it natural and musical at the same time is the challenge and the fun." Musicians just don't study their music. They play it. A coach, reading the lines of the other characters in the scene, helps an actor simulate an audition. So many obstacles can interfere with an actor's concentration when he walks into audition. The only thing an actor has control over is his mastery of the material. Being well rehearsed allows an actor to perform with confidence.

Why are a coach's choices better than yours? They aren't always. But a coach can be a second pair of eyes. A coach may spy a joke you missed or an impulse you had (but didn't follow). A coach allows you to simply act and not analyze. An actor who is analyzing or watching himself during the scene is not fully present in the material. So, what makes an excellent audition? Bartlett says, "Spontaneity above all. Bringing yourself to

AUDITION HINTS

What separates the good actors from the bad actors and the good writer from the hack, is that good actors can take a hack script and make it blossom into more than that writer deserves. The good writer can watch a bad actor make him or her seem like a hack. The point is, it's a synergy. A good actor will read a difficult piece of writing, like Brecht, Albee or Neil Simon, and even if they don't understand the writer's point (and if they don't understand Simon, there are other lines of work), their own uniqueness will embellish it because the words are there. Do not fuck up or add to the words. Writers hate that. They might not tell you to your face, but they do. That can come after you get the job (unless it's Simon and he'll fire you in a New York minute.) And a good writer will create characters that are vivid, even in their dullness, for an actor to wrap his or her minds around. If an actor says of a script, "But there's nothing for me to grab onto" he or she is saying, "Please fire me." Find something. If the actor makes a writer see something they hadn't thought of before, he'll take credit for it and hire you, even if you're thinking inside, "This is shit".

Ian Praiser, Writer, *Alf, Suddenly Susan, Caroline in the City*

the material, which is often written formulaically."

Choosing a coach for a sitcom should depend on whether that coach is an EXPERT in the field of sitcoms. Just making good acting choices is not enough. Sitcoms are different from other material because their aim is to make people laugh! Sitcom writer, producer, creator Nancylee Myatt (*Night Court, Social Studies, The Powers That Be, Living Single*) was asked to describe the difference between sitcoms and other material. She replied, "It's funny. If your script doesn't make people laugh, and I mean out loud, not just smile, perhaps you should write a drama." So, make sure your coach has a sense of humor. Your immediate reward will be making him or her laugh!

THE AUDITION

How does an actor get an audition appointment? After an agent receives notices from Breakdown Services, he submits his clients for the roles. The casting director sets up appointment times. The actor auditions for the casting director. Then the actor sometimes auditions again (a **callback**). Then the actor sometimes auditions again (final producer session). Then, in the case of a pilot, the actor auditions again ("going to network"), maybe on tape. Before this final pilot audition, an actor signs his contract called a "test deal."

Actors should foster relationships with casting directors. The secret is how to do this without being a pest. The best sales tool an actor has for this purpose is the reputation of doing consistently good work. There are workshops where actors pay a fee to meet casting directors.[14] They usually involve doing a prepared scene or pairing up with another actor in the workshop to read a set of sides. These workshops DO NOT come with any job offers or guarantees. They are merely a way of getting a casting director to see your face and view a sample of your work. After one of these workshops, a casting director may agree to look at a sample reel of you work. Sample reels should never exceed 5-7 minutes. You're lucky if a casting director will watch more than 2 minutes. Sending postcards or flyers alerting a casting director that you are in a play, performing standup, or appearing on an episode of an upcoming show is a great way to keep your face or name in front of them. Quoting good reviews or mentions in newspapers or magazines gives them an unbiased assessment of your work. Invite them, but don't ever expect casting directors to actually come to an event. They couldn't possibly see everything. You just want it on their radar that you're out there working.

Casting directors are asked to vouch for an actor's reputation. They should know that you're cooperative, professional, and ON TIME! It's also helpful when they know you have a life. An articulate or funny comment made about current events, a recent movie, or a book you just read may leave a more lasting impression than bragging about your latest gig. An actor who talks only about himself

14 To prevent scams, the Casting Society of America supports the regulations that the State of California sets up on how these types of workshops should be run.

and his career is a boring, boring, boring.[15] One sitcom writer interviewed for this book commented on actors giving bad writing notes. He followed this insult with "I can say this safely because actors don't read books that aren't about themselves." The perception that actors are self-absorbed is hard to live down.

At the same time, it is important to note that the audition is NOT the time or place for long chitchat. An actor should come in, ascertain with whom he is reading, do the material, thank the casting director, and leave. Casting director Beth Goldstein (*The Naked Truth, The Hughleys*) also offers some other advice: "If you don't connect with the character and know you'll give a poor audition, pass on the audition. If you are sick, don't come in: chances are you'll give a bad audition and can get everyone else sick, plus you might have the good fortune of being able to reschedule when you are well. In both cases remember: better not to be seen than to be seen poorly."

AUDITION HINTS

Always bring a picture and resume...even if your agent tells you that the casting director already has it on file. Be on time or early for your audition! Don't make a mountain out of a mole hill- Some actors are under the mistaken impression that the longer you're in the audition room, the better shot you have a booking the role. Wrong. Go in, do your scene, and get the hell out so we can talk about you while the audition is fresh in our minds. Don't feel the need to shake everyone's hand when you both enter and leave the room. Don't second-guess your audition: If you have a bad start on the first line, ask to start again. Otherwise, shake it off and keep going. And don't ever finish the audition and then ask to do the scene again because you were unhappy with your performance. It just shows that you were insecure with your choices the first time around. If the Producer or Casting Director asks you to read again, make sure you take their direction. Don't ignore it.

Marc Hirschfeld,
Ex.VP Casting, NBC Entertainment

PROPS AND COSTUMES

Actors often ask about wearing a costume or bringing a prop to an audition. Wearing something that gives the flavor of a character is often helpful. Wearing a costume is trying too hard. For example, a loose fitting garment would be better for a pregnant character than a pillow or pregnancy suit. Similarly, a black shirt and dress pants would give the flavor of a minister rather than an actual clerical collar. NBC's Marc Hirschfeld thinks this is the most common audition mistake: "An actor should dress to indicate the role, but don't come in wearing a uniform. If you're auditioning for a steel worker, don't come in wearing a hard hat. Wear casual clothes, blue jeans, work shirt."

Then there are always exceptions to the rule, and it all comes down to being comfortable. Actor William Forward (*The Gilmore Girls, Babylon 5*) found he got more work in his own comfortable, nice, casual wardrobe than when he tried for a look. His jeans and cashmere sweater booked him a job as funeral director: he was the only actor not wearing black. His khakis and sweater did not prevent

15 There are many jokes told about actor narcissism. One story tells of an actor going on and on about his last role and then realizing that he's been talking only about himself. The story ends with the actor saying, "Enough about me...what do you think about me?"

him from being cast as an Ivy League admissions director: it helped him stand out from the sea of tweed. Forward said, "Dressing in what suits you can show them you are a confident actor, not trying desperately to please."

With props, think substitution. Our rule of thumb is, if it's something you normally carry, you can use it. We have seen cell phones, water bottles, and pens substitute for anything from a gun to a cattle prod. If an actor commits to that prop, his audience at a casting session will believe it too.

Casting director Beth Goldstein also advises, "Do not bring unnecessary props. Small props are fine such as a cell phone, candy bar etc. Guns are tricky. The two times I've seen them brought in, the actors actually booked the job! If you do choose to bring it in, show everyone in the room, BEFORE THE AUDITION, that it is not real or loaded. At no time during the audition do you point the gun at anyone in the room. My director on a film actually responded to the actor who brought in the gun because many other actors had a hard time pantomiming having the gun."

Auditioning is hard. The pressure can be excruciating; the stakes are high: landing a pilot can lead to six years[16] of continued employment plus syndication. As if auditioning's not hard enough, respect for actors can be sometimes less than it should be. We have heard two great pieces of advice about auditioning, one, enjoy yourself, and two, don't replay it! Marietta Diprima (*The Hughleys, Dear John*) loves to act. She says, "Auditioning as an opportunity. I'm a character actor. Auditioning is my chance at creating my own little repertory theatre company!" Moreover, she "gets to play all the parts... one audition at a time." An audition is the first, last, and only time an actor gets to create a character without other people's input. Diprima says, "It belongs to you! You go in, you do it, you do it right, and whether they cast you or not, you KNOW that you did it." Marietta believes in living or dying by her choices because they're hers.

Sitcom audiences know the late Betty Garrett as Irene Lorenzo on *All in the Family* and *The Jeffersons* and as Edna Babish-DeFazio on *Laverne and Shirley*. Garrett, a lovely actress, a very funny lady, and a wise sage, said, "I treat an audition as a performance. I just get out there and enjoy myself. And if I get the job, that's just gravy!"

Try to remember: They have a problem (casting this role) and you have the solution. You are the doctor. You're there to fix the problem. Don't go in to be funny; go in to be the character. Don't hit the jokes too hard; let the material do the work for you.

Always give your auditioners the benefit of the doubt. They're fallible. Remem-

16 Actors sign contracts before they audition for a pilot that contracts them for the first six years on a sitcom series. The goal of most series is to produce enough shows so that all episodes produced can be sold into syndication. Syndication means lots of residuals. The target number for a syndication package is 100 episodes. That's five seasons of 22 episodes a year. The sixth season is the last season to make more shows without renegotiating with the actors. In the case of a mega-hit like "Friends," renegotiations are done earlier than six years in good faith because the show has been such a financial success.

ber they're people, too. Scott Bakula (*Men of a Certain Age, Enterprise, Quantum Leap, Murphy Brown*) shares a perfect example:

> I'm a theatre guy. When I came to L.A., after 10 years in New York doing mostly musical comedy, the sitcom world was a natural fit for me. I loved and understood the live audience, and I loved the sense of performance, of getting ready for "Show" night! I was lucky enough to land the guest-starring role on the "Designing Women" pilot, which was an exciting, complicated, but very visible introduction to the L.A. scene. People had started to know who I was when I went into an audition later that year, an audition that I've never forgotten.
>
> It was to replace the lead in a pilot that had been picked up already. (I won't name names because this is about the audition process). I went into a room to read for the Executive Producers and Writers, one of whom was sitting down in a big, soft chair, and never got up. I plowed into the scenes but couldn't help but notice that as I went on, the man (who had never gotten up), sank lower and lower into his chair and that by the time I was done, he was basically fully reclining. He said "thank you" from the reclining position and I left; immediately called my agent telling them I almost put the guy to sleep, the whole thing was a disaster, what a rude S.O.B., etc., etc., etc. Oddly enough, to my surprise, I got the job.
>
> Turned out he was the Executive Producer and his back was out, and he was in terrible pain at my audition. Hence his posture and attitude. The moral of course being that you never know what will happen at any given audition. Every one is different. You need to stay positive, as positive as anyone can, during that mind-bending, necessary evil of "the audition".

Replaying an audition can be destructive. Do not waste time re-running your last one in your heads, worrying if you made the right choices or chitchat. Actress Kate Zentall warns about such obsessing. "Auditioning should be like going to the bathroom," she begins in her own irreverent way. "Just do your business, flush, and then forget about it!"

Nevertheless, actors have a lot of valid questions after they leave the room. One is "Who were all those people?" Another is "Did they like my choices?" And "Would they have validated my parking?" The answer to the last question is definitely no.[17] The people in the room might include the casting director, a casting assistant that reads the scene with you, the producer/writer who wrote that episode, the show runner, the line producer and the director.[18] If you're audition-

17 Not-yet-cast actors are at the bottom of the food chain. Directors and writers often get their parking validated.

18 For some unknown reason, a lot more male producers show up when a girl in a bathing suit is being cast.

ing for a series regular, network and studio people may be there as well. On rare occasions when the audition is for a particularly important series regular, the series' star might be there to read. As an actor, don't try to get everyone's name. Just focus on the work!

Richard Lewis, actor/writer/comedian and author of *The Other Great Depression* suggests:

> Find yourself in every role. The best screenplays are generally written--at least the personal ones--by writers who know their subject matter first hand. To me, I need to find the part of me that is very much a part of whomever I am playing to make it real or I'm through. This holds true in the auditioning process. What's the point when you usually have one shot not to do it your way? Even if you don't get the role and that can be for a zillion reasons that have nothing to do with you or your talent, if you drive home after an audition knowing you didn't do it the way you truly believed was the way to go, to me, it's a waste of time. And on screen, obviously directors can do take after take but all I can say is I hope that you never find yourself in a position where you cave in to a direction that you feel, in your gut, is so wrong. Trust me, months later when it airs or in a year in the darkened movie house you will cringe and all you had to do is not do it. It's your career and your "being" up there, regardless of the role so be compassionate to your instincts and yourself because sadly, it's a world of a lot of ego-trippers and power hungry people who need to justify their creative existence. Well, guess what, so do all of us, so fight for what you believe in!

The best feedback on your choices is the laughs that you can earn from the people in the room. Stick by your choices. Trust us, if there is interest in casting an actor, someone will offer an adjustment if it's necessary. The choice is yours whether to take the offer. The changes may be asked for immediately in the casting room. Be open. If you want extra time to rethink the scene, you can ask to go into the waiting room and return shortly. More often, feedback gets filtered through an agent. You may be asked to change something for a callback. If no requests are made, *do the scene the way you did it the first time.*

Casting director Beth Goldstein suggests, "Don't invade the reader's space. It makes the reader feel uncomfortable and it's difficult for us to see you so close up. If you can't play the character from across the room, you can't play it. Do not have actual physical contact with the reader during the audition. If the character you are playing is supposed to kiss the other character, SKIP IT and any other inappropriate contact. The only time this is acceptable is if you are told to do it, perhaps for a screen test."

Increasingly, auditions are being videotaped. If someone making a casting choice was not able to attend the audition, or would like to review an audition, this can be a very valuable tool. Actors are asked to **slate** their name. This means announcing your name as a first thing on the video tape to identify yourself. Such as "Ashton Kutcher, Endeavor Agency."[19] The casting director or assistant who is reading will usually stand right next to the camera. Play the scene to the person, not the camera. Playing to the lens will give the appearance of breaking the **fourth wall.**[20] If an actor knows that an audition is going to be taped, we recommend rehearsing as if there were a camera in the room.

Casting is the most important single task of a sitcom. Producer Peter Engel says that, "Casting is the key to television." Engel continues, "In the perfect casting situation, when you see the right actor come in, there is no one else in the world. You know 'that is the person I wrote it for,' there's no one else!" If a show is not cast well, it doesn't matter how well the script was written, how masterfully it was directed, how beautifully it was lit and shot, or how stunning the designs. What matters is can these characters come into TV viewers' home every week and consistently entertain them. That's why the actors on hit shows make mega-bucks. Actors are treated like royalty on sitcoms. A show is identified with the faces that make them laugh every week!

Some stars define a series. Mark-Paul Gosselaar who stars on *NYPD Blue* starred on the original *Saved by the Bell.* Engel describes the talent of Gosselaar as "awesome. He understood it, he got it. He *was* 'Saved by the Bell.' He was the most popular kid in the school and the biggest geek was his sidekick." Engel talks about casting him, "I said to casting director Robbin Lippin, if we don't find a Zack, we don't have a show. When Gosselaar walked in the room, I said, 'If he can speak English, he's got the job' because he had a sparkle." Even though in real life, Mark-Paul was nothing like the character he played, he had the ability to become Zack. "And nobody else did! Mark-Paul could look you in the eye, lie to you, and you knew he was lying to you and you still loved him. Brandon Tartikoff likened the Zack character to the early sitcom character Bilko."

Actress Kate Zentall offers a realistic picture:

> Chances are you will be auditioning for a smaller guest-star role, a probable one-episode gig. Chances are your character will be there to further the plot, create situations to be overcome by the series regulars. Chances are your ability to be unique and interesting and sincere, and charming will get you the part. Chances are also that once you do get the part you will notice that it gets progressively smaller and less funny with each day of rehearsal. Chances are you will take this personally. Do not do this.

19 Of course, once you're as famous as Ashton, you'll get offers without auditions and will never have to slate again.

20 Fourth wall is a theatre term referring to the imaginary wall through which the audience is watching. Breaking the fourth wall in theatre is when a character speaks directly to the audience. Breaking the fourth wall in television is when the actor looks directly into the camera lense and appears to be talking directly to the viewers. *Malcolm in the Middle* and *Bernie Mac* regularly used the device for effect.

> The very charming and funny thing that got you the part may very possibly be excised from the script by taping day. You often become a straight man to one of the regulars. It hurts, but so does childbirth, strep, or other unfortunate conditions of life. The more you anguish and worry, the worse it is all around. You are a hired hand, a professional. Watch, listen, be a good guest, a helpful participant. Know your place. Be a grown up.

GETTING THE JOB–WRITER

The Pilot

A writer gets a job on sitcoms in an entirely different way: he gets read and then he pitches...or in the case of a **pilot**, he just pitches. A pilot is the very first episode of any television show. It is the model on which a series is based. The cast, the scenery, the "look" and style of a show are set during a pilot. Pitching is telling your idea: your idea for the pilot or your ideas for future episodes.[21]

Nearly always, a writer pitches his pilot to a network in the hopes that that network (or another) will like the idea enough to order a script. The game in Hollywood is to be one of the individuals who gets to pitch. That game is often set up by only the most powerful of agents, or by a producer or studio with a track record, or a manager with a hot client. Comedian D.L. Hughley sold his pilot *The Hughleys* based on his pitch. His already successful stand-up career got him the pitch meeting! If a writer has a hit show on the air, his chances are far better to get the opportunity to pitch.

Before the network pitch, a studio will often get involved. Touchstone's Stephen McPerson explains that, "We find a writer we like, or have an idea that he likes and wants to develop, and pitch that to the networks."

It can also happen the other way. The network can ask a producer to develop something they have in mind. Peter Engel gives an example about his series *Saved by the Bell.* "NBC's Brandon Tartikoff wanted me to do a Saturday morning show.[22] The premise really was six kids 'who were starting high school: the wondrous wonder years.' The pitch was telling these kid's stories from the opening bell at eight o'clock on Monday to four o'clock on Friday." Peter and his writers laid out the show for Tartikoff, who asked, "What shall we call this?" Writer Tom Tenowich suggested *Saved by the Bell.* The title cleared[23] and the next day a sign was up.

The last and most unusual way to get a show on the air is to write a spec pilot. This does not involve pitching. Howard Gewirtz did this with *Oliver Beene.* Even though a network might buy a pilot idea and commission a script to be written, it does not guarantee that the pilot will get produced. Once a pilot script is

---

21 Writers also pitch individual jokes as part of an ongoing rewriting process.

22 NBC wanted to capture 10 – 13 year old market. Research said it would never work.

23 Shows use an outside contractor to check for legal clearances or conflicts

bought, the next step is getting a commitment from a network to make it. Many pilots are made each year. Few actually make it to the air. The way a pilot makes it to the air is with star power or audience testing. Over the years, we have seen some very funny pilots not make the schedule while another, not so sharp pilot with a major star in the lead, gets the pickup. A recent trend in sitcoms is for networks to buy shows that they have produced by a studio "in house." For example, CBS network owns CBS Productions. When it comes time to sell that product into syndication,[24] CBS reaps more profits because it is both the buyer and the seller.

A pilot script is different from other episodes in that it must entertain while containing more expository information than a normal script. A pilot has to introduce all the regular characters and the basic premise of the show. When viewers watch a sitcom from week to week, there's a familiarity with these characters. The pilot lays the foundation for this. When test audiences view a pilot,[25] they give specific feedback on how much they like each character. Characters are often re-cast if the audience test group is favorable toward the show but unfavorable toward the actor.

Getting staffed on a pilot (AND DOING A GOOD JOB on that pilot) often will ensure a job for future episodes of that show if it gets on the schedule.

GETTING THE JOB–WRITER

Staffing

Getting the writing job on an existing series is another matter. First a writer gets read, then he pitches. **Getting read** means an agent submits writing samples of his writer client. This may be scripts that have been produced or speculative scripts from popular shows on the air. Every year, there are different shows in vogue to write as spec scripts. The writer has copied the format of the show and supplied his own story using the regular characters and some guest stars. It shows what the writer can create for an already existing show. Not any show will do. There is a practice that only certain shows are worthy of copying. For years it was great to have a *Frasier*, but now everyone has a *Frasier*, so it might be better to do a *Modern Family*. Writers need multiple writing samples if they want to go to a new show. Writer/ producer/ creator Nancylee Myatt advises the aspiring sitcom writer. "Writers write. Write something. Then write something else. Then another thing. Until you have so many samples from different genres that you'll be covered for any opportunity. By genre I mean: a family show, a popular at that

24 This is where sitcoms make huge profits! It's like selling something twice, but the second time you have no production costs other than residuals.

25 Pilots are viewed by test audience private screenings in different cities. Each audience member has a dial, which they turn up if they like something, and down when they don't. Some of them are interviewed in depth right after the viewing. The results are crucial to determining whether a show continues. A show can live or die by the turn of a dial.

time workplace comedy, a 20-something ensemble, etc. Because invariably the spec script you have will be from the one show that the producer who can give a job hates."

For writers, a job interview is the next step. "I'm looking for people with passion for what they are doing," says Peter Engel. "People came in like Leslie Eberhard (*USA High*). Who is this guy? Why does he want to work for us? I had read his 'Frasier[26]' which was totally wrong for us, but when he came in, there was so much enthusiasm...and he had done his homework. Knowing what we're doing, that's what it's about!" During the interview, the writer may have to pitch stories for the series. These are multiple ideas for episodes. When a writer successfully pitches his ideas for an already existing series and gets hired, it is called **staffing**.

When Engel looks for a writing staff, he "casts the room." "I try to cast a room with diversity, and I don't mean diversity female/ male, black/white. I mean diversity in ages.[27] I wanted to get a diversity of ideas so that the older guys could teach the young guys and the younger guys could teach the older guys. I cast the room like I'd cast the show. It's great because you don't have just one point of view!"

Engel has read many spec scripts. "What I'm looking for in reading a writer is finding something that pops off the page. Yes, I've read this kind of scene a hundred times, but this is a different attack on it. For instance, I read Jeffrey Sachs's (*9 to 5, City Guys, Hang Time*) script of *The Wonder Years*. Obviously, my doing all these young adult shows, *The Wonder Years* was a good sample. I didn't want to read *Homicide*. Jeffrey Sachs' script talked about a bully who Kevin (Fred Savage) could not avoid. He had to fight him after school at 3 o'clock. Jeffrey dealt with leading up to the fight and then the confrontation, and how Kevin got out. Jeffrey treated it differently, and that's why I hired him. I was looking for something that was very real emotionally but treated differently or uniquely."

GETTING THE JOB--DIRECTOR

Directors being considered for sitcom jobs also interview. Instead of a spec script, an agent sends over an already produced episode on CD or a sample reel of a director's work. For the newcomer this may be a student film, commercial etc. Director Steve Zuckerman (*Everybody Loves Raymond, Friends, Murphy Brown*) says,

> If you put together a reel or show someone an episode, it doesn't show too much about you. It looks the same as the other episodes of that show. What it doesn't show is how the week went. Did you do it on time? Did you do the shots or did the TD or AD do them? By the time it is ed-

26 In this case a produced episode; not a spec script.

27 Tomes have been written about ageism in the TV business. Mr. Engel seems to have walked to the beat of his own drum for which we applaud him.

> ited, all sitcoms look the same. But my agent said I had to give them a reel so you try to give them something that they are looking for. They might be looking for a lot of physical comedy. That will help. If you are up for a single camera show, you might have an episode with some single camera elements.

WRITING CAREER TRACK

My advice to anyone who wants to become a writer of sitcoms (or any other form of writer) can be summed up in three words: write, write, write. The difference between people who talk about being writers and those of us who are writers is the difference between a blank page and one that is filled with words. I carve out a space every day to write, if not on a project or script, then in my journal. Learning to create with words, like making music from piano keys requires practice. It's a use it or lose it proposition. Writers write.

As a kid I was a television addict–still am. Back in the days before VCRs, I used to write out the story in dialogue of a favorite series I'd seen the night before. By the time I was in high school, I would amuse myself by making up my own "episodes" of my favorite shows. When I had my first interview with an agent and he asked to see my material, one of the things I gave him was an original sketch I'd written for The Carol Burnett Show. *That sketch landed my first job, a summer replacement series produced by the writers from the Burnett show. To my good fortune, we all learned I could write more than just "pretend' sketches and was ultimately brought on staff of* The Carol Burnett Show.

Rick Hawkins
Writer, *Major Dad, Sister, Sister*

Picking the right style of show is as important as the right quality of show. In addition to the ability to actually produce a good finished product, a director is judged on whether he can handle the cast and crew. Being at the helm is great responsibility and there are many big personalities involved.[28] A producer takes a big leap to hire an unknown or unproven quantity. For this reason many journeyman directors "observe" on a sitcom in order to gain familiarity with a show and more important gain the confidence of the regular director and producer. A verbal vote of confidence or recommendation can make all the difference as to whether a young director gets a break. Director Michael Lembeck (*Friends, Mad About You, According to Jim, Babby Daddy, Hot in Cleveland*) has very generously helped many careers this way. Writer/director/actor Jonathan Prince (*American Dreams, Dream On, Throb*) agrees. He told a theater full of Director Guild members that the key to employment in this industry is "who you know." He said "Mentors," he said, "get you in the door."

There are also training programs sponsored by the studios or networks. ABC and Disney, in association with Touchstone Television, have fellowship programs for both writers and directors. Warner Brothers has a long history of developing writers. Writer Nancylee Myatt (*Night Court, Social Studies*) talks about that program:

> I believe the Warner Bros. Writer's Workshop originally started as a minority program for the studio. The studio would choose writers who

28 Madeline Cripe when talking about a director's responsibilities includes "walking on egg shells and talking to the actors....who will occasionally listen."

met the minority criteria with an eye to putting them on the shows that were being produced by Warner Bros. Writers and producers who were working on Warner Bros. shows at that time taught the class. I ended up teaching there a couple of years when I was working on the lot. The studio would help place the graduates on their shows, pay the writing salaries -- that way everyone got a break. When I went through the WBWW in the late 80's it was still geared toward minorities somewhat, but was starting to open the doors to all writers who turned in a good sample which rose to the top of the very tall stack of submissions. I hit the minority status on two levels -- I'm a woman and a Native American (and yes I can prove it, I'm a card-carrying member of the Cherokee Tribe. Being a woman has been much easier to prove over the years). And I had the good fortune of having producers who were running shows for Warner Bros. recommend me to the workshop. I had been their writer's assistant and they told the studio that if I got into the class and showed promise they would hire me. It all came down that way and they gave me my first job on "Night Court." Of course, everyone who got hired out of the workshop had to then prove they were worth keeping around -- because the studio was only paying our salaries for the first 13 weeks as a term writer. After that, the producers had to keep us on as staff writers and pay the salary from the writer's budget on the show. It's my understanding that the program is still going on -- but is no longer focusing on minority hires and making no promises about staffing. And once you get accepted, you have to pay a fee to the workshop. I understand Disney has a similar program. So it took a while, but the studios have finally figured out a way to get writers to pay them for writing.

GETTING THE JOB–DESIGNERS AND CREW

Department heads and designers are hired at the very beginning of the preproduction period. That period is usually about six to ten weeks for a series and may be just a few weeks for a pilot. To save time, the heads and crew from a show that is just finishing its season might be hired to continue as the staff for a pilot that is being done by the same production company. For example, many crewmembers from the already running *The Hughleys* worked on the new pilot *One on One*, both for the Greenblatt Janollari Studios. When *One on One* got on the air, the crew members who only worked two days a week were able to do both shows simultaneously for the years that both shows were in production.

After the show runner, director, writers, and department heads are set, the line producer fills all of the approximately one hundred positions it takes to make a sitcom. Line producer Coral Hawthorne (*Reed Between the Lines, The Hughleys*) clarifies, "I let the department heads choose their own staff. I just have veto power." She goes on to explain that she rarely exercises that veto and that it is rare for a department head to not have recommendations.

So how does one get to know that department head who uses people they know? Any way you can! A common route is starting as production assistant or PA. Madeline Cripe started out this way.

Work breeds work! It is easier to move laterally from a position in the company. Script supervisor Kit Wilkinson "took the only job available" and explained her other interests to her employers once she was already in the job. Oscar winning producer Jana Sue Memel believes it's all about relationships. "There are a lot of qualified people in this business; it's assumed you can do the job well, or you wouldn't be considered. The deciding factor is whether the person hiring feels comfortable with you." Costume designer Emily Draper (*Oliver Beene, Grace Under Fire*) explains about breaking into her field: "I do think you have to be willing to work on almost anything to get experience and connections. You also need to try to get into the union by working in a costume house or on a movie that goes union. Usually, if you keep working hard and are easy to get along with, you will keep working." Director of photography Bruce Finn (*Eight Simple Rules*) gives this advice, "Befriend and call huge volumes of business potential clients." Writer/producer Rick Hawkins (*Sister, Sister, Major Dad*) credits luck and nepotism: "Almost everyone in show business had had someone to give them a break, lend a hand, or teach them the ropes. If not, they were just lucky enough to be in the right place at the right time."

There is a popular cameraman in Hollywood named Vito Giambalvo. Actors love him. Producers love him. Crews love him. Why? Vito has a great laugh. When Vito sees a scene, he is the best audience anyone could ask for. Line producers hiring **below-the-line**[29] staff have kept Vito employed continuously for 30 years because they want him and his great sense of humor around ... and he's a great camera operator. **Above the line**[30] are the actors, director and producers or as Second Assistant Director Marcia Lapin wryly defines it as "the people who get big **residuals**."[31] Residuals are payments negotiated by a union for re-use of a TV show. When a line producer is staffing, it is a crucial time for resumes of all personnel to be already at his or her disposal. Keeping in touch year-round is the smartest thing to do so you don't appear at the last minute, too hungry for the job. People can smell panic in Hollywood.

Designers and below-the-line crew interview for jobs. Even for well-established people it is sometimes difficult getting a foot in the door. We recommend

29 Below the line refers to the crew and production staff. Some are paid only for the weeks they work. Others are "carried" and receive payment for the weeks that a show is not in production and on hiatus.

30 Above and below the line staff are either under contract to the studio, sign a production company deal-memo or get paid by the day.

31 Screen Actors Guild-AFTRA, Writers Guild and Directors Guild negotiate payments for reuse on behalf of their membership. Second Assistant Directors get a MUCH smaller residual payment than Directors. According to Teri Benton of the DGA, only the sitcom director earns a residual for Free TV, syndication, and foreign reuse. Below the line Guild members share a percentage of video sales and Pay TV rights only.

always asking someone to make a call on your behalf for that entrée or recommendation. If that person knows you well, and likes your work, it will make a difference in whether you get the interview. Remember, ONLY YOU CAN GET THE JOB!

PRE-PRODUCTION

If you land the job, all departments have a certain amount of pre-production work that begins with reading the script. The production designer is drawing up blueprints for scenery and getting it built within the production's budget. A copy of the production designer's set plans[32] are sent to the director and lighting designer. The designer must understand the physical requirements of shooting four cameras simultaneously (see Chapter 5), creating a space that fulfills the requirement of the script, and finally understand what aspects of the scenery will enhance the comedy. More confined spaces, for example, make a scene funnier than a wide-open area. The production designer supervises the set decoration department in selecting all furniture, rugs, drapery, etc. Ann Donahue in a *Daily Variety* article entitled "Sitcoms set in their ways" writes:

> The look of the family sitcom was established in the late 60's and early 70's with *The Brady Bunch* and *All in the Family*. Little has changed since: There's a couch in the middle, a staircase to nowhere and a swinging door that provides fodder for comic entrances and exits.

In that same article Donahue quotes Multi-Emmy winner John Shaffner for *Friends* who acknowledges the challenge.

> The sitcom set is a vernacular that everybody recognizes... Doing sets for multicam is like that line from Ginger Rogers...you have to do everything on three walls that movies get to do with four walls. Ginger Rogers had to do everything Fred Astaire did, but backwards and in high heels.

Donahue also quotes art director Roy Christopher (*Frasier, Murphy Brown*) who explains that the usual set design is the fallback that makes it easiest for thesps to time their lines.

> You want it so they can go down the stairs, say their line, and head out the front door. On *Frasier* we have Niles' beautiful Montana apartment, and to walk through the front door and go to the kitchen it's about 40 feet. The writers are always telling me. Roy, it's really hard to fill all that."

The wardrobe department can begin shopping or pulling wardrobe once the

32 See the sample plans in the appendix.

actors are cast. The lighting designer can hang a general lighting plot before the set is loaded in. The properties (props) department will shop for specific props for the show and have an array of general props available for weekly use. The script supervisor does an initial timing of the script. The camera and sound equipment is usually rented by the line producer. The editor can use either rented equipment or rent space and time at a post production house. The camera, sound, and editing department have limited pre-production work.

Pre-production generally has an ease to it because less is going on. Hours tend to be more regular and for some departments nonexistent if there is nothing that can be done ahead of time. A master list is generated from the office-with the name and contact information of each crew member. When you get it, make sure your information is correct. Our last piece of advice is take it easy during pre-production because production will be more hectic and pressured.

Sitcom Vocabulary Quick Review

Read these sentences. If the director gave you these notes, would you instantly know what he meant? If not, go back and review the explanation in this chapter.

We don't have to worry about overtime because he's **above the line**.

This is a **below the line** *problem.*

There was no information on it in the **breakdown**.

Let's see what she does at the **callback**.

The only one who should be **cueing** *is the script supervisor.*

Don't break the **fourth wall**.

Getting read *on that show is harder than childbirth.*

Did they refer to a sister in the **pilot**?

This is not what was **pitched**!

Syndication would mean more **residuals**.

Let's leave it up to the **show runner**.

We aren't going to use the **sides**, *turn to page 15 in the script.*

They're done **staffing**.

Is everyone looking at the **table draft**?

Sitcom Insider

One of the aspects of directing that has always been very important to me is preparation. When I first receive a script, I read it through from beginning to end. In doing so, I get an overall sense of the story to be told. How does it move from point 'A' to point 'B'? Is the story told through a specific point of view? How do the events in the story impact each of the characters? What makes it funny?

I read the script again. Then I read it a third time. I make note of all the production requirements; props, set dressing, set design, wardrobe, lighting, camera, special effects, etc. If there is anything about the script that is confusing to me, I make a note of it so that I can talk with the writer to clarify his or her intent. I also note script changes I will suggest to the writer. At the same time I block the action of each scene. I decide on where actors will be at the beginning of each scene, when and where they will move and why. I create 'business' for them to do. I stage scenes in each set and vary the playing areas as much as possible to allow for visual variety.

I love to walk onto the set and have my game plan. If a prop master asks me where to put a hand prop, I have an answer. If a special effects team asks me which kitchen sink drain needs to be practical, I know immediately. If the director of photography asks me where I plan a lighting change, I can give him the details.

I'm right there with an answer when an actor looks at me and says, "Where do you want me?" "What am I doing in this scene?" "Why am I moving here?" I never consider my plan written in stone. I use it as a jumping off point. If an actor has a good suggestion about some other approach he or she would like to try, I try it. If rehearsal should reveal better choices, I go with them. If an actor tells me something's not working for him or her, I always have some alternate plans ready to go.

A director must have the wisdom and confidence to recognize a good idea, no matter where it comes from. I once listened to what a stand-in had to say about a particular piece of business and I incorporated it into the scene. It got a huge laugh and I gave him credit for coming up with it. It improved the show in more ways than one. The audience thoroughly enjoyed it and as a member of the crew, he felt appreciated.

For me, preparation is very important. Having a plan, along with a back-up plan or two, has proven invaluable to me. I've found that by working this way, I can maintain my vision for how I want to tell the story and at the same time, create a secure collaborative atmosphere on the stage.

Andrew D. Weyman, Director
Roseanne, Ellen, Two and a Half Men

Sitcom Career Profile

ROBI REED
CASTING DIRECTOR

Robi has an amazing ability to find great acting talent. Her sessions are an embarrassment of riches! She is creative yet discerning and is well liked by actors because she treats them with respect.

What shows have you worked on?

Girlfriends, In the House, Sister, Sister, Roc, In Living Color, A Different World, Out All Night, The PJS, The Robert Guillaume Show, Sparks, Good News, The Kirk Franklin Show.

What are your responsibilities?

I'm responsible for casting all principal roles (speaking parts) in each show.

Did you have specific training in this field?

My training primarily was on the job training. I interned in a casting office for a short stint before receiving my first paying gig as a casting coordinator on a movie. I did, however, study acting and directing in school and received my BA in Speech Communications and Theatre. I believe both areas are invaluable to the casting director.

How did you get your first job?

I knew the production coordinator on a feature film. She hired me to work as her assistant - so I was assistant Prod. Office Coordinator. I did well, however, it wasn't my desired area. On her next film - the Casting Director didn't have an assistant - I met her and she hired me. That was 19 years ago - and I've been working ever since. Interestingly enough - that same Casting Director and I are still good friends - and when she's in LA (She lives in NY) we often visit comedy clubs together.

What advice would you give someone who wants to do what you do?

Preparation. You can never be too prepared. Take and acting and directing class - it will help you in your casting sessions. Intern in a casting office to gather experience. Most Casting offices want actual experience. See lots of movies and television. Go to plays, showcases and comedy clubs. Don't ever limit yourself - and keep an open mind. I've discovered many people who are 'stars' today. Everyone needs a break. What is five minutes in the room when it can change someone's life. If you become bored - get out of it. You'll stop being good at it.

What do you like best about your job?

Helping people achieve their dreams.

CASTING DIRECTORS
Union: None
Typical Weekly Salary: $2000-6000
Hours Per Week: 60-84

Chapter 2 MONDAY (EXCEPT WHEN IT'S NOT)... THE TABLE READ

In this chapter:

- How to survive the table reading
- How to best utilize the rehearsal
- Dos and Don'ts when working with a star
- Set stage etiquette
- How to identify jokes in a script
- The role of the script supervisor
- Advice to the aspiring comedy writer
- Career profile of a costume designer

Arriving for the Monday table read of a new show is always exhilarating. It's a new script and a new story! It's often a different director and writer from the week before! A new guest cast is arriving. There are new **swing sets**[1] being erected and **dressed** (decorated) on stage. Each Monday is a new beginning.

A Monday table read doesn't always take place on Monday. Most sitcoms run on a five day schedule: table read on Monday, rehearse on Tuesday and Wednesday, camera block on Thursday, and film or tape on Friday night. There are any numbers of reasons to alter this schedule. The stand-up comedian, who is the star of the show, may have a gig on Friday night or be flying to the city where he or she is performing. Executive producer Michael Jacobs (*Charles In Charge*, *Boy Meets World*) doesn't work on his Sabbath, which begins on Friday night at sundown so his shows always shoot on Thursdays. A very common reason for altering the schedule though is to accommodate the studio who may have more than one show on the air. For example, Robert Greenblatt and David Janollari are hands-on executive producers. Until Greenblatt started running Showtime (and now NBC), they attended the taping or filming of every episode. When they had two shows in production, they couldn't be in two places at once on Friday night. Finally, since certain members of the crew such as camera operators only work on two days of the sitcom week, they try to work two shows

SITCOM RULE

Hold for laughs. *Laughs are an important part of Sitcom rhythm. Actors must wait to deliver their dialogue or business when the audience is laughing.*

---

1 These sets are new to this particular episode. On some very busy shows, the crew actually "swings" them into a space between two regular sets. See the set plan in the appendix.

each week of the season. They also can't be doing two shows on the same days. A good camera crew is worth the change in schedule. Therefore, the most typical schedules are Monday through Friday or Wednesday through Tuesday.

THE PRODUCTION MEETING

An hour before the cast arrives to read the new script, there is always a thirty to sixty minute production meeting. The production manager **(UPM**[2] or Producer may be his official title) sits at the same table with the **show runner**,[3]director, and all department heads to discuss the upcoming episode. Usually, the assistant director[4] **(AD)** runs this meeting. The AD will go through the script page by page discussing anything that is relevant. Each department head has previously read the script and marked it for their individual needs, highlighting the places where the dialogue or stage directions calls for anything pertaining to their department. They pose questions during the production meeting.

For example, on one episode of *Fresh Prince of Bel Air*, there was a gag where Will Smith burns down the kitchen. All the department heads had lots of questions for director Madeline Cripe. "Will we be doing this in front of the audience or pre-shooting?" "Will we need props and costumes for the next scene that look as if they have burned?" "Will we be burning the actual set or building a duplicate?" "Will a representative of the fire department have to be on set?" "Will the special effects person need to have a safety meeting with the cast and crew?" "How will we keep characters in the next room from knowing the kitchen has burned?" Cripe explains further:

> One of the biggest issues was one of reality. (Although reality is usually stretched to the limits in half-hour sitcoms.) The *Fresh Prince* set was designed so that the kitchen opened directly into the living room. After the kitchen burned there were scenes to be played out in the living room. These characters would look directly into the burned out kitchen and supposedly not see it. (Let's not even discuss what they would smell.) In discussing this issue with the producers and set designer the solution was a shutter panel and sliding shutter doors. This piece was installed for this one episode, never to be seen again in the Bank's house. We should all be so lucky to have a set department at our disposal.

---

2 Unit Production Manager, Directors Guild members since 1964.

3 This is the executive producer who actually runs the show. He is usually the head writer.

4 The director's assistants evolved differently in film and live television (which became videotaped television). Film shows have an assistant director, second assistant and sometimes a 2nd second AD. Taped shows have an associate director, stage manager and second stage manager. The new 24P digital camera systems (which is really tape) use both hierarchies, depending on the studio. The new DGA contract will change the title of technical coordinators to associate directors.

ARRIVING AND SEATING ASSIGNMENTS

As the production meeting is winding down, the cast arrives for the table read. For a guest cast member, locating the table read is not always easy. The table read is in a different location from where that actor auditioned. It is often in a different location from where that actor will be doing the show. Security differs from studio lot to studio lot. At some studios, the parking lot is a good ten-minute walk from the sound stage. *Allowing enough time to get on to a studio lot is mandatory.* It is much harder to get laughs at the table read if you've kept everyone waiting.

If the production meeting is taking place on stage, anyone arriving for the table read should keep their conversations to a minimum. If the reading will take place in a conference room, don't enter until the meeting is over. This may seem obvious, but many an actor has opened a conference room door, only to have 30 people turn around and glare at them for his interruption. This is usually avoided by posting a note on the entrance saying "Production Meeting In Progress." If you are early and there is no sign, but the door is closed, wait.

There is usually assigned seating for the cast at a table read. As a guest actor, you will want to ask the AD, "Where do I sit?" There are probably 60-75 chairs in the room. You will not be welcome in most of them. A network executive doesn't necessarily want you overhearing a conversation he is having about the strategy for sweeps week[5]. The writers may be discussing a future script. It's a great idea to greet and thank the casting director who was instrumental in getting you the job.

Actress Kate Zentall describes her feelings as a guest actor and gives some valuable advice:

Sitcoms are great for any actor because it's a job. You can only pray the writing is good and the all important show runner is hard working and writes true to the character you have developed--which is a combination of what the writer had in mind and hopefully was flexible enough to take your input. I have had joyous times and miserable times on sitcoms. Recently, four years into Curb Your Enthusiasm, albeit no script but a tight outline, although I am able to ad-lib--the star is a brilliant writer and producer and allows the best to come from you as an actor. Many other shows I have done there are oftentimes the writers versus the actors mentality and if there isn't a strong show runner with a vision and a lot of clout an actor gets notes from what seems like an army of people and that's before the director. It's more fun doing drama on TV as you usually deal more with your director and not a ton of writer-producers who for better or for worse have their two cents and it can at times get very frustrating and hard to focus on what you, the actor, and the talent behind the role really wants to do. There is so much luck involved in getting a good role and having producers and directors more into the scene than the power. If you get the former scenario, consider yourself blessed and enjoy every moment as one day you'll get directions that only visitors from outer space "might" understand.

Richard Lewis
Actor/Writer/Comedian and
Author of *The Other Great Depression*

5 This week is defined by the key ratings periods. Networks battle for their share of the television viewers. The shows airing during sweeps week may be stunt cast (casting big name star) in order to attract an even larger audience.

Few things are more exciting than anticipating your first day on the set, that initial "table read." Chances are you have had yet another script delivered (*delivered!* At like 11 PM! By a friendly human who has found your abode without needing directions!) -- and what a feeling to walk onto the same lot you trod only a few days before for the audition, when you were not quite so sure you belonged. But belong you now do. You even get to park with the big boys. If you have any theater experience, the thrill notches up a few points, because sitcoms are the closest thing to theater television has, and what a luxury to have a *whole week* of rehearsal time. So you find the soundstage, step into the darkness, and .... huh? Where are you exactly, what are all these flats and clusters of furniture, and where is everyone? Are you even in the right place?

You probably are. First thing is to find an AD (assistant director). Ask anyone, and you'll be pointed right. The 2nd AD is usually in charge of keeping track of you, and it is your responsibility to find him or her and check in, and not vice versa. Chances are you will be on time (you'd better be), but ahead of the rest of the cast (that's their prerogative, but not yours). You'll be pointed to the coffee and donuts. Make yourself comfortable, and wait. Cheerfully.

As the cast drifts in (and they may all be there already; it depends on the kind of set and show and how long it's been running; usually the more well established a show is, the looser the atmosphere}, you will probably be introduced, or they will do it themselves. And then there's the star. It's usually someone you feel you have known onscreen for years, but remember this: That star has not known *you*, and despite how much like a play this seems, it is not like theater, where you all instantly become one family. The hierarchy is very much there.

Stars carry the show, and despite all the red carpets and entourage and assistants, the pressure is on. Some of them are remote and "difficult"; others create a more relaxed ambiance and joke around. But make no mistake -- either way, they are on the line, and they are working hard. Even when it doesn't look that way. Years ago when I did a *Cheers* episode, Ted Danson was easy and funny and relaxed and instinctively seemed to understand how his mood set the tone for the rest of the set. It took me a few days to see how he used his charm and grace and humor to serve the needs of the show; it greased the wheels and created a wonderful counterpoint to the slightly nerve-wracking end-of-day rehearsals in front of the producers and writers. Years later, when I guested on *Becker*, his MO hadn't changed much. But he was working harder than ever -- though he still made it seem effortless. And the unwritten rule had also not changed: Respect the delicate web of privacy around him, and take your cue from him. I have watched some sitcom guests breezily, cluelessly violate this, sometimes never realizing their gaffe, and sooner or later it catches up to them. Do not interpret an easygoing facade as an invitation to conversation or engagement. Keep your distance, respect the star's space.

Series regulars usually take the same seats; the director and executive producers are seated nearby at the head of the table configuration. The AD will try to place you close to the other actors in your scenes. You'll get a strong sense of the show from the amount of banter that goes on before starting. On a successful show, people may be discussing the houses they're buying. On a friendly show, people may be discussing their weekend. On a show with declining ratings, there is little chatter except for cell phone calls to agents. The AD will signal when everyone[6] has arrived and the table read will begin.

The table read is the first time the writers will hear their whole script read aloud by the cast. Now they get to hear it from the mouths of the people playing the characters that they created. They want to hear what they wrote, exactly how they wrote it! This may be the only chance to hear their vision before everyone starts "improving it." (Read Chapter 3 SITCOM INSIDER Michael Kaplan.)

READING THE SCRIPT

Everyone is settled for the reading. The show runner or director will congratulate everyone for their hard work on the previous episode (unless it's the pilot), then introduce the guest actors, and finally the director starts the table read with the title and author of the episode. Then the performance begins!

Broadway and daytime drama veteran Marilyn McIntyre (*Gemini*, *Search for Tomorrow, One Life To Live*) describes the enormous pressure she felt at this moment on her first sitcom, *Who's The Boss*: "You look up and see the amount of people in the room and you have this realization: they're looking right now to see if what they've written is funny, and if you're funny doing it. The pressure is intense."

While the actors read their parts aloud, and the director reads the stage directions, the studio and network executives are making notes on content and structure. The writers are noting when a joke has **landed** or scored (gotten a laugh). This may be simply a check mark in their script. These laughs are important! The sitcom rule, which begins this chapter, states **HOLD FOR LAUGHS**. If an actor tries to speak his next line while the people at the table read are laughing, no one will hear the information in that next line. Holding for laughs may seem unnatural but it is essential to sitcom rhythm. This rule applies not only at the table read, but the entire week.

6 Network executives, studio executives, the entire writing staff, non-writing executive producers, the cast and guest cast, the casting director, the parents of child cast members, the teacher, the department heads, the script supervisor and the director's team all attend the table read. There might also be people that you won't see again until shooting like publicists, executive assistants and the postproduction teams.

Laughs are noted because everyone wants to know what works and what doesn't. In addition, the script supervisor is timing the actual reading and then adding a reasonable amount of time for staging and full audience laughter. This timing will guide the extent and length of the re-write. Script Supervisor Ellen Deutsch (*The Golden Girls, Malcolm & Eddie, Regular Joe*) says she reads the script at least twice before the table read and times it for the anticipated action and business.

The crowd attending the table read might be the toughest audience the cast has all week. They must do their best to sell this story to everyone. Nothing will infuriate a writing staff more than a half-hearted performance at a table read. A guest cast member is expected to duplicate what he did "in the room" at the audition. This performance got him the job! This is sometimes a challenge, especially if the part has been substantially re-written.

This is only the first of many challenges for the guest star. Regan Burns (Star of Spike TV's *Oblivious*) whose sitcom guest appearances include: *Curb Your Enthusiasm, Mind of the Married Man, The Ellen Show, 3rd Rock From the Sun, Titus, Suddenly Susan,* and *The Drew Carey Show* shares: Guest starring in a sitcom can best be described as asking for a girl's phone number, calling her up, asking her on a date, going out for a romantic dinner, finding out you have a lot in common, continuing to seeing her, falling in love, deciding to move in together, empty out a drawer for her, introduce her to the folks, planning the wedding and then finding out she left you for your best friend. Oh, and this all happens in five days!"

It's also important that the guest actor look the same as when he or she auditioned. Changing a hairstyle or dressing weirdly doesn't make the best first impression.... and this is the first time many people on the show have seen you. While we're on the subject of changing your appearance... *DON'T*! Even if you're a series regular. On one sitcom, a very hip, youthful cast arrived at the table read, after a week off, with three new tattoos, two body piercings and one change in hairstyle and color. The cast was read the riot act after the reading. On another sitcom, a hairstyle change (and unwillingness to change it back) caused a permanent rift between a star/executive producer and his studio head...also an executive producer. Remember that actors are hired not only for their talent but also on their appearance. You are under contract to play a character. Don't screw up and do anything that changes that without first consulting the show runner. That includes extreme sports on weekends. The writers don't want to accommodate a full leg cast unless they have to.[7]

Not radically changing appearance has to do with how the shows air. They are not necessarily programmed in the same order they are made. If the show is lucky enough to re-air for years to come, it is disconcerting to the audience if the characters look different every time they turn on the TV.

7 Stage and TV actor Jon Cypher broke his leg in a theater accident during *Major Dad*. Producer Rick Hawkins wrote it into the script. Cypher made his performance in a wheelchair and with a cane even funnier.

NETWORK AND STUDIO NOTES

Body casts, hair-dos, and tattoos aside, the cast is usually dismissed from the room after the reading. The show runner, his second in charge, and director (with the script supervisor to write his notes) stay for notes with the network and studio executives. This can be very tense. The writing staff has created what they think is a worthy product. The "**suits**"[8] may disagree. Now the tearing apart begins. When asked for comments about notes after a table read, one writer told us "I'm not going to say much about network and studio executives, because a few of them can read, and I hope to continue working."

The tone of this comment is common in sitcoms. Sitcom writers are some of the smartest, wittiest, most creative individuals you'll ever meet. They are well read, well educated, and socially and politically astute. They are proprietary about their responsibility for the literary content of a show. They consider themselves artists. Network and studio executives often possess these same qualities but ultimately they are the money-people, and report to a corporate entity. Many writers feel the "suits," who are asking for changes to "their" script, don't know dick[9] about writing!

Another writer warns, "Never make an enemy of a network or studio executive. Network and studio executives never die or lose their jobs. They just keep trading places. So that enemy you make at NBC today will be your enemy at FOX tomorrow. They also never forget or forgive..."

It's not all bad. *Home Improvement's* Carmen Finestra explains it from his point of view, "Notes are given by the network and studio, often in collaboration with the producers and writers, i.e. if the network and studio have a problem, generally a compromise or solution gets worked out."

A show sometimes works well with complete cooperation and artistic vision from its network and studio. After the table read for *All About The Andersons*, a pilot developed by Warner Brothers Television Network, there were no notes. Comedian Anthony Anderson along with his co-creators Marco Pennette and Adam Glass walked away from the table read with complete confidence that they had written a pilot that the WB would support.[10] Stories are rarely told about great situations like this because it's easier to be funny relating a story that has a good guy and bad guy. In most of the stories you hear on stage, the suits are the bad guys. When the writers are considered the bad guys, they just stop getting hired and start telling funny stories![11]

---

8 Suits are so named because of the odd uniform they wear.

9 Dick is a technical term with a *k* sound.

10 The WB nurtured and developed this script from the beginning.

11 Although we are not sure he has ever been out of work between the late 1940s to the late 1990s, Leonard Stern of *Get Smart* and *The Honeymooners* fame has assembled a book of notes from studio and network executives, called "A Martian Wouldn't Say That!"

While notes are being given, the rest of the writing staff goes to the writer's room and begins the rewrites. Some changes are obvious from the reading so they waste no time getting started even though the show runner will have more changes from the network and studio meeting. Writer Nancylee Myatt describes the process in the writer's room: "A bunch of adults with arrested development will sit around a table and pitch jokes. Whichever joke gets the biggest laugh in the room will land in the script. Unfortunately, the best joke is usually the filthiest joke and cannot be said on network television. Thank God for cable."

Guest actors are usually shown to their dressing rooms during notes. Wardrobe fittings may begin during this break. The **load-in** of this week's set continues on stage.

After the meeting, Carmen Finestra tells us, "Producers and writers go upstairs and begin the rewrite. Some producers and writers may pair off and divide scenes, while others concentrate on coming up with new stories for future episodes. Work on existing drafts for future episodes may also occur at this time."

REHEARSAL

On stage, rehearsal begins...or sometimes the actors are sent home. Finestra says that this is rare unless the entire script is being changed.

Whether to rehearse or not is the choice of the director but it is dictated by many factors. Reasons for going home include: giving the stage to the crew to complete the new set's load-in, everyone is exhausted because they shot an episode until late last night, this show (usually in its third of fourth season) normally and efficiently rehearses only four days a week, or the star of the show has a 2 o'clock tee time.

The more years that a show is on the air, the more comfortable the regular actors are with playing their characters. The writers have been writing their dialogue to fit closer to the actors' own personalities. These shortened weeks makes it harder for a guest actor to discover the finer aspects of his character.

THE SETS

If rehearsal begins on this day, actors may be working on a half built or improvised swing set. If you spot anything that appears unsafe on the set, report it to the AD immediately! The sets that are used every week are called the **standing sets** and remain in place for the whole season. Although inviting,[12] sets are never to be used as a lounging or eating area. Often, a "Hot Set" sign will remind you.

UTILIZING THE REHEARSAL

Every show rehearses differently. Monday may be the time that the director allows the actors to explore the material more on their own. If this is the case, it is the perfect opportunity for the guest actor to try anything different from his

12 The sets are supposed to appear inviting to the TV audience. If they do, the set decorator has done his job well.

audition choices. Actor Regan Burns suggests being a "guest star can be one of two things. Either your chance to feed stale straight lines to the star of the show who gets all the zingers; or, an opportunity to seize the moment and make the role memorable as your own." He continues, "The process from the initial audition to the martini[13] shot on Friday night is grueling, boring, exciting, frantic, stress inducing and well worth every second of it. Granted, as long as you didn't get written out in one of the 25 rewrites since the script was first delivered to your door."

Stage actors are always surprised at how quickly scenes are rehearsed on sitcoms. This week, the director has about twenty or so hours to rehearse what is essentially a short two-act play. He then has about the same amount of time to film it.

> *Be proud of even the smallest role on a sitcom. Many would kill to be in your shoes saying, "I have a package for Chandler."*
>
> Regan Burns, (Host of *Oblivious*)

Guest actors, explore your relationship with the cast and director. Try to fit in! If this show is easy going, flow with it. If the cast seems very private, don't invade their space. Michael Lembeck, Emmy-award winning *Friends* director, calls this "taking the temperature of the room." Remember that these people are a family (or at the very least, a working unit) and you are a guest. Remember your manners. On most shows, the series regulars will come up, introduce themselves, and welcome you to their show. Sometimes it is less pleasant. Just remember you don't always have the inside scoop, and the cast may seem aloof because they don't want to air "family" laundry. Or maybe, as Kate Zentall says,

> "They are simply preoccupied, with (a) the size of their part that week, (b) the size of their paycheck after recent contract renegotiations, (c) the size of the audience share that week, (d) the size of their new house, (e) the size of their butt. The point is, you never, ever know, so do not take it personally, or let it affect your performance in any way. And speaking of performances. Remember the scene you nailed and the great laughs you got at the audition? Be prepared for those lovely lines to morph and even be whittled away by shooting day. The script changes daily. You might have been hired because you were funny, but you may notice that you are increasingly becoming a straight man for the regulars. That's normal. You may even start to feel like an exchangeable Lego part. That's also normal. And if you can accept that and still have fun and take pride in your work, you just may have a career in sitcoms."

WAYS OF WORKING

Actors have many different ways of working. As perennial movie butler Arthur Treacher described his acting theory: Say the words, take the money, go home.

13 Completing the last shot on any production signals that IT'S TIME TO PARTY!!!

Actors who do this earn instant respect because they know what they're doing, don't demand a lot of attention for doing it, and have a life to go to when they've done it. Katherine Helmond is also from the simplicity school. She told us, "I don't have high-flown ideas about acting. I just work by doing."

Other actors have complex ways of working. Some need to do a scene repeatedly, trying to find the core. Others are looking for every opportunity to add a new joke or modify an existing one. Some actors need repetition to help then learn their words or to work the words and movement together. Others don't want to move much at all. Gerald McRaney (*Simon & Simon, Major Dad*) minimized the number of props he had to handle. At home on stage, screen, and TV, he always considered rehearsal time a private time for actors and their director to rehearse. Very much an artist, he would seek the truth of a character's core and the integrity of a script's story within a safe environment where actors were free to try things (that means often failing) in an effort to make the show the best it could be. When the words "closed set" appear on a sound stage door, he expected them to be respected.

Matt LeBlanc of (*Friends, Joey, Episodes*) is quoted in *Daily Variety* saying, "I'm more confident, which is one of your biggest assets as an actor especially in comedy. In comedy, you have to be unafraid to hang from the tree branch naked in the high wind and you have to be absolutely unafraid to look ridiculous and silly."

Some actors have to work beat-by-beat so their character logically and organically progresses from moment to moment. Some are selfish; some are generous. Some are easy. Some are difficult.

The late motion picture and TV actor Richard Mulligan (*Little Big Man, Soap, Empty Nest*) was questioning every direction and note that the director was giving him during one rehearsal. He stopped in the middle of second-guessing the director and said to him, "I love what you are doing, but I need to do this." Challenges and struggle helped Mulligan feel that the scene was fully explored for its potential.

We asked Robin Bartlett, (*Mad About You, Powers That Be*) about the challenges of working on a sitcom. She remarked, "Don't ask! Well, okay. I was in a sitcom with an unnamed movie star. It was a terribly pressured situation; the difficulties were myriad. Staying focused on my own work was the only solution. Otherwise I would have been pulled into the drama and very unfunny world of the woman I was working with."

CELEBRITY/COMEDIAN-DRIVEN VERSUS ACTOR/ENSEMBLE-DRIVEN

Shows are divided into two genres: an actor driven show or a comedian driven show. The first builds on the established talents of that person, for example, comdians such as Jerry Seinfeld, Tim Allen, Roseanne Barr had established audiences and uniquely identifiable material from their stand-up careers. Their hit sitcoms were designed to appeal to these target audiences and expand from there. Hip Hop artist Eve and Chef Emeril Lagasse were given opportunities to move into a sitcom after their success in their individual fields. The expectation is always that they will bring a built-in audience.

An actor/ensemble driven show starts with a premise before a star. Although a well-known comedian, actor, or celebrity may very well be cast in the leading role, this genre always begins with a writer premise. *All in the Family* is a perfect example of a character driven show. Plotlines came out of the characters that the writers created and the themes that the show wanted to explore. Howard Gewirtz talked in the *Miami New Times* about finding his characters for *Oliver Beene*. "I really wrote a lots of it based on people in my world – my mother and father provided inspiration, as did my brother. Our actual family dynamic was significantly different, but it was a starting-off point, and the material breathed for me." Tim Goodman of the *San Francisco Chronicle* speaks of another successful comedy. "The vision that made *Sex in the City* so attractive to viewers is back. The great majority of these stories are believable, the characters fleshed out in a way rarely seen (especially in a comedy) and the writing crisp and fun as ever." We whole heartily agree with Goodman but we don't actually consider *Sex in the City* a sitcom format.

Originally, the position of the script supervisor was that of a secretary, taking director's notes to give the editor. It soon became a position with a lot more responsibility. I can't tell you the amount of times that I have had fellow crew members come to me and say, "You have the toughest job on the show." I believe because the position is held primarily by women, the industry still does not value it. I have always said my job is like that of the anesthesiologist, there are times that it looks like you are not doing anything but when all hell breaks loose, you better know how to fix it.

Marcia Gould, Script Supervisor *Wings* and countless others

In our opinion, the best sitcom writing combines the best aspects of both joke based and character based genre. Here is one of our favorite character driven scenes from the pilot *Style and Substance* by Emmy award winning writer Peter Tolan. Jean Smart played Chelsea, Nancy McKeon played Jane, and Heath Hyche played Terry.

Sitcom Exercise

Read this scene and find the jokes! Identify things that make you laugh. You already know how to identify words with K sounds and patterns of three. In addition, look for character driven jokes. Understand that Terry is a somewhat inefficient male secretary, Jane an insecure but ambitious office manager, and Chelsea an empire-building superwoman, founder of a Martha Stewart-like company. We have identified the first two jokes for you with a ✓✓✓ where we think the audience is expected to laugh. You can find all the jokes identified in the appendix. Don't cheat!

```
                STYLE AND SUBSTANCE - PILOT
                           (B)
INT. CHELSEAS'S OFFICE - LATER THAT MORNING (D-1)
```

(CHELSEA, JANE, TERRY)
CHELSEA IS LISTENING TO TERRY, HER YOUNG MALE SECRETARY, RUN DOWN A LIST OF PHONE MESSAGES. CHELSEA MAKES HIM NERVOUS.

TERRY
Francine Messinger called and said thanks for the padlocks.

CHELSEA
That's Nancy Kissinger, and she's thanking me for the gravlax. ✓✓✓

TERRY
Right. Franklin Carter called...

CHELSEA
Frank Langella. ✓✓✓

TERRY
Okay. Needs advice on planting an urban garden.

CHELSEA
An herb garden. Breathe, Terry.

TERRY
Okay. Ken Klein called...

CHELSEA
Kevin Kline?

TERRY
No.

CHELSEA
Calvin Klein?

TERRY SHAKES HIS HEAD NO.

CHELSEA (CONT'D)
Kelly Klein. Carol Kane. Carol King. (A BEAT) Beverly Sills?

TERRY
Yes. You're good at this.

CHELSEA
Thank you. Terry. Much better today.

TERRY
I thought so too.

TERRY EXITS AS JANE ENTERS.

JANE
Hi, Chelsea. Listen I don't want to be a bugaboo, but have you had a chance to sign that budget agreement yet?

CHELSEA STARES AT HER FOR A SECOND.

JANE (CONT'D)
Jane Sokol. From Ferber Communications?

CHELSEA
Jane, please. I know who you are. What a darling suit.

JANE
Thanks. I really need you to sign that agreement. Being put in charge of your office is the first major assignment the company's given me, so I want to keep Mr. Ferber happy happy. So sign sign.

CHELSEA
I'll look at it right away.

JANE NOTICES A PURSE ON THE DESK.

JANE
We have the same purse.

CHELSEA
Really?

JANE
Yes. It's exactly the same purse.

CHELSEA
How about that?

JANE

I mean...it's the same purse. (A BEAT) That's my purse, isn't it?

CHELSEA

Why don't we talk about something else? (PICKING SOMETHING UP FROM THE DESK) Oh, look. A recipe for flan.

JANE

Chelsea. You have my purse.

CHELSEA

Don't get upset, Jane. You're new here, I want to get to know you. You know the old saying. The fastest way to get to know another woman is to look in her purse.

JANE

Here's another old saying. I want my purse back.

CHELSEA

You have something to hide?

JANE

No.

CHELSEA

I'd let you look in my purse.

JANE

I doubt that.

CHELSEA

I would.

JANE

Right.

CHELSEA

Go ahead.

JANE

Where is it?

CHELSEA
At home. But if it were here, I'd let you look at it.

JANE
Chelsea, this is a major invasion of my privacy.

CHELSEA HOLDS OUT A SMALL JAR OF JAM TO JANE.

CHELSEA
Jane, I'd like you to have this. It's a jar of my lovely homemade preserves. I hope you like rhubarb.

JANE
Do you honestly believe that giving me a little jar of jam will make this okay?

CHELSEA
I have a bigger jar.

JANE
That is so not my point.

CHELSEA
Oh, I get it. There's a jam hater in our midst, is there?

JANE
Oh, please. I love jam.

CHELSEA
I wish I could believe that.

JANE
I am crazy about jam.

CHELSEA
You do not seem jam friendly to me.

JANE
(AFTER A BEAT) Okay. Okay. You want to look in my purse? You go right ahead. This is unbelievable.

CHELSEA
Oh, pooh. You really know how to take the fun out of things.

CHELSEA STARTS DIGGING AROUND IN THE PURSE.

CHELSEA (CONT'D)
Somebody clips coupons.

CHELSEA TAKES A COUPON OUT AND GRIMACES.

CHELSEA (CONT'D)
Macaroni and cheese? From a box?

JANE
It's filling and inexpensive.

CHELSEA
I can't argue, Jane, but if those were the only criteria for nourishment, there'd be a lot more recipes for dirt. (DIGGING) Lip gloss, rouge...I see tweezers. Eyebrows on the march, Jane?

JANE
Are we done yet?

CHELSEA
Oh, Jane. Jane, Jane, Jane...

CHELSEA REMOVES A PACKAGE OF HOSTESS SNOBALLS FROM THE PURSE.

CHELSEA (CONT'D)
Hostess Snoballs? Why, Jane?

JANE
I like them. They're fun.

CHELSEA
Have you heard the expression, "You are what you eat?" Add bangs and a business suit, this is you, Jane.

JANE
I'll be going now...

JANE GATHERS UP HER PURSE AND STARTS TO EXIT. CHELSEA HOLDS UP A SMALL PHOTOGRAPH.

CHELSEA
Who's this?

JANE
Give me that, please.

CHELSEA
Brother?

JANE
None of your business.

CHELSEA
Friends?

JANE
I'm not telling you.

CHELSEA
Fiance?

JANE
(A BEAT) No.

CHELSEA
You paused.

JANE
Darn!

CHELSEA
What's his name?

JANE
Why would I tell you?

CHELSEA
Because I really think you want to talk about it. Mint?

CHELSEA HOLDS OUT A SMALL CONTAINER OF MINTS.

JANE
(GRABBING THEM) Those are mine. Chelsea, I appreciate your trying to be friendly, but I'm not going to discuss my personal life with you.

CHELSEA
He looks like a Paul.

JANE
I'm here to do a job. It's a job I take seriously.

CHELSEA
Doug? Dennis?

JANE
There's a line between business and personal...

CHELSEA
Tony? Mike?

JANE
I'm a professional, and I'm going to maintain a professional...

CHELSEA
Chuck?

JANE
(END OF ROPE) Steve! Steve! The man's name is Steve! Are you happy now?

CHELSEA
I knew you wanted to talk about it.

JANE
I don't! This is the office. The office is where we talk about office things. My ex-fiance is not an office thing.

CHELSEA
Your ex-fiance?

JANE
Darn!

CHELSEA
What happened? He hit you, didn't he? (TO THE PHOTO) You bastard.

JANE

This is really inappropriate, How would you like it if I just waltzed in here and started asking you about your divorce? Which by the way, I would never do. I know it must've been difficult and I hope you're okay.

CHELSEA

(THROWN) I'm sorry?

JANE

I said I hope you're okay.

CHELSEA

(COVERING) Well, yes...of course I am. My husband wasn't giving me what I needed, he was a lox, I kicked him out. Let's get back to you.

JANE

Look, I need that agreement signed and on my desk by the end of the day.

CHELSEA

I'll look it over right now. Jane, if I upset you, I'm sorry. It was wrong to take your purse.

JANE

Okay. I'll be in my office if you need me.

JANE EXITS AND CLOSES THE DOOR BEHIND HER. CHELSEA TAKES OUT THE SNOBALLS AND TAKES A BITE OF ONE. JANE ENTERS.

JANE (CONT'D)

Where are they?

A BEAT, THEN CHELSEA MAKES A MUFFLED RESPONSE.

CHELSEA

Where's what?

CHELSEA HANDS THE REMAINING SNOBALL BACK TO JANE.

FADE OUT.[14]

14 Used by permission of Touchstone Television. All Rights Reserved.

THE ACTOR/DIRECTOR RELATIONSHIP

Monday's are the first chance for the actor to work with the director. Some directors are more effusive than others. An actor should assume that the director is pleased with what an actor is doing unless the director asks the actor to change it. A needy actor who constantly needs an "Atta boy" is a pain in the neck. The director has too many things to think about without being the personal cheering section to one individual. Conversely, directors can be the best audience in the world. They are an actor's best allies on the set. They have heard all of the notes from the 'suits' and the show runner and can help the actor satisfy everyone's needs. No one appreciates talent, craft, and dedication from an actor more than a director. It only makes him look good!

Director Steve Zuckerman (*Everybody Loves Raymond,* series director *Empty Nest,*) gained his first notoriety on and off-Broadway. He has been described as an "actors' director." He explains this in his own words:

> Being called an "Actor's Director" means that I came from the theater and I can read. I can read a script and know about the structure and about the writing. I'm good at knowing what the moments are and knowing what the writer's intent was. No matter how good an actor is, they really approach it from: "Bullshit...bullshit...bullshit...my line!" They also really don't read the stage directions. They might not be getting the meaning of something and I can point our what the intent of a line is. They really appreciate that."

Joe Regalbuto (actor-director *Murphy Brown* director *The George Lopez Show*) regularly works on both sides of the relationship. That has brought him a unique perspective,

> During the very first episode of *Murphy Brown* that I directed, I was so concerned with technical considerations that I forgot that I was also in it as an actor. I finally realized that in the scene we were staging, I was the weakest link.
>
> As an actor in the scene, I was thinking only about what my character wants. As a director, I had to also look at the 2nd, 3rd and 4th characters' needs. I had to know the perspective of everything in the scene. The experience of directing has enhanced my acting. I now see how my part fits into the whole. It has opened me up as an actor. It has settled me into my place.
>
> Actors come in arms out and eyes wide open hoping that the director will see what they are trying to do and will help. Actors can usually find out in thirty seconds if that help is coming.

THE REHEARSAL TEAM

The group attending the actual scene rehearsal is small. It is a close team and generally feels like a family. This group includes the actors, director, AD or stage manager, script supervisor, on set prop person and on set decorator. That's it. Others come in and out all day, but this is the core team. And they trust each other. On a show where a director is doing the whole season (directing all the episodes), that director will often request his team. These are the individuals whom that director trusts with seeing the rehearsal process unfold. Script supervisor Kit Wilkinson describes this from her point of view:

> As a script supervisor you need to have the ability to focus on multiple details, understand the actors and their processes so as to help not hinder, and have a sixth sense about when to contribute and when to keep quiet. The rehearsal week early on is a small group--actors, director, AD, and you. It's intimate. But there is no training that really aids with this sensitivity.

STAGE ETIQUETTE AND WRAP

If the rehearsal day is long enough there may be lunch break on Monday. All cast and crew should report to the set (not dressing rooms) to see what's up first after lunch because the anticipated scenes may or may not be rehearsed in order. Never assume that you know what is being scheduled next, because it will change! Reporting to the set every morning and after every meal break is general courtesy. After telling the AD that you have arrived, actors that are not needed will be dismissed to their dressing rooms. That is where the AD expects to find you unless you tell him otherwise. Rounding up actors for the next scene is an easy task *IF* the AD knows where to find you. In some cases it is simply an announcement over the PA system into the dressing rooms. Others choose to call actors individually on their phones or knock at their dressing room doors. However summoned, an actor should drop what they are doing and come immediately to the set.

After rehearsal, actors may have wardrobe fittings. Work will continue on sets. The prop master is arranging the rental or purchase of key props. The AD's continue their paperwork and planning for the week. Writing is still going on in the writers' room. Carmen Finestra tells us, "Rewrite usually lasts until 9 PM or 10 o'clock (or into the wee hours if there are real problems, occasionally that happens. Be sure to sleep well over the weekend.)"

At the end of each workday, actors sign out and crew fills in their time cards. Be sure to know the **call time** for the next day. That's when you are expected to be on stage ready to work. Don't assume that because your day is done, everyone else's is as well. It takes many hands to make a sitcom. All departments are integral to the final product. A simple acknowledgement from an actor leaving for the day to a crew member who is still working is always appreciated. It says that the actor knows that although he is in front of the camera, there is huge supportive network behind him. Actor/comedian D.L. Hughley was always loved by his crew because when he arrived he would always greet everyone often with a kiss on the cheek or handshake. When he left the stage for the day, he'd thank everybody for their efforts.

Sitcom Insider

ADVICE TO THE ASPIRING COMEDY WRITER

Three things are important:

1. **Read.** *And not just Variety. Read good books---classics with expressive language and nuanced characters, as well as modern fiction that features humorous description and dialogue. Richard Russo is a good choice. If you want to be a good writer, you have to know what good writing is. Don't sit at home only watching television. Much of it is not good. If George Santayana were alive today, I'm sure he'd say, " Those who watch bad television are condemned to repeat it."*

2. **Live.** *Before you can write, you have to live. The best writing comes from life experience. Plato said, "The unexamined life is not worth living." A psychiatrist amended that saying, "The unlived life is not worth examining." I agree. Go to concerts, theater, lectures, play with your children, hug your mate, listen to them and engage them fully. If you don't presently have someone in your life, try to enjoy meeting someone. Not just at singles bars or clubs. Do volunteer work, with causes you care about. Invite friends to your place, not to watch videos, but to talk and exchange views. Don't get bogged down in discussing "the business." It just cuts you off from the real world -- the world where people work, struggle, cry, laugh, love and hate. If you just want to be a hip cynic, who disdains life, your writing will reflect it. It'll be clever, but not memorable. People who know how to write character and emotion are the ones who keep collecting the residual checks.*

3. **Write.** *Then write some more. Writers become better writers by writing. It's no secret. You have to sit down at a desk and pound it out. Gene Fowler said, "Writing is easy. You just sit in front of a blank page until the blood pours out of your forehead." Keeping a journal might help. It's a good way to start the day. Write everything you saw and heard. Build up your writing muscle any way you can.*

Carmen Finestra, writer co-creator *Home Improvement*

Sitcom Vocabulary Quick Review

Read these sentences. If the director gave you these notes, would you instantly know what he meant? If not, go back and review the explanation in this chapter.

Take it up with the **AD**.

What's your **call time** *tomorrow?*

Is the kitchen **dressed**?

The joke didn't **land**.

We won't pre-tape anything in the **standing sets**.

Have the **suits** *arrived?*

Is the **swing set** *secure?*

Did the **UPM** *approve that?*

Who was the **show runner** *on that series?*

We'll rehearse as soon as the **load in** *is finished.*

Script Supervisor's Monday Tasks

- ✓ *Come to table reading having prepped the script.*
- ✓ *Time the reading.*
- ✓ *Report timing to executive producer and director.*
- ✓ *Go to note session, take any notes for director if needed.*
- ✓ *Rehearse.*
- ✓ *Notate blocking in your script.*
- ✓ *Time each scene.*
- ✓ *Act as liaison between stage and office.*

Sitcom Career Profile

EMILY DRAPER
COSTUME DESIGNER

We met Emily when she was a costume assistant on a delightful sitcom called DOMESTIC LIFE created by Howard Gewirtz and Ian Praiser. It was one of those gems that never made it past 10 episodes despite its excellence. Emily reunites with Mr. Gerwirtz on OLIVER BEENE. She now heads the costume department and brings the 60's to life in her historically accurate, yet highly creative designs!

What shows have you worked on?

Oliver Beene, Grace Under Fire, Normal Ohio, Oh Baby, many others, many pilots...assistant on *General Hospital.*

What are your responsibilities?

I am responsible for reading and breaking down the script, renting, fittings, hiring and overseeing costumers, and the budget. I also have to please the actors, producers and network!

Did you have specific training in this field?

No. I got my first experience in Equity Waiver theater, AFI Films and friends' short films-any way possible. There was never any pay on these jobs!

How did you get your first job?

My first job was as a costumer on a pilot called *MR SUCCESS.* I was hired by a friend: Howard Gewirtz. He had to foist me onto them - but they ended up liking me.

What do you like best about your job?

Shopping, working with great costumes, working with producers and actors. I love clothes! I love that it all comes together quickly! I love the whole process!

COSTUME DESIGNER INFO
Union: IATSE Local 892
Typical Weekly Salary: $2400-$3000
Hours Per Week: 40-50

Chapter 3 TUESDAY...REHEARSAL/PRODUCERS' RUN-THRU DAY

In this chapter:

- How to collate a script
- Identifying the setup and punchline
- Advice from a sitcom writer
- What to do while holding for a laugh
- Dos and Don'ts of staging
- How to stay focused as a character
- Surviving a run-thru
- Career profile of a script supervisor

Why did they change it?" is the most frequently asked (or thought) question on Tuesday. The table read went well. The jokes got laughs. Now, lines are gone when you get the first rewrite. There may be an entirely new script, a new first act, or at least several new jokes.

The reason for the changes can mostly be found from the discussions on Monday's meeting after the table reading.[1] Considerations about character development, plot clarity, and general direction for the series caused the writers to spend many hours working on the pages that you now have. Notes were given by network, studio, and countless other people yesterday. They all have their own needs and desires. Writers must address all these notes. At the same time, they want to rewrite for their own satisfaction of playing with the story and making it all fit together.

So, "Why *did* they change it?" Sometimes your line is gone, simply because the script was too long. Look at the page count; is it shorter? Sitcoms are programmed to the second. The writer is aware of how much of a thirty minute time slot is set aside for the opening credits, the show, ending credits, and commercials. The length of the material that is being rehearsed is probably only twenty minutes or less. Each sitcom has this time adjusted for its specific network, time slot, credit length

> **SITCOM RULE**
> ***Don't move on the joke.*** *The joke is most important. Moving on the joke distracts the audience from listening to the punch line. Moving after the joke gives a place for the audience to laugh without missing dialogue.*

---

1 Nearly everyone involved with the show was asked to leave the room for those notes. The director was there and can explain some of the more perplexing changes.

and transitions. Most shows try to end up about one and one half to two minutes "long" at the end of the week. This gives the director and producer the ability to tighten up the pace in editing and remove the occasional lame joke or two. *Seinfeld* was notorious for coming in as much as seven minutes long. This gave creator Larry David the freedom to take out quite a bit of material and keep only the crème de la crème[2].

The script supervisor timed yesterday's reading. To that timing was added about two minutes for the "laugh spread." This is the anticipated extra time expected from a full audience's laughter. An additional two minutes is added because actual staging and camera transitions usually take longer than just the director reading stage directions.

There are a myriad other reasons for script changes. After yesterday's rehearsal, the director may have made requests based on difficulties in staging. For example, on *Frasier*, Daphne might have been given the stage direction: "ENTERS AND CROSSES TO KITCHEN." As happens occasionally, an actress might be pregnant and her character is not. In this case the director could suggest she, "ENTERS HOLDING DRY CLEANING AND CROSSES TO KITCHEN." The prop should hide her bulging belly. He may have found something during rehearsal that will tell the story better or in a more visual way than what the writer described on paper. The director may have told the writers that a scene just wasn't working or asked for help in a certain area to better serve an actor.

The script may be shorter because it was too expensive! Revised cost estimates of the sets, props, wardrobe, and special physical effects were discussed in yesterday's production meeting.[3] Line producers who keep track of the physical costs of the production make requests to cut entire scenes! Sometimes there isn't money in the budget to build another set. At times, there isn't enough room to squeeze another set on the soundstage. Marsha Scarbrough, in that *Written by* article, writes about the "No Fat" episode of *Everybody Loves Raymond*: "Because there is not enough room on the stage for both the pharmacy set and the bedroom set, the bedroom scene is eliminated." The line producer's responsibility is to bring the show in on budget. Everyone can love a scene but sometimes it's just gotta go! A *Seinfeld* script described a set once then explained that the scene took place in the dark. We have to wonder if this was written to alleviate the cost or space concerns over another set.

Finally, the reason for script changes could be that the star didn't want other cast members to be funnier than he is. Although neither of us worked on the series *Cybill*, it was rumored that there was friction over the script almost every

2 One of our favorite activities is watching that great sitcom and hoping to catch George go into Jerry's bathroom and then see him again on the couch without coming out. Excising jokes could leave a mismatch or two.

3 Maybe budgets haven't been turned in yet, but the line producer wishes he had them!

week of the production between the star Cybill Shepherd and the **second banana**[4] Christine Baranski. Once something like this is anticipated, the writers spend much of their rewrite trying to avoid this situation.

A typical Tuesday call time is 10 a.m., with the producer's run-thru scheduled in the mid to late afternoon. That is approximately four or five hours of actual rehearsal, an hour for lunch, and time for the run-thru and notes. Because the majority of in-depth rehearsal takes place today, use that time wisely.

> *During the day, prior to the run-through, writers are working on future scripts. Producers are also busy editing prior episodes, casting, meeting with potential writers for episode assignments. This happens every day of the week.*
>
> Carmen Finestra , Co-creator and Executive Producer, *Home Improvement*

THE NEW SCRIPT

The writers–there can be as many as fifteen of them–work around a conference table with an assistant making each change on a computer. Many writers are looking at the large computer monitor visible to everyone. This scene somewhat resembles a hospital's late night emergency room with its motley characters. However, this room feels like *American Idol* with writers competing with each other, performing new jokes that will replace the old. The head writer has the final word.

We know about a couple of exceptions to this collaborative writers-room system. We have been told that Susan Harris almost exclusively wrote the majority of *Soap* episodes. Her scripts had a wonderful emotional base with a wacky style. She had a couple of other writers working along with her during the four-year run of that show. It was evident because of her distinctive flair which scenes she completely wrote and which were written by other fine writers such as Stu Silver who had his own distinct funny voice.

The very talented Aaron Sorkin also worked as a lone gunman...on two shows at the same time! You can't argue with the results: *The West Wing* and the sitcom *Sports Night*. Show runner Tim Doyle had just finished working on the **wrapped**[5] *Ellen*. Doyle and most of his writers were available to aid sitcom newcomer Sorkin, the feature film writer and playwright. Doyle told us that Sorkin essentially didn't need much help. If you missed Sorkin's comedic voice on *Sports Night*, rent *The American President* or *The Newsroom* for a real treat.

Sometimes the new script or new pages are delivered to the actor's door. It is

4 Second Banana is a term from Burlesque. Today, Burlesque brings to mind strippers. Before television, it was a major form of comedy for the masses. Phil Silvers starred in Broadway's homage to Burlesque *First Banana*. He was a natural to move over to star as Sgt. Bilko in the hugely popular early sitcom *You'll Never Get Rich*. Baranski was the second character of importance hence the name second banana. Despite Baranski's distinguished Broadway career and comedic chops, it was Shepherd who brought "name value" to the show because she was a more recognizable movie star at that time.

5 Wrapped means completing the days work, and episode, or in this case the entire series.

usually late in the evening when the writers finish this first rewrite. A production assistant stays with the writers to make the deliveries. If it is too late, the delivery might be made by another assistant who comes in at dawn for that purpose. Actors should not leave their houses or apartments until they have checked around their front door or gate for a package with these pages.

If there are fewer changes, the scripts will be left on the stage. Department heads will often get the script delivered to their office or know the designated spot on stage where new scripts are usually left. When in doubt, ask the script supervisor who can always track down the new script. Always assume that there are pages to incorporate. If you need extra time to assimilate new dialogue or prep before rehearsal, consider getting to the set before your actual call time. All departments need to read their new script....all of it!

COLLATING

To begin, check all scenes for changes that affect you. READ THE WHOLE SCRIPT! Sometimes you've been added or deleted from scenes. To help you find changes easily, there are usually asterisks (in the margin) at the place on the page where there is a new line or word. If the entire page is very different, the asterisk will be at the top. If you have not received a completely new script, **collate** the new colored pages into your old script. This means putting the script in order. This can be daunting if you've never done it before.

Here's what you need to know to collate a sitcom script properly. All changes keep to the original page numbers. If page 4 has new dialogue, it replaces the old page 4. If there are now too many lines to fit on page 4, they will continue to an "A" page with the same original number. Page four will now be two sheets: 4 followed by 4A. If there are cuts, the original numbers are accounted for with a hyphen. You might see page 28-31 as the designation of the original page twenty-eight and the missing scene after it. Each show has their own color system for each set of changes. The first rewrite is probably printed on pink paper. The next is blue, then green, goldenrod, etc.

> *My job is to train the writer's assistant as to what is needed or not needed a script for the stage. For me, the writer's assistant is the most overworked and under appreciated job on the show. The hours are terrible and the mistakes are there in black and white. Many have had little sleep and very little leeway given to them. So, I guess part of my job is to tell them I understand and that there is nothing that cannot be fixed.*
>
> Marcia Gould,
> Script Supervisor, *Wings*

If you have to collate on the set, find a place where you can spread out. Work from the beginning to the end sequentially. Be sure to clean up after yourself. Most stages have a recycling bin for old pages. Then, if you haven't done it yet, READ THE NEW SCRIPT!

GETTING THE MOST OUT OF REHEARSAL

If you are an actor and your script is complete, take the time to study it. Today is your day to do most of the rehearsal for the entire week. Theater veterans are used to a long rehearsal schedule that slowly reveals the subtleties of their character and the plot. Sitcoms have only three days in which to rehearse the script as a stage play. Dramatic television actors are often surprised that sitcoms are much more like theater than they are like episodic series[6]. Standup comics often discover how rehearsal can be helpful to creating a rich character and performance. Others don't value that time and want to keep their performances "fresh".

Bill Cosby disdained long rehearsals. He let his stand-in, Samuel L. Jackson[7], work much of the rehearsal to allow the other actors their time. Audrey Meadows once told us that Jackie Gleason would only rehearse *The Honeymooners* scenes one time. If you watch the reruns closely, you will occasionally see Meadows feeding Gleason his forgotten line. Brett Butler of *Grace Under Fire*, would often say, "I don't know why you are taking this long to rehearse. I can *learn* a script in a couple of hours." She knew the intricacies of her character, since the series was based partially on her life.

Guest actors, who are only working on one episode, need to realize that they have to help create their new character in very little time. Robin Bartlett suggests, "Don't overwork the material. It is usually thin enough to be weighted down by too much thought. This does not mean that it isn't worth the time. I think of sitcom as the vaudeville of this era. At its best it is both common and full of wit and wisdom."

SET-UP, PUNCHLINE, OR PIPE?

The better you know what the scene is about and the better grasp you have on the words you say, the more profitable your rehearsal will be. Sitcom dialogue can be broken into three categories: the **set-up**, the **punchline**, and the **pipe.** A student of comedy can tell the difference.

The set-up is the statement or premise that has to be understood for a joke to get a laugh. It immediately precedes the punchline. You will see that this construction is very precise. There are no extra words or thoughts to get in the way of this premise.

The punchline is the other half of the formula. It is the funny part, but will not be funny without the set-up. Here is an example of a classic set-up and punchline:

```
                    MONICA
(NOTICING HIS TIE) Oh, honey I thought I told you
not to wear that tie.
```

6 Dramatic television actors will often shoot scenes with little or no rehearsal.

7 Jay Sandrich, the Director of *Cosby*, impressed with Jackson's acting ability as Bill's stand-in, kept trying to get the producers to let "Sam" play a small part in an episode. It never happened. With all of that sitcom experience, we were not surprised at how many laughs Jackson got in the feature film *Pulp Fiction*.

WILLIAM
I thought you meant just that one time.

MONICA
No, darling, I meant never.[8]

The set-up and punchline make up the jokes; everything else is pipe or exposition. The set-up is also known as the **feed** because it comes before or feeds into the punchline. Pipe is simply information that helps audiences understand the story. It also can serve as a set-up for something that will be coming later. It could be dialogue such as, "So your brother is coming over. I hope you guys can get along for a change." This establishes a premise that won't be paid off right away, but is important to know when he shows up and there is a series of jokes based on the idea of sibling incompatibility. Each of those jokes will have their own immediate set-up and punchline.

Pipe is found in abundance in the first scene of a script, or in the first script of a series, called the pilot. Hiding the pipe is the challenge of most pilots. Due to the expository nature of these lines, they are the parts of the script that don't get laughs. Many actors complain that all they are doing is **laying pipe** in such scenes. They feel like a laborer rather than an artist since they are not involved in either the front half or back half of the actual joke. Actor Anthony Anderson (*All About the Andersons*) cleverly disguises the pipe explaining his character's move from New York to Los Angeles in the pilot episode of his show. The secret that Anderson knew was to play the needs of the character. The audience heard a lot of background information disguised as a heated discussion.

Analyze the structure to understand how to deliver it. You should be able to find the **operative word** that is key to each sentence's meaning. That word is not always the funny word but it is usually the premise by which the joke is based. Understanding this script construction is critical so that each line can be framed or presented by the actor in such a way that will make the audience laugh.

As we begin to breakdown the structure of comedy, we have to admit that over-analysis can be the death of comedy for SOME people. Many naturally funny people will start morphing into a homogenized standard sitcom caricature if they are not careful. Our experience has shown us that MOST newcomers who don't naturally see the structure and hear the rhythm desperately need to understand these sitcom basics. The best way to learn that is to read a lot of sitcom scripts and identify exactly what makes them funny.

Here is a classic scene from the pilot *Luis* by Will Gluck. The very talented actor Luis Guzman plays a gruff but good-hearted owner of a Spanish Harlem donut shop. The character Greg is Luis' daughter Marly's live-in boyfriend.

8 From the episode "Invasion of the Gold Digger," written by Keith Josef Adkins from the series *Girlfriends*, created by Mara Brock Akil. Used by permission of Paramount Pictures Corporation.

Sitcom Exercise

Read this scene. Identify the **set-up** *and* **punchline** *for all the jokes. We've done the first two for you. Complete the rest remembering that for every* **punchline**, *there is a* **set-up**. *You know where the answers are.*

LUIS - "PILOT"

INT. DONUT SHOP - DAY

(LUIS, GREG, MARLY)

GREG KISSES MARLY. HE NOTICES LUIS WATCHING AND BREAKS IT OFF.

GREG

Oh, I guess I shouldn't kiss your daughter in front of you, huh?

LUIS

You can kiss my daughter in front of me. You just can't kiss my daughter in front of me without a job.

GREG

What else can I do in front of you if I get a job? Grab her ass?

LUIS

A good job, yes.

GREG

What can I do for eighty-five grand and a dental plan?

LUIS

You make eighty-five grand a year, you can grab my ass.

GREG

(RE: GREG'S SMALL HANDS AND LUIS'S LARGE ASS) I don't think that's possible.

LUIS TAKES A BEAT THEN LUNGES AT HIM.

GREG (CONT'D)

You know, Luis, most artists don't achieve success until after they're dead.

LUIS

How 'bout I make you successful right now? (THEN, RE: GREG'S DONUT) Did you pay for that?

GREG

Of, course.

LUIS

(MENACING) Did you?

GREG

Yes!

LUIS

(MENACING) Did you?

GREG

Marly, can I borrow a dollar? (THEN) I'm kidding. Of course I paid for it. I mean, come on. (LOUD WHISPERS) Marly. Dollar bill. Quickly!

LUIS

I don't get it. She's a smart girl. What does she see in you?

GREG

Maybe a guy who loves her, who's sensitive, talented, and from time to time (OFF LUIS) not afraid to show fear. (LOUD WHISPER, TO MARLY) Dollar...bill. Now. If you love me!

MARLY BRINGS HIM A DOLLAR.

GREG (CONT'D)

Here you go.

LUIS

I don't understand you. I mean, how can you let a woman pay your bills?

```
                    GREG
It'd be a hell of a lot easier if you didn't bring
it up all the time. (THEN, RE: DOLLAR) Do I got some
change skating my way, how does that work?

                                      CUT TO:[9]
```

HOLDING FOR LAUGHS

After studying the script, go back and make a note when a punchline is your **cue**. The cue is the last word spoken by another actor before the next actor's line. It is critical to have an awareness of when the audience is laughing. They can't hear the next line if it is spoken under a laugh. Actors need to get used to this rhythm of the sitcom. Remember the sitcom rule **HOLD FOR LAUGHS!**

Emmy nominated director Jim Drake (*Golden Girls, Buffalo Bill*) was directing a little-experienced actress in a scene on the classic *Sanford*[10]. During rehearsal he kept warning her about the need to hold for the laugh that she would get in the middle of her own speech. He explained that she needed to give the audience time to appreciate her joke before she continued. Finally, she seemed to understand. On the night of the taping before the live audience, she got to the joke and got the big laugh that Jim predicted. Happily, she held for the laugh. As the laugh was diminishing, before she finished her speech, she turned to the audience and took a bow...Not exactly the activity Jim was hoping for during that laugh.

Holding is waiting...and so much more. Holding requires the actor to remain involved in the scene. The actor must remain in character as well.

If you are an actor, decide if your character knows that the joke is funny. That might call for a different reaction than if the joke was an insult to your character and funny only for the audience. The proper reaction can add much dimension to the comedy of your performance and the scene. It is important for you to discover what your character is thinking during the pause for the laugh. This moment should be a genuine organic moment of the character rather than just an actor waiting for the laugh to end. On *Major Dad*, Beverly Archer (who played "Gunnery Sergeant Bricker") could always be counted on for an extra or prolonged laugh when you cut to her **deadpan**[11] face. Ms. Archer had made the character choice that Gunny took her job very seriously. Her stern reaction to anything humorous was always a sure laugh! Regan Burns who has been a guest star on dozens of sitcoms says, "During any comedic argument, I always

---

9 *Luis* © 2003 Twentieth Century Fox Film Corporation. All Rights Reserved.

10 This is the 1980's series that followed the classic *Sanford and Son* and *Sanford Arms*.

11 The human face has been referred to as a "pan" since the 19th century possibly because the face is broad and shallow like a fry pan.

hunt for the 'deadpan.' That one line that seems to be most powerful when just delivered flat. It's important to find the different levels."

Similarly, Lisa Kudrow of *Friends* extends laughs by her character's naiveté, bewilderment, or ignorance of something said to her. Observe Kudrow thinking, in character, while she waits for the audience laughter to subside. Matt LeBlanc also of *Friends* constantly gets laughs while his character tries to decipher what has been said.

A FEW PRELIMINARIES

Rehearsal on Tuesday will resemble a play rehearsal. Rehearsal will be on a set that may or may not be completely built. For example, the Living Room walls may be standing, but there may not be a front door. Folding chairs are often substituted for a car set. Actors should use rehearsal props whenever possible even though they are holding a script in their hand. The prop department provides both real and rehearsal props. You should always ask if the prop will be different from the one you are using.

Scenes may be rehearsed out of order on Tuesday. This is common practice in the film and television industry. If there are child actors in the episode, their limited time[12] on the set needs to be optimized. All of their scenes may be rehearsed back-to-back even if they are not sequential in the script. The star might have an interview with the press in the morning and needs to have a later call, if this is the case. Any scene, that the star is not a part of, would be scheduled early.

It is an actor's job to keep track of what takes place in the scene. The script supervisor is keeping an official record if an actor ever has a script question. Ellen Deutsch calls herself and fellow script supervisors the "logic police." However, even the best script supervisor doesn't have the benefit of the organic acting process, which reveals a moment that doesn't ring true because of a gap in emotional logic. This talent comes with an actor's ability to behave in character sequentially from moment to moment.

This is the day to make sure that there is a proper through-line for each character.

If you are an actor, ask yourself a few questions: Does everything make sense? What changes are made as each scene progresses and how do these make me change? Did my character have information earlier that would be necessary for my scripted behavior in this scene? Any problems in continuity should be brought to the attention of the director. Since there have been, and will continue to be, changes in the script, some things fall through the cracks. Bringing attention to the problem, can remedy these inconsistencies.

There is a difference between being creative and helpful and being thought of as a selfish performer.[13] As a guest actor, you should also be sensitive to

12 Nearby are a classroom and a studio teacher whose responsibility it is to protect the child from abusive working conditions.

13 The term "selfish performer" is actually never used on the set. These people are always called "pain in the ass."

monopolizing the rehearsal time. If you have something that you think could help, don't hold it back... but find the right time to share it. If the director agrees that it is important, he will bring this to the attention of the writers. They care very much if it causes the story not to work-unless it means losing a really good joke...and then some writers will excuse the logic by telling you that they are taking "comedic license."

By contrast, writers may seem almost uncaring about long-term character continuity. For example, you may come across a line that states your character is meeting his sweetheart at the high school reunion. You may remind the writers that in the pilot, you had a line about not dating in high school. You may be told, "Nobody will ever remember that!" The prevailing attitude is that most of the audience doesn't keep track of these details. Some shows have had a change of careers for some of the characters without any explanation. Next-door neighbors appear and then are replaced in the very next episode. Diana Canova's son in *Throb* went from tall thin blond actor Paul Walker[14] to shorter, stockier, dark-haired Sean DeVeritch. Other shows are very strict about the show's continuity and every detail fits together like a giant puzzle.

The actors will put every scene on its feet. It is their time to get familiar with props and the set. It is also a good time to get to know the rehearsal crew. The prop master will give out each hand held prop just before its scene. Props should be returned to the prop department after each scene. Props are the items that are identified in the script to be used by a character. Everything else in the set is part of the set dressing. For any questions about the set or if an actor wishes to use some set dressing as a prop, a set decorator is on hand during all rehearsals.

If you are an actor, become familiar with your props. They are an adjunct to your performance. Let them help rather than hinder you. Ease with props takes repeated rehearsals even for seasoned professionals. On an episode of *Charles in Charge* guest star, John Astin[15], needed to use a medicine case as a part of his scene. He spent his entire lunch hour of Tuesday's rehearsal working at loading and unloading the case (with the permission of the prop master). He worked it repeatedly until the movement was habitual to the character. It became so fluid, that the character and his case were the delight of the show.

STAGE GEOGRAPHY

An actor should be aware of his physical position in relation to his fellow actor and his audience. In order to share the stage with his fellow actor, the

14 Paul Walker went on to star in non-comedic action features such as *Varsity Blues, Pleasantville, The Fast and The Furious* movies, and *Timeline*. He has been called "the next Steve McQueen".

15 Prior to many guest appearances including *Charles in Charge*, John Astin has had a distinguished career as the star of long running sitcoms such as *I'm Dickens, He's Fenster, The Addams Family* and *Operation Petticoat*. His resume goes all the way back to an appearance in a dance sequence from the film *West Side Story*.

physical relationship between them should be **50/50**. This means that each actor is equally visible to the audience. If both actors are facing each other, they mirror each other's position while both attempt to turn their downstage shoulder outwards toward the audience. The audience isn't there on Tuesday, but an easy way to gauge this relationship is by looking at the **set-line**[16]which lies **downstage**[17] at the edge of the set. This line is called the proscenium line in the theatre. The actors are standing at a slight angle to each other. The upstage shoulders of the actors are closer to one another than the downstage ones. An easy trick is to always lean on your upstage leg. This gives the effect of opening you up to the audience for better viewing, and as we'll learn in Chapter 5, better viewing by the cameras.

During rehearsal, the script supervisor is keeping track of all dialogue changes made with the director's approval. Actors should call out the word "line" to ask the script supervisor to **feed** the words. She is also recording blocking notes and can refresh your memory about movement and continuity during the scene. The A.D. or stage manager will be keeping everything operating properly on the stage and often give you your entrance cues. Cue lights are sometimes set up backstage in order to cue silently.

The crew is an actor's friend. Everyone needs to treat them respectfully. Everyone on a sitcom is part of a creative team. Each individual is providing his expertise. Often, a crewmember is over qualified for his job. He may have surprisingly long and distinguished credits in similar or complimentary positions. For example, prior to becoming a prop master, Ron Woods (*Eight Simple Rules, Dave's World*) acted at the renowned Oregon Shakespeare Festival. He has been known to fill in for a missing actor during rehearsal and give quite an excellent performance!

Out of respect to your fellow craftsmen, no personal food or drink should ever be brought onto the set. Cell phones and pagers should be set on vibrate. No one should ever lounge in a set when it's not in use. Space allowing, there is always a table and chairs in front of the center set to use for collating, going over your lines, and relaxing.

Each scene will be rehearsed a number of times, until the director is satisfied with it. Notes may be given after each completed scene or the director will stop and start in order to figure out the best way to execute the scene. ACTORS SHOULD USE THIS TIME TO EXPLORE! USE THIS TIME TO ASK QUESTIONS! Remember the rule: **DON'T MOVE ON THE JOKE**. This pertains to your and other character's jokes. Actually, it pertains mostly to the punch line. Nothing should distract the audience from laughing. Any movement or gesture will take

---

16 The set flooring, painted or real, is easier to use as a guide than the often-asymmetrical walls.

17 Downstage is so named because when stages (not audiences) were raked (tilted), the lower part of the stage was closer to the audience for better viewing. As the actors walked away from the audience, they literally were traveling up.

their attention away from hearing the funny part. There are always exceptions. D.L. Hughley knew this rule and would purposely defy it to prove his skill at comedy...he always got the laugh!

STAGE BUSINESS AND BLOCKING

Actors, write down your blocking! It is also a good idea for the director, his assistants and a must for the script supervisor. You can use the shorthand of an up arrow when you rise from a chair, a down arrow when you sit and an X for when you cross the room. Always use pencil because things are always changing. Play with the other actors! Find your moments! Create your own **business**! Business is any physical action: any movement or gesture. It may support dialogue or exist on its own. Business can make a character memorable as in the example of John Astin and the medicine case. Some actors have been hired just for their **shtick**.[18] An extreme piece of shtick is a pratfall. Actors hired for their shtick are expected to enhance their performance with more physicality than most. If Jim Carey were doing sitcom, he'd be known for his shtick. Michael Richards of *Seinfeld* brought humorous physicality of his character "Kramer" to an art form. This was well planned, expertly executed, inventive work!

Seinfeld director of photography, Wayne Kennan remembers Richards as a very hard worker who would toil all day long on his physical business, "He would be constantly trying different ways of entering and exiting through Jerry's apartment door. By the end of the series, the bottom of the door was completely beat-up and almost black from Kramer's shoe marks." Kennan watched as Richards developed one piece of physical business when he sat down at a barstool. Kennan said, "Michael didn't smoke and it was pure genius the way he worked with that cigarette and beer. His hilarious antics fit really well in the sitcom arena."

Actors have to find the appropriate business for their character. Most business is naturalistic such as a mother unloading grocery bags and putting the food away in the kitchen cabinets. Actors should make their energy and activities fit their character. It may, however, be more than real life and more than a dramatic character would do. On one episode of *Girlfriends*, actress Tracee Ellis Ross invented a piece of business for her character who was cooking pasta. Her character Joan was angry with William (Reggie Hayes) for betraying her. Ross punctuated her line by broadly snapping the dry pasta in half and depositing it into the boiling water at the end of her line.

JOAN

You know what? I was wrong. This isn't about Monica. She doesn't owe me anything. This is about William, and how he betrayed me as a colleague and a friend.

18 Shtick is the old Yiddish term for piece or routine. It described the physical comedy or little dances of vaudeville.

```
        We are more than friends, we're like family. You
        don't turn on family -- unless you're Fredo Cor-
        leone. And like Fredo Corleone, his ass is going
        down.
ON THE GIRLS' REACTIONS, WE:

                                        FADE OUT.
                          END OF ACT ONE[19]
```

This ended the act with a huge laugh!

ADVICE: WORK HARD BUT KEEP IT FUN

Sitcom rehearsals are usually a lot of fun. Everyone needs to stay loose. You may be very good at your job, but if you bring tension to the set, you won't last long in sitcoms. That goes for both actors and others. We knew an individual working in a prop department who was militaristic in efficiency. She made her fellow crew members tense, the actors nervous, and drove us crazy. The laudable attention to detail was overshadowed by the tension created.

Crew members, feel free to laugh! Remember this is a situation comedy. The actors love having an audience during rehearsal. The television audience wants to laugh as well; otherwise, they'd be watching a drama. That being said, rehearsals also have a serious intent. As an actor, this is the time to practice the scenes so that you will perform it, retaining what you rehearsed, at the producers run-thru later this afternoon.

THE PRODUCER RUN-THRU

The producer run-thru is a performance for the writers. Scarbrough defines the *Everybody Loves Raymond* experience. "They watch the cast perform the script 'on its feet' in the sets." Scenes are done in order. Actress Catherine MacNeal (*Cheers, Night Court, Designing Women*) admits:

> When I did my first sitcom, I got very nervous before run-thrus for producers or the network. I worried that if I didn't land the joke, it would be gone the next day. But once the audience arrived, I loosened up and felt like I was back in the theatre, theatre with retakes. With every job, I reminded myself that it was "theatre" and tried to carry that feeling of freedom into every run-thru.

The writers are the audience. They will laugh... a lot. They will also take a lot of notes to aid them in the second rewrite that evening. Actors, you will hear a lot of pencils writing during the run-thru. Don't assume that they are writing

19 From the episode "Invasion of the Gold Digger," written by Keith Josef Adkins from the series *Girlfriends*, created by Mara Brock Akil. Used by permission of Paramount Pictures Corporation. All Rights Reserved.

criticisms of you. They usually are marking the script for places that need writing help. These markings are their own shorthand. They might spot a place where a joke is needed and write **JTC** meaning joke to come, **LTC** meaning line to come, or some other mark.

Executive Producer Peter Engel was so noted for his two notes **punch** and **replace**, he received solid gold cufflinks of those words as a warm hearted gesture from one of his writers. Punch means to refine the joke to make it better; replace means to come up with an entirely new joke. These two instructions may be only marked in the script by a check mark, but the producer or writer knows that this is a place to review during the re-write. If a joke has been checked in a script, a writer or writer's assistant will say, "I've got it marked."

The more successful a run-thru, the earlier the writers get to go home. For that reason, there is a lot of pressure. Concentrating on the scene and remembering everything practiced in the rehearsals is expected. This is not the time to add anything new. Directors don't like surprises. One of the most important skills for a sitcom actor (this applies to almost everyone in all positions) is to be able to reproduce the exact same performance many times in a row. Once you have arrived at a desired choice, stay with it. If an actor wants to try something different, do it in rehearsal. It is the director's prerogative to keep it or not. If a prop person has a different prop from what was used in rehearsal, he should check to see if the director wants to use it during run-thru. A wardrobe person that wants an actor to wear wardrobe during run-thru should also run it by the director.

HOLDING SCRIPTS, NOTES, AND SIGNING OUT

Today, scripts should be held even if an actor knows his lines word perfect. There is no expectation that an actor be **off book**[20], so there will be little sympathy if lines are muffed or cues are wrong. The writers want to hear it the way it was written! If they don't have this opportunity, they won't know what to change. Actors should think of this as a performance and dress appropriately for the character. Women should wear make-up. Everyone's hair should be out of his or her eyes. NO GUM! NO HATS! NO SUNGLASSES!

Notes will be given at the end of a run-thru. Actors may or may not be included. Sometimes notes may contradict each other. The director will decipher what is needed. Actors should write down notes if they have less than perfect memories. Carmen Finestra explains what happens to the writers after a run-thru. "Tuesdays are often considered a "punch up" night, where concentration is given to making the jokes better and funnier. Sometimes certain writers, who

---

20 Off book means an actor no longer needs to carry a script in his hands because he has memorized the words. This makes it easier for him to act, handle props, and move about the stage more freely.

are known as great joke writers, are hired for this one night.[21] Obviously, any structural or motivational changes to scenes, if necessary, are also made."

Actors sign out with the 2nd A.D. or Assistant Stage Manager. The crew hands in timecards. Actors may be needed for costume fittings before they leave. Now is a good time to find out what the procedure is for having guests at the Friday audience show. Ask the **second**[22] whom to notify about your guests. Guests are usually given priority seating. The crew doesn't sign out, but submits daily time cards. Props, Script supervisors, directors, their assistants and some other crew members may have additional hours to complete their work after the run-thru.

Hope you had a good time! Tomorrow is the last chance to concentrate on just the play before cameras make it into a teleplay. Rest...and come back ready to refine what you've already begun!

---

21 Bob Smith, who had worked as a joke writer for Johnny Carson's *The Tonight Show* served as a "punch up" genius on several Carsey-Werner shows including *3rd Rock from the Sun, Grace Under Fire, and That 70s Show* all at the same time.

22 DGA position of Second AD or Second Stage Manager.

Sitcom Vocabulary Quick Review

Read these sentences. If the director gave you these notes, would you instantly know what he meant? If not, go back and review the explanation in this chapter.

That piece of **business** *gets in the way of the punchline.*

You jumped the **cue**.

When you **collate** *your script, omit page 24a from the new pages.*

A **deadpan** *reaction will get a bigger laugh.*

Cross **downstage** *on that line*

The **punchline** *didn't pay off because the* **feed** *wasn't clear.*

Stand **50/50** *with him.*

Hold *for the laugh!*

Don't worry we'll have a **JTC**.

Disguise the fact that you're **laying pipe**.

He's the **second banana** *on this show.*

You don't need to be **off book** *today.*

Pace it up and get through that **pipe**.

The writer's will **punch** *it.*

If it doesn't work, we'll **replace** *it.*

Check with the **Second** *before you go to lunch.*

The **setline** *is farther downstage.*

The **set-up** *is too far away from the* **punchline**.

What is the **operative word** *in that line?*

Can you come up with some **shtick** *for this scene?*

What week were you **wrapped**?

Script Supervisor's Tuesday and Wednesday Tasks

- ✓ *Make sure all actors, DGA team, department heads etc. have revised script.*
- ✓ *Read Revised Table Draft.*
- ✓ *Transfer blocking notes that apply.*
- ✓ *Possible informal reading of revised script with actors and director.*
- ✓ *Rehearse*
- ✓ *Stay on book (script) in order to prompt actors of their lines if needed.*
- ✓ *Advise actors of dialogue if they are having difficulty.*
- ✓ *Time producers' run-thru.*
- ✓ *Take any notes for the director during run-thru.*
- ✓ *Report time to execs.*
- ✓ *Go to notes, record any notes for the director.*

Sitcom Insider

NOTES ON WRITING SITCOMS

As jobs go, being a writer on a sit-com can be a fantastic way to make a living. You're well paid, well fed, and, in most cases, have a lot of fun. A writer on one show I worked on used to say that when he came home from work and his wife asked how his day was, he had to lie. Because, if he told her the truth – that he spent the day laughing and eating and bullshitting with his friends – she would become resentful over being left at home to do the truly hard job of taking care of the kids. In fact, being a sit-com writer is like being a calf raised for veal. And I mean that in a good way. You're kept in a confined space, and fed all day, with the added bonus that when you've been sufficiently fattened up, the slaughter is only metaphorical.

One downside should be obvious: it's hard to get a job on a sit-com these days, as there are fewer and fewer being produced, and budget cuts on those that remain on the air have reduced the number of writers being hired. In any given season, most job openings are on new shows, and most new shows get cancelled before the end of the season. But if you're lucky or talented enough to be working on a show, it can be a lot of fun.

It can be, that is, as long as you don't look to your writing on the show to provide fulfillment to your creative urges. And therein lies the other downside. On most sit-com staffs, the room (meaning the ten or so writers acting as a group) breaks (meaning outlines) a story for an episode (meaning episode). Then one writer goes off to write one or two drafts of the episode. That episode is thereafter referred to as that writer's episode. As in, "We're shooting Michael's episode this week." If you believe this – that it is really your episode -- you're going to have your heart broken. You spend two weeks or so pouring your heart and soul into the script, and then bring it back to the room. The room then re-writes the script. There's a certain feeling of being violated, and not a damn thing you can do about it. And the room re-writing one's script is just the beginning of the process. If a writer is able to make it through the room rewrite with most of his script in tact, then he gets to watch the actors read it and hear the network and studio executives give notes on it.

I've been lucky enough to work on a couple of shows where a well-written first draft can make it all the way to shoot night without being messed up. But this is the exception. All too often, scripts are changed and not always for the better. And even if the changes in your script are all for the better, chances are you don't realize it. Chances are, you think the brilliance that you achieved in your first draft is much better than what ended up getting shot. And sometimes the changes are just lateral, because the process is all about re-writing, whether it's necessary or not. And so, the writer of the script is often left missing his draft, even if he knows, deep down, that the re-write is better.

It helps, if you want to work as a writer on a sit-com, to enjoy the food and the camaraderie, but to look elsewhere for creative fulfillment. Write a novel or a play on the side. Or your own spec pilot or screenplay. Something that's yours, that no one else can touch. (Unless, of course, you actually sell it, and then you'll have to get notes from somebody. But don't worry, that'll never happen.) Enjoy the show as a fun job and not as an outlet for all your creative urges, and you'll have fun.

Michael Kaplan, *Frasier, Girlfriends, Roseanne*

Sitcom Career Profile

KIT WILKINSON - SCRIPT SUPERVISOR

There was one season where Kit was offered 12 different shows! Everyone wants to work with her! Besides being an incredibly gifted script supervisor, she is great fun to be around. She has a goodness and honesty that you can always count on!

What shows have you worked on?

I worked in Accounting and as a Writer's Assistant on *Kate and Allie.* (NY) I also worked as a Writer's Assistant the first season of *Golden Girls.* I was Script Supervisor on *Charles in Charge, The George Lopez Show, The Norm Show, Cybil, and The Torkelsons.* I was a Technical Coordinator on *The Drew Carey Show* and Associate Director on *The Fresh Prince of Bel Air.*

What are your responsibilities?

As a script supervisor, I am recording and keeping track of information for the actors, director, and writers and finally on show day, for the editor. I make changes in the script - mine is always the most accurate written version of the script at any given moment. I communicate write-ins from the stage to the writers and vise-versa. I mark down blocking for actors and director's reference. I note props and continuity. On show day, I keep a marked script of takes and the material covered, number of cameras filming, word flubs or other mistakes, and record these notations in my script which is then handed over to the editor.

Did you have specific training in this field?

No. All my training was on-the-job...and through observation. I worked first in accounting, then in script processing, and finally was given the opportunity to script supervise.

How did you get your first job?

I talked the coordinating producer into letting me pay bills because it was the only job available. I explained my interest in writing and was eventually moved over to Writer's Assistant.

What advice would you give someone who wants to do what you do?

Find a producer willing to give you a shot. Work in some other capacity to start, pay attention, make friends, let 'em see how smart you are, and organized and efficient and never stop expressing you interests and goals. Editors have helped me a lot. They evaluate your work very critically because your notes facilitate their work. And make friends with directors...often the choice of script supervisor is left to them.

What do you like best about your job?

Variety: every day is different. Autonomy: very seldom does anyone tell me how to do my job. Witnessing the creative process.

SCRIPT SUPERVISORS
Union: IATSE Local 871
Typical Weekly Salary: $1500
Hours Per Week: 40-54

Chapter 4 WEDNESDAY...REHEARSAL/NETWORK RUN-THRU

In this chapter:

How a sitcom is structured
Why sight gags make us laugh
The magic of misleading
Traps to avoid as an actor
Writers' room etiquette
How to set up a callback
Why actors get fired
Career profile of a sitcom director of photography

Wednesday is about refining! Just as a writer edits what he writes, an actor refines his performance as he rehearses. At the very least, this means learning the text and getting "off book." At its very finest, refining means honing a performance so that every moment is believable, every joke pops, and all this work looks effortless.

This seemingly effortless performance will be for the network at the end of the workday. That's why the food is better today! Everyone is trying very hard to make the network enjoy this run-thru. A tasty nibble from the **craft service**[1] table may put the suits in a better mood after a long day. It also demarcates the office from the stage. Hopefully, the stage feels more like a place to be entertained rather than a place to work. The goal is for the network executive to sit back and enjoy the show!

When the actors arrive on Wednesday, the crew has already been busy. Most of the sets and props are in place. Costumes have been bought or rented.[2] The script has undergone another revision. The actor is responsible for noting all these changes just as he did for the previous rewrite... and more!

Occasionally, Wednesday will begin with a table read if the script has changed significantly and the writers want to hear it aloud. Otherwise, everyone leaps into rehearsal. Scene by scene, the director will convey any performance notes that the producers requested after the

SITCOM RULE
Faster is funnier. *Pace and energy causes dramatic material to be more comedic.*

1 "Craft service," usually one or two people, provides snacks and (sometimes meals) for the crew working on stage.

2 On the groundbreaking sitcom *Soap*, Judy Evans designed and constructed much of the wardrobe for each episode.

Tuesday run-thru. Each scene will be rehearsed a number of times. The scenes with few changes will take very little time and others may take an hour or more per scene. The stand-ins are present, writing down blocking as they watch the actors rehearse. With most of the props and sets completed, everyone gets a real sense of how this episode will actually look. Repetition is the actor's friend. It not only gives the actor a chance to mold his performance, it allows the other actors to know what to expect from their fellow scene mates. It also allows the crew to know how to plan appropriately.

On many sitcoms, the level of acting expertise varies. Producer Peter Engel talks about how to get the most out of an actor, "We'd give them boundaries and stretch them within the boundaries. We never asked more of an actor than he or she could do." There is an excellent opportunity for the sitcom novice to learn from rehearsing or watching. We believe that recognizing types of jokes is the key. In the previous chapters, we looked at the construction of jokes: divided into a setup and a punchline. We identified the easy to spot jokes that have *K* sounds or patterns of three. Now we want to look at the overall structure of a script and talk about other specific kinds of jokes common to sitcoms.

SITCOM STRUCTURE

Sitcoms classically are two-act teleplays[3]. A short scene called the **teaser** precedes the first act. This scene introduces the theme of the episode. If it appears before the opening credits to entice or tease the audience into not changing the channel and watching the entire episode, it is called a **cold open**. The networks try to get the viewing audience to watch their channel without switching after the previous program ends. They sometimes make the teaser so "cold" or unanticipated that it may start immediately as the other show ends, not even a station break to separate them. The advertisers use the time after the teaser to air their first commercial break.

Next is the first act, which introduces the A and B stories. Sitcoms have usually two stories going on simultaneously. The A story is the main plot, always involving the lead character, usually introduced in the teaser. The B story is the secondary plot, often involving a secondary character, which may or may not echo the theme of the A story. The number of scenes in the first act varies from episode to episode. Some writers like the energy derived from many short scenes. Others will write three or fewer scenes per act[4]. Most scenes end with a final joke called the **blow** (big joke) or **button**[5] (smaller joke). If an actor is not

---

3 Increasingly, sitcoms have three acts to allow for another commercial break.

4 Peter Tolan's brilliant pilot script for *Style and Substance* starring Jean Smart actually only had two scenes in the first act. Shows with fewer (and therefore longer) scenes are more dependent on the strength of the writing and the ensemble cast for pacing and performance. *Style and Substance* had no problem filling these shoes.

5 "Button" can also refer to some verbal or physical emphasis given to the end of any joke.

giving enough energy to a blow or button, he is instructed to "**punch it up**." To punch it up means to give a joke greater emphasis or to hit it harder. The blow or button must be punched up to let the audience know that the scene is over and that the story is moving on. The added energy or emphasis also helps bring out the FUNNY. Of course, going too far can kill the joke. Developing skill means knowing the difference.

The first act concludes with an **act break**: the dividing point in the story. It is usually punctuated by a twist in the plot that makes the audience want to come back after the second commercial break. It is also a moment that should be a major dilemma for the lead character and at the same time be very funny. It occurs about half way through the show[6]. The number of scenes in the second act also varies. Writer Michael Langworthy (*The Drew Carey Show, 8 Simple Rules*) simplifies it: "Sitcoms build to a strong act break. The dilemma gets worse in the middle of Act 2." This intensifying of the dilemma is often referred to as the **wrinkle**. Everything gets solved and the second act often winds the A and usually the B stories. The second act winds up the A story.

There is a third commercial break after the second act. The show concludes with the **tag**: a short final scene before or during the end credits. Since the story has already concluded, the tag is icing or a confection. Although it may be a place to conclude the almost forgotten B story, its main purpose is to leave the audience laughing! Sometimes it has been used just to show outtakes from the filming or it is a place to revisit a very funny joke that occurred during the show. For example: In "The Helmet" episode of *According to Jim* written by David Feeney, Jim (Jim Belushi) says he doesn't know what he did to deserve his wife Cheryl (Courtney Thorne-Smith).

```
                                JIM
          The only thing I can come up with is when I was ten,
          I gave a hobo half a hot dog. I mean, I guess I've
          done other good stuff, but that's the one that re-
          ally stands out.
```

In the tag this is revisited.

```
                                 TAG
FADE IN:

INT. LIVING ROOOM/FRONT DOOR - NEXT DAY (DAY 6)

(JIM, OLDER MAN)
```

6 Not counting the opening and closing credits, there is roughly about 20 minutes of actual script per episode.

SFX: DOORBELL.

JIM CROSSES AND OPENS THE DOOR REVEALING AN OLDER, SOPHISTICATED MAN.

JIM

Hi.

OLDER MAN

Hello. You probably don't remember me, but years ago when I was down on my luck, you saw it in your heart to give a poor hobo half a hot dog.

JIM

Oh, my god. That was you!

OLDER MAN

Yes. And because of that single act of kindness I turned my life around and now stand before you a benevolent millionaire.

JIM

And you're here to reward me.

OLDER MAN

Why sir, your reward is the joy of knowing you helped a fellow human being. And no amount of money could ever --

JIM SLAMS THE DOOR AND TURNS AROUND.

JIM

(CALLING) Hey, Cheryl, when's dinner?

AND WE:

FADE OUT.

END OF SHOW[7]

Many experts understand the reasons that comedy makes people laugh. They range from Dr. Jonathan Miller, a comic and physician who performed with Dudley Moore and Peter Cook on English TV in the 1960s. He has actually lectured on the medical and brainwave functions that apply to comedy. Others

7 Used by permission of Touchstone Television. All Rights Reserved.

may simply say "I know it when I see it." It helps everyone working on a sitcom to have some basic understanding of how jokes work.

TWO CATEGORIES OF JOKES: PHYSICAL AND VERBAL

The specific kinds of jokes common in sitcoms can be divided in two broad categories: physical jokes and verbal jokes. Both are steeped in history. Physical jokes date back to vaudeville where performers were known for slapstick[8] routines. These silly antics took great physical discipline and timing. Verbal jokes still emulate the rhythm and style of the Borsht Belt comics that performed in the primarily Jewish resorts in the Catskills. Producer Peter Engel would say, "Take a wasp kid, teach him Jewish rhythms and you've got a star." He sites Mary Tyler Moore and Cary Grant as prime examples of people who understood this rhythm." Rob Reiner echoed the same idea to Elaine Dutka of the *Los Angles Times*: "My dad (Carl Reiner) filtered Jewish neurosis through a goyish personality with Dick Van Dyke and came up with a hybird that worked." Sitcom legend Dick Van Dyke elaborated on that when he told us, "Carl had a unique ability to pick up the cadence and personality of each actor. He immediately found Morey's (Amsterdam) and Rosey's (Rose Marie) pattern and he ended up making Rob (Van Dyke) Midwestern... all with the Jewish neuroses."

Sitcoms were one of the first forms that filled the fledgling medium of television when it began coming into thousands of households in the 1950s. TV tapped the established writers and performers of that day, who had developed their rhythms through their many live performances. After all the decades since, audiences may have no connection to the beginnings but still respond to the style. It is now the style and rhythm of the sitcom. The language and rhythm slowly evolves with every new show, but the emphasis is on "slowly." If an actor is having a particularly difficult time finding the rhythm of a sitcom line, a simple trick is to say the line aloud in a thick Yiddish accent. It will often reveal the writer's intention for the joke. Imitate the rhythms used by the late Henny Youngman in his signature phrase. "Take my wife...please." After the actor has a feel for it, it's simple to just drop the accent. Dick Van Dyke echoed a similar idea, quoting writer Bill Persky, "Think British, write Yiddish."

Rhythm is essential especially in **patter**[9] between two actors. Take this example from "Daddy's Lil' Girl" episode of the *The Hughleys* written by John D. Beck & Ron Hart

> On Home Improvement *we invited a small audience of 20 regular people (usually gotten from the Universal Tour) to give the actors a feel for a live audience's reaction, and also to give them energy. It's always more fun to perform in front of real people.*
>
> Carmen Finestra , Co-creator and Executive Producer, *Home Improvement*

8 Two hinged paddles were slapped together off-stage to emphasize a physical hit.

9 Patter is glib or rapid talk used to attract attention or entertain. The word derives from praying the paternoster (The Lord's Prayer) or praying mechanically.

from the series *The Hughleys*, created by D.L. Hughley and Matt Wickline.

```
                         SALLY
Who is Little Romeo, anyway?

                         YVONNE
Not little. Lil'.

                         SALLY
Little.

                         YVONNE
Lil'.

                         SALLY
Little.

                         YVONNE
Lil'.

                         SALLY
I don't really care anymore.[10]
```

PHYSICAL JOKES

There are many great comics and some are great physical comics.

Some physical comedy is as simple as turning your head. Here are three physical jokes that all involve turning your head. They are the **slow burn**, the **double take** and the **spit take**. They are all a type of **sight gag**. This means you have to see it (as opposed to hear it) to get the joke. For example, in a slow burn, Character A is looking away from Character B. Character A hears Character B say something Character A doesn't like or agree with. Character A slowly turns his head until his eyes land on Character B. Think of *The Honeymooners*. Jackie Gleason, playing Ralph, would hear yet another inane comment from Art Carney, playing Norton. Ralph would slowly turn his head until his eyes landed on Norton. Norton would react appropriately - shamed or ignorant of his stupidity. Jackie Gleason was a master of the slow burn. Art Carney completed the joke with his reaction to it.

The double take and the spit take both require a quick turn of the head. With a double take, Character A is not focused on Character B. Character A turns towards Character B (for any number of reasons) and sees something that doesn't immediately register. Character A begins to turn away and go about his normal routine then quickly whips his head back to stare at Character B. These

10 *The Hughleys* © 2001 Twentieth Century Fox Film Corporation. All Rights Reserved.

two turns of the head constitute a double take.[11] A double take can also be done when Character B is an animate object. Imagine a character walking into his bedroom to get ready for bed. When he left the room this morning it looked normal. He walks in the door yawning, glances at the room, and then looks down as he begins to unbutton his shirt. Suddenly he registers that all the furniture is gone. His head shoots back to the room he just glanced at and stares at the empty room. He has just done a double take to the room. Surprise is key to making an audience laugh. In this example, the audience is waiting to see the character's reaction. The first part of the take shows no reaction. The quick timing of the second turn is what catches the audience.

A spit take involves...well...spitting. Similar to the two previous kinds of take, in a spit take a character is dissatisfied, unhappy or surprised with what he sees or hears. His reaction is so violent that he spits out what he has just put in his mouth as the information registers. This works better for everyone involved (including the audience's sensibilities) if it involves coffee or some other liquid. Regardless, the wardrobe department must be prepared with two or more copies of the same clothing. This is called **doubling**. Spit takes are so big a reaction that they don't often find their way into sitcoms. They are much more common to sketch comedians, like the late Milton Berle.

Many sight gags are not specifically written in the script. But through script analysis, you can find opportunities to use physical business. Here is the beginning of the same episode of *The Hughleys*:

```
FADE IN:

INT. DARRYL AND YVONNE'S BEDROOM - MORNING (DAY 1)

(DARRYL, YVONNE, SYDNEY, MICHAEL)

DARRYL IS ASLEEP. SYDNEY THROWS OPEN THE BEDROOM DOOR.

                              SYDNEY
          Dad!

DARRYL'S EYES POP OPEN.[12]
```

Both D.L. Hughley and Ashley Monique Clark, who played Sydney seized their opportunities. Clark by emphatically throwing the door open and loudly screaming her line; Hughley by bolting up, not knowing what hit him.

Dick Van Dyke shared with us that occasionally the writers would just add the

11 Again we site Michael Richards physical comedy. He could make a triple take work!

12 *The Hughleys* ©2003 Twentieth Century Fox Film Corporation. All Rights Reserved.

stage direction "Dick does what he does" and left it to Dick's physical creativity and tenacity to invent a piece of physical business. Van Dyke told us, "I often went to the set on Saturdays to work with the props and furniture to find ways to create physical humor. Other times I would just find things at the spur of the moment. Carl Reiner saw my love for physical comedy, so Rob Petry became a klutz."

Actors worry about going "over the top" in trying to get laughs. It is all a matter of commitment to character choices and levels. Real life is not generally entertaining enough to put on television.[13] If an actor's energy is strong enough, his dialogue becomes dramatic. Amp it up a little more and it will become funny, especially if the line has sitcom construction. When you go too far, then it becomes "sketchy" or over the top.[14]

Situations can also border on going "over the top." One of the more famous episodes of *The Mary Tyler Moore Show* was the Chuckles The Clown funeral. You would think that it is tough to get laughs at a funeral. However, the very tension of the event leads an audience to want to relieve this by laughing. The very last episode of *9 to 5* centered on a funeral and again there were big laughs. Actors, directors and writers all have to walk the line to find the right level that keeps this in the arena of situation comedy and not slip into sketch comedy. A *Girlfriends* episode dealt with Jenifer Lewis falling off the wagon. Her drunken portrayal had the perfect balance needed for the necessary pathos without losing the funny.

There are plenty of other sight gags: a character walking into a door, a blender exploding, an oven billowing smoke, or a garbage disposal spitting back at you. All of these depend on the element of surprise. One of the most famous sight gags comes from the *I Love Lucy* episode[15] where Ball did a TV commercial for "Vitameatavegamin." Every time she had another spoonful, she would react accordingly to the bad taste or to the alcohol content that was rapidly affecting her. Using the element of surprise, another sight gag from that same episode was Lucy's talking head appearing in the empty TV console's "screen." The sequence ends with sparks flying and smoke billowing from a TV, another sight gag.

VERBAL JOKES

Verbal comedy tends to be more intellectual than physical comedy. It can be as simple as the use of alliteration (Lucy's "happy peppy people" or "poop out at parties"), a pun "especially if it's pun-expected," or simply funny sounding

13 So-called "reality" shows are carefully presented in an entertaining way. They don't resemble our lives.

14 There was a dueling scene with umbrellas in a sitcom entitled *Over the Top* performed quite brilliantly by Tim Curry and John Ritter. Staged by Michael Lembeck, it was brilliantly funny and not "over the top."

15 This *I Love Lucy* episode and others are available through CBS Broadcasting Inc.

words ("big booty"). These jokes depend on sound. Desi Arnaz would often rapidly vent his frustration with Lucy in Spanish or mispronounce a word such as "experience" as "sperience." These were sure laughs for Desi.

One of the most common verbal jokes used on sitcoms is a **mislead** which takes the audience in one direction with information or an idea then surprises them by going in another direction. The point between the set up and punchline when the information goes in the other direction is called the **turn.** A turn can be accompanied by a physical turn, change of vocal pace, or change of body position. This physicalization accentuates the turn and enhances the comedy. In the "I've Got Friends I Haven't Used Yet" episode of *Becker*, Ted Danson (Becker) reunites with Kelsey Grammer who plays Becker's old friend Rick Cooper. Grammer flawlessly executes not only one but two turns within a single speech:

```
                         BECKER
Any more surprises?

                         RICK
No, no, no... oh wait a minute. There was...oh no,
that wasn't you. That's it.[16]
```

Aided by Danson's sarcastic set-up, Grammer does his first mislead with "No, no, no." He immediately does a turn on "oh wait a minute. There was..." This serves as another mislead so that Grammer can do his second turn on "oh no, that wasn't you." He then punctuates it with "That's it." Watch these skilled professionals. Their light, yet skilled, touch with comedy is a joy to behold.

Another popular joke in a sitcom is a **callback**[17], which is a reference to previously, mentioned material or piece of business. Sometimes whole jokes are repeated. Sometimes a specific word or piece of business is repeated. Every time Lucille Ball had another taste of the "Vitameatavegamin," either by spoon of swig from the bottle, it was a callback. Callbacks give the audience a chance to enjoy a joke again. Sometimes they occur within the same scene; sometimes in a later scene. The key for a callback that occurs in a later scene is that the first time the information is mentioned, it must be big enough to be memorable. The following example is from the episode "Invasion of the Gold Digger," written by Keith Josef Adkins from the series *Girlfriends*, created by Mara Brock Akil. The girls are trying to come up with a plan to get even with William's (Reggie Hayes) gold digger girlfriend Monica (Keesha Sharp). After Joan (Tracee Ellis Ross) suggests that they need to get rid of her, Lynn (Persia White) suggests her idea for doing away with Monica.

---

16 From the episode "I Have Friends I Haven't Used Yet," written by Ian Gurvitz, from the series *Becker*, created by Dave Hackel. Paramount Pictures Corporation. All Rights Reserved.

17 This is different from the callback an actor gets after an audition.

LYNN

"Officer, I don't know how that radio fell in the hot tub."

White not only gets her laugh on this joke but memorably sets up a callback for the tag where Monica is in the hot tub sitting across from Lynn. Monica wears an eye mask so she can't see Lynn's hand inching towards the radio. The show ends with another huge laugh as Monica reminds Lynn.

MONICA

(WITHOUT REMOVING THE MASK) Lynn, you're in the hot tub, too.

ON LYNN'S "DAMN SHE'S RIGHT" LOOK, WE:

FADE OUT[18]

Here is another example of a callback from "The Helmet" episode written by David Feeney from the series *According to Jim* where Cheryl (Courtney Thorne-Smith) and Dana (Kimberly Williams) are discussing an Internet auction where Cheryl is posing as a man:

ACT ONE

SCENE C

INT. KITCHEN - DAYS LATER (DAY 3)

(CHERYL, DANA)

CHERYL SITS AT THE COMPUTER. DANA ENTERS AND READS THE SCREEN. THEY AD-LIB HELLOS.

DANA

(READING) "I hear that, my man. You marry them right away they try to change you." (TO CHERYL) You're still writing SPIFFYTOOL405?

CHERYL

Yeah. That helmet's as good as mine. Men are so stupid.

18 Paramount Pictures Corporation.

DANA

So you guys are becoming friends.

CHERYL

How could we not? We both could stand to lose a little weight, we've both been thrown out of Bulls games for mooning the ref, and our favorite beer is "the next one."

DANA

You're not going to go out cruising chicks together are you?

CHERYL

It's fascinating being a guy. He tells me stuff he'd never tell his wife.

DANA

Like what?

CHERYL

Get this...he buys sports stuff off the Internet and hides it from her in a tool cabinet in his garage.

DANA

That poor woman.

CHERYL

Please, she's a sap. You can't feel sorry for women like that, Dana. They bring it on themselves. (OFF WATCH) Oh, it's twelve-thirty. I gotta go meet Jim. (THEN TYPING AND READING) "Well, the ol' ball and chain is calling. Nag nag nag."

DANA

Hey, tell him an off color joke. Guys love those.

CHERYL

I don't know any.

DANA GRABS THE COMPUTER AND PULLS IT IN FRONT OF HER. SHE STARTS TO TYPE.

DANA

You don't know any? You're married to an off-color joke. Check this out. It's about a sailor and a parrot who meet the Pope. I heard it at a gas station.

CHERYL LOOKS AT IT, THEN CHUCKLES.

CHERYL
I get it. The parrot's Jewish.

DANA
What? No.

CHERYL
Oh. I don't get it then.

AND WE:

CUT TO:

The Jewish parrot returns at the act break:

JIM (O.S.)
Hey, Cheryl, I heard a great joke today about a sailor and a parrot meeting the Pope.

CHERYL REACTS AS JIM ENTERS, PUTTING ON HIS JACKET.

JIM (CONT'D)
Wanna hear it?

CHERYL
Oh, uh...no. I've already heard that one.

JIM
Oh.

AS THEY HEAD OUT.

JIM (CONT'D)
The parrot's Jewish, right?

FADE OUT:

END OF ACT ONE[19]

An exact and immediate callback is called an **echo.** Mocking someone is an echo. Jane Leeves, of *Frasier* fame, got great mileage from her English accent in

19 Touchstone Television. All Rights Reserved.

an earlier series *Throb*. While discussing an automobile with Diana Canova, Jane simply repeated the word "car" in Diana's American accent and got a big laugh. Like a callback, when a writer uses an echo, he has to be sure the audience has registered the information the first time that information is mentioned. The echo may be in the same scene or many scenes later on in the script. If the audience doesn't remember it, in either case, we say, "The callback is too far away."

The previously sited episode of *Girlfriends* begins with this echo:

```
                    WILLIAM
Joan, guess who got the Thatcher-Dunwoody case?
Three hints. He's tall. He's devilishly handsome.
And he's not you.

                    JOAN
William, every junior partner in the firm has been
fiending for that case. How did you get it?

                    WILLIAM
I told you. I'm tall. I'm devilishly handsome and
most importantly, I'm not you.[20]
```

In this case, Hayes echoed himself.

Writers often employ **irony** in sitcoms. An example that Webster's New World Dictionary gives to illustrate irony is "calling a stupid man 'clever'" or saying that "the firehouse burned." These jokes are usually very straightforward and depend on the audience's intelligence. Punching these kind of jokes is not advised. Irony is very specific because the meaning of the words used is the opposite of their usual sense. *Fraiser* is known for its "smart humor" in the way it uses irony. Literary reference, the use of alliteration or personification in constructing the language of jokes adds to this style. In the hot tub, Keesha Sharp accentuated the comedy accentuating the alliteration and using the *T*s in "hot tub too."

The two final types of jokes we'll discuss are the **understatement** and the **twist**. Understatement employs irony. It deliberately states the truth inaccurately or too weakly in order to make the audience laugh. Most jokes that are understatements are accompanied by the **subtext** "Duh!" Subtext[21] is what an actor is thinking while he says the line. It is his silent or hidden message. Subtext is an important tool for an actor not only when understating something but whenever a character is thinking something different from or more complex than

20 From the episode "Invasion of the Gold Digger," written by Keith Josef Adkins from the series *Girlfriends*, created by Mara Brock Akil. Paramount Pictures Corporation. All Rights Reserved.

21 Sub meaning "under" and text meaning "wording." Duh!

what his actual words (or lack of words) allows him to say aloud. A **dichotomy** is another literary tool employed, as part of an understatement, to evoke humor. It divides an idea into separate classes thereby bringing out the funny in the comparison. These jokes are usually delivered very straightforward and depend on the audience's intelligence. Punching these kind of jokes is also not advised.

Many jokes are entirely based in character, for example, insults. An insult is based on information that one character feels about another. A running joke on *The Hughleys* was to see which ethnic or social group Darryl could insult that week. Over the course of four seasons, he insulted gays, the physically challenged, Little People, Republicans, Democrats, Asians, Hispanics and many more. Every time he got a laugh!

Since much of comedy is based in insult humor, much care needs to be taken in assuring that the joke-tellers are still likeable. An audience will not laugh at real pain. They have to know that everyone will be all right. It is a hard line to walk at times. Insult standup comics, like Don Rickles, have always used phrases like "I kid" throughout their performances. Dabney Coleman (*9 to 5, Buffalo Bill*), Ted Knight (*The Mary Tyler Moore Show, Too Close for Comfort*) and Ed Asner (*The Mary Tyler Moore, Lou Grant*) were always actors that could play the part of the curmudgeon but still be likeable. Every writer, producer, director and actor tries to create character that the audience will care about. Even main-character villains must have human qualities that can be understood, so that they are somehow sympathetic. It is much more critical with comedy.

Some jokes are word-based like a pun or play on words. Other jokes build on a previous punchline. This is called a **topper**. If the topper is not funnier than the original joke, it is not worth doing.

Some jokes are based in story such as a twist or a surprise. It usually is an unexpected plot point. It is much the same as a turn, but not in the classic sense. Turns must have an immediate setup. Twists often do not. The following twist, a play on words, was delivered by Elise Neal on an episode of *The Hughleys*.

```
                    YVONNE
I know. I heard your version of "The old woman who
lived in a show, who only had two children because
a career is important too."[22]
```

Twists sometimes merely steers the story in another direction. When Bret Butler's character Grace in *Grace Under Fire* saw her father-in-law in a bar during one episode, it got a small reaction. When Grace and the audience realized that it was a gay bar, the laugh was big. Classic act break material!

22 *The Hughleys* ©2001 Twentieth Century Fox Film Corporation. All Rights Reserved.

Sitcom Exercise

Read these scenes and find the jokes. Next, identify the type of joke it is (turn, run of three, "K" sound, call back, echo, understatement, twist. pun, etc.). Here are two scenes. The first from the "Home Improvement," *pilot based the stand-up comedy of Tim Allen. Wilson was played in the series by Earl Hindman.*

```
                    HOME IMPROVEMENT
                        "PILOT"
                        ACT TWO
                        SCENE 2
EXT. BACKYARD-DUSK (DAY 2)
SPFX: BARBEQUE SMOKE FROM WILSON'S YARD
(WE SEE WILSON BARBEQUING. TIM SEARCHES FOR THE DISHWASHER PARTS)

                          TIM
          What a mess.

                         WILSON
          Hi, ya, Tim!

                          TIM
          Hi Wilson. Mmm. Smells good. What are you cooking?
          Baby back ribs?

                         WILSON
          Squirrel.

                          TIM
          Squirrel. What's that taste like?

                         WILSON
          Sort of like chipmunk. By the way, a couple of those
          bolts landed in the birdbath.

                          TIM
          I was a little surprised by the torque on that
          compressor.

                         WILSON
          I tell you, Tim, this is what it's all about. Catch
          of the day cooking, sun setting, men standing around
          the campfire, telling stories.
```

TIM
Can I tell you one?

WILSON
Campfire's lit, good neighbor.

TIM
Jill didn't get the job she wanted. I tell her not to feel bad and she gets angry at me.

WILSON
Hmm.

TIM
And then I tell her what to do, she gets all bent out of shape and storms out of the rooom.

WILSON
Sounds like you were having an asymmetrical conversation.

TIM
Asymmetrical. How do you spell that?

WILSON
Let's just say one-sided.

(TIM DOES A KNOWING GRUNT.)

WILSON (CONT'D)
You see, Tim, by nature, men are problem solvers. But Jill didn't want you to solve her problem.

TIM
She didn't?

WILSON
No. She just wanted you to listen while she shared her feelings.

TIM
Just stand there and listen? That's like doing nothing?

WILSON

Sometimes the best thing you can do is nothing.

(TIM DOES AN UNDERSTANDING GRUNT)

TIM

I get it. Jill got mad at me because I didn't listen to her.

WILSON

No, she got mad at you because you blew up the damn dishwasher.[23]

Here is another scene from the Style and Substance *pilot. The character of Mr. John was played by Joseph Maher. Trudy was Linda Kash.*

STYLE AND SUBSTANCE

"PILOT"

ACT ONE

(A)

FADE IN:

INT. OUTER LOBBY - MORNING (D-1)

(JANE)

CAMERA STARTS IN CLOSE ON A BEAUTIFUL FLORAL ARRANGEMENT ON A TABLE IN THE OUTER LOBBY (THE SHOW TITLE WILL BE SEEN HERE). CAMERA PANS UP AND WE SEE THE SIGN ON THE WALL: "CHELSEA STEVENS, A DIVISION OF FERBER COMMUNICATIONS." WE FIND JANE TALKING ON HER CELLULAR PHONE.

JANE

Everything's under control, Mr. Ferber. You sent me to run things here, that's what I'm doing. No, Chelsea hasn't signed the budget agreement yet. Yes, I did promise I'd have that signed by the end of my first week. Yes, that would be tomorrow. Yes, I'm aware I'm saying yes a lot. Yes. Mr. Ferber, I've just had a little trouble pinning Chelsea down, but I will pin her. Consider her pinned. Yes. Thank you sir.

23 From the pilot episode of *Home Improvement* created by Matt Williams, David McFadzean, and Carmen Finestra. Used by permission of Touchstone Television. All Rights Reserved.

JANE CLICKS OFF, GROWLS AND EXITS INTO THE OFFICES.

INT. PRODUCTION OFFICES - CONTINUOUS (D-1)

(CHELSEA, JANE, TRUDY, MR. JOHN, TERRY, OFFICE EXTRAS)
JANE ENTERS AND CROSSES OVER TO WHERE TRUDY IS MAKING HERSELF A CUP OF COFFEE.

JANE
Hi, Trudy. Have you seen Chelsea?

TRUDY
Not yet. She hasn't signed your budget thing, huh?

JANE
I'm getting desperate.

TRUDY
Jane, let me give you some advice. When you deal with Chelsea, you always, always have to remember one important thing.

JANE
What's that?

TRUDY
She's a freak.

JANE
She's not a freak.

TRUDY
Oh, yes, she is. Last Christmas, she made a gingerbread house? It was built to code. There was a guest gingerbread house in the back.

JANE
Okay, she's a little obsessive, but she's built a very successful business. The magazine, the television show...

TRUDY
It's a great big freakdom.

JANE

Then why are you here?

TRUDY

Because I'm the best food stylist in the world and Chelsea knows it.

TRUDY OPENS HER PORTFOLIO AND FLIPS THROUGH IT.

TRUDY (CONT'D)

My award-winning chocolate sundae.

JANE

That ice cream looks delicious.

TRUDY

Thank you. It's lard. I can recreate any dish for photographic purposes. I use whatever it takes. That chocolate sauce?

JANE

It looks good.

TRUDY

Quaker State motor oil. That's thirty weight, if memory serves. (TURNING THE PAGE) This is my fettuccine alfredo.

JANE

The noodles look real.

TRUDY

Oh, they are.

JANE

How about the sauce?

TRUDY

Sears Weatherbeater house paint. And that's one coat, Jane.

<u>MR. JOHN</u> CROSSES OVER. HE'S A DAPPER MAN IN HIS FIFTIES.

TRUDY (CONT'D)

Perhaps we should ask Mr. John.

MR. JOHN

Ask me what?

TRUDY

Do you think Chelsea's a freak?

MR. JOHN

No, I don't. I've been designing for Chelsea Stevens for ten wonderful years, and I believe her to be the apotheosis of taste and style.

TRUDY

She's not in yet.

MR. JOHN

She's a freak. (TO TRUDY) Let's tell her about the gingerbread house.

TRUDY

I already did.

MR. JOHN

(TO JANE) It had plumbing. Guy and I still talk about it.

JANE

Guy?

MR. JOHN

My life partner. I'm sorry if my frankness shocks you, Jane, but I'm proud of my relationship and I don't hide the fact.

JANE

I'm fine.

MR. JOHN

Well. I know you've come from the Midwest...so if I do say anything that makes you uncomfortable, I hope you'll speak up.

JANE

It's not a problem. I am an adult.

MR. JOHN

Thank you, Jane. It's like I was saying to Guy in the shower this morning as we were lathering up...

JANE

Oh, dear.

MR. JOHN

Too much?

CHELSEA STEVENS, THE JUGGERNAUT OF STYLE AND TASTE, ENTERS FROM THE OUTER LOBBY. SHE CARRIES A SMALL WICKER BASKET COVERED WITH A RED-CHECKERED NAPKIN.

CHELSEA

Good morning, everyone!

STAFFERS ADLIB GREETINGS.

CHELSEA (CONT'D)

This morning before breakfast while I was restocking my trout pond and shearing my lamb, I realized I wanted to tell you all how much I appreciate the hard work you do. But then later, while I was airing out my quilts and making prosciutto jerky, I reminded myself that we can always work harder. I guess what I'm trying to say is...be more like me. And one more thing. In the magazine, on the show...no more kiwi. Kiwi is over. If I could talk to a kiwi, do you know what I'd say? I'd say "Get out, get a shave, you're through." No kiwi. Let's all say it.

ALL

No kiwi.

CHELSEA

Thank you. And the big news. My divorce becomes final today, so I think we all knows what that means.

A BEAT, THEN SHE PUTS THE BASKET ON THE TABLE.

```
                              CHELSEA (CONT'D)
            That's right. I made scones!

CHELSEA DISAPPEARS INTO HER OFFICE.

                              MR. JOHN
            She seems down today.

                                              DISSOLVE TO:[24]
```

PLAYING A JOKE

Recognizing a joke and playing a joke are two different skills. Many an actor is born with an innate sense of comedy. He may be able to deliver any of the jokes we mentioned above without being able to identify them. He may simply feel them. He may be funny without knowing why he's funny. Some actors feel that overanalyzing may trip them up in performing because they begin to "over think" the material. A person, who has an analytical approach to comedy but without the mastery of how to perform them, may be better suited to writing or directing than to acting. Our advice is to go with whatever works for you. Actor/ director/ playwright Carlos Lacamara (*Brothers Garcia*) advises:

> Keep it real. We've all seen examples of big, wacky acting on sitcoms, but the best actors keep their performances honest. Create your character and be true to it. Forget about being funny. One of the easiest traps to fall into is trying to repeat a laugh. If you get a laugh in a rehearsal, then you imitate your line reading to get that laugh again, you often get rewarded with silence. Forget about the laugh. Be true to the character and the teleplay. Listen and react. The laugh will take care of itself. And bring a sweater. Those stages are cold.

We think Lacamara's advice is good...for SOME actors. If being conscious of the comedic requirements takes you out of the scene, you won't get laughs. We're not trying to confuse you. Sitcom acting requires a light touch. You must understand the inherent rhythm, feel the timing, and hear the music of the words but not punch them too hard. If the audience sees the joke coming a mile away, you have lost the element of surprise, which is what causes their laughter. Find the level that works for you. For example, jokes that have funny words, alliteration, or *K*'s and *P*'s play themselves.

It is easy to fall into some traps. Lacamara pointed out the most fatal one: repeating. EVERYTIME AN ACTOR SAYS HIS WORDS, IT SHOULD HAVE THE ILLUSION OF THE FIRST TIME. Be present! Listen! Good actors know that this means staying in the moment. Watch Ted Danson, Michael J. Fox, Kelsey Gram-

24 Used by permission of Touchstone Television. All Rights Reserved.

mer, Mary Tyler Moore. They are brilliant comic actors with huge bodies of work that can teach you volumes.

Other traps are specific to comedy because comedy uses the element of surprise. The first trap is called **tipping the joke**. Tipping the joke is giving away prematurely what is about to come. It's also called **telegraphing** or **giving it away**. Actors often tip the joke by laughing before the punchline or reacting to a line before replying to the line. This robs the audience of the surprise, which the punchline will reveal. This may seem like you're robbing the character of his natural reaction. We suggest building into the character that he hears the information but waits to reveal his feelings with dialogue. Let the line be funny. The writer will appreciate it! That being said, there are exceptions to this. Sometimes the simple reaction that occurs when an actor is listening is funnier than the line that the writer wrote.

So many jokes are character based. Lacamara mentions creating a character and being true to it. Most sitcoms have characters whose jokes are based on the same premise. For example, on *Cheers* Nicholas Colasanto created the Coach character who always misunderstood information. Woody Harrelson's character trait of naiveté worked the same way when he replaced Colasanto after his untimely passing. Choose well when creating a character. Know what will best serve the comedy.

In Chapter One we talked about the sitcom rule **COMEDY COMES IN THREES.** To play a joke that is a run, the secret is to not telegraph that the joke is coming. List the first two items and then make sure they hear the third because that's the funny part.

Another comedy trap is leaving too much air between lines. The sitcom rule at the beginning of this chapter states that **FASTER IS FUNNIER**. An easy way to keep the pacing fast is to **cue bite** or take out the pauses between the lines. It is also called **picking up the cues** or **dovetailing** the lines. The only time an actor shouldn't cue bite is after a punchline, when he should be holding for a laugh. After two days of learning staging, memorizing cues and lines, it is easy to forget that this stuff isfunny. The goal is to pace up and energize the dialogue but stop to wait for the laughs.

THE DIFFERENCE BETWEEN TUESDAY AND WEDNESDAY

The Wednesday rehearsal will be different from the Tuesday rehearsal: it will probably be more fun because more things are working. This is due to the writers pinpointing places in the script where they could help with the writing. Another factor is the actors and director are now more familiar with the material as they incorporate the changes and refinements. If a particular scene is still proving problematic, the director might ask the show runner to come to the set. The problem scene or section will be shown to the writer. Writing changes may be done on the spot[25] or the writer may go back to his office and send down new pages as soon as the rewriting is done.

Every cast has a different relationship with the writers. Some are adversarial some are collaborative. Writer Michael Kaplan (*Girlfriends*) says, "All too often, scripts are changed and not always for the better." Director James Burrows (*Cheers, News Radio, Will & Grace*) suggests that the most important function a director has is to break down the barriers between actors and writers. On shows where an actor holds a writing title or executive producer title, that actor may be more vocal about rewrites. The ultimate goal is to create the best show possible. Ideally, this is done within a respectful, creative environment.

Many sitcom casts do a **speed-thru** of the lines before the run-thru begins or before a scene begins. In a speed-thru, an actor recites his dialogue at a quicker speed than normal (sometimes devoid of meaning). This serves two purposes. First, it refreshes and reviews the dialogue (especially if there have been changes) and it let's the actors discover that saying a line simply faster enhances the comedy.

On that last funeral episode of *9 to 5*, executive producer Michael Kagan was cast[26] as a minister and for the first time joined the actors in rehearsals. Just before a run-thru, the cast wanted to play a gag on him by telling him that they always do a speed-thru at that time. They then proceeded to run the lines at a speed that was so lightning-fast that Michael would have trouble just keeping up. After a good laugh, everyone realized that the one thing that the show had been missing was extra pace. The run-thru and the show played much better when they split the difference between how they were doing the lines and the newfound energy. Let us repeat once more **FASTER IS FUNNIER**!

THE NETWORK RUN-THRU

Besides pacing the show, an actor must also pace himself. The goal for Wednesday is doing an excellent network run-thru. The "suits" are the buyers of our product. Whether an actor is in every scene or just one, he must time his day so that his energy is peaking for this performance. For some actors this means, "saving it" for run-thru. For others, it means attacking every scene at performance level all day so they can see what that feels like. Most casts will get a short break before run-thru. This is a good time when an actor might close his eyes and regroup or focus. Another actor may have that afternoon tea or coffee to bolster his energy. Others may seek out the script supervisor or dialogue coach to run lines. Another actor may find that visiting[27] with producers or studio and network people, who are arriving for the run-thru, clears his mind for a good performance.

---

25 The script supervisor will be noting all the changes made.

26 Michael must have liked acting so much that he now acts full time.

27 Better known as "kissing ass."

This break between rehearsal and run-thru is when the rest of the crew is getting ready for the run-thru. The on-set crew is doing everything possible to make the run-thru flow as smoothly as possible. The on-set crews are the people who are there to support the daily rehearsals. It includes the assistant directors, or stage managers, the script supervisor, the onstage prop person, the onstage decorator, and the dialogue coach. The rest of the department heads are winding up whatever they're doing so they can attend the run-thru.

The network run-thru begins the moment the last network executive arrives. The AD or stage manager quiets everyone down. Some people will be standing; some people will be sitting in chairs right in front of the set. Crewmembers will either be "on the floor" or in the audience bleachers. Someone from the lighting crew will usually bring up basic show lights[28] in each of the sets as they are used. This is different! All week we have been using fluorescent work lights.

The script supervisor will be timing the scene in order to answer the first question that usually is asked after run-thru: "How long are we?" The lighting director is noting what areas of the set are specifically being used. As soon as run-thru is over, his crew lead by the **gaffer**[29] will do the **hanging** of extra lighting instruments in those areas noted for this episode.

In order to facilitate a smooth run-thru, actors must anticipate where they need to be. The show is run in order from top to bottom so there are no surprises. While the network execs on the soundstage floor are walking to the next set and stagehands move their chairs, the prop master is distributing hand props and doing last minute adjustments for the next scene. The AD or stage manager is reviewing his or her checklist to see that everyone is in place for their first entrance to the next scene. Actors, DON'T make the AD or stage manager have to look for you! Delays in the run-thru, due to anyone not being ready, is unacceptable. It ruins the flow of the show for everyone.

After the run-thru, the show runner meets with the network and studio executives to get notes. Their opinion counts. Usually the rest of the writing staff returns to the writers' room and begins work on the obvious fixes. The set crew immediately gets to work on finishing the set. After notes, the actors sign out and get their call times for the next day. There may be some pre-shooting done on Thursday. The actors and the crew will be told Thursday's schedule, which scenes will be camera blocked, and which scenes will be pre-shot.

With luck, the note session with the network will be brief. If their notes from Monday have been addressed, they may have a few additional requests, praise the work that has been done thus far, and leave. That is the best-case scenario. The worst-case scenario may involve a massive rewrite or recasting a guest star. Yes, this means someone may get FIRED!

---

28 Show lights are instruments hung especially to light the set as opposed to general fluorescent lighting that exists in the soundstage for everyday use. Show lights are hotter and more concentrated.

29 The gaffer is in charge of hanging and focussing the lighting instruments. He is an expert electrician.

GETTING FIRED, NO, WAIT, NOT GETTING FIRED

Getting fired is the actor's worst nightmare.[30] It happens often enough on sitcoms that actors live in fear until they get their new script on Wednesday night and check to see that their name is still there. In our experience, there are two main reasons for getting fired: miscasting and not being very good. Miscasting is NEVER the fault of the actor. In fact, an actor that gets miscast must have been pretty darn good to get the part in the first place.

Not being very good is trickier. It doesn't necessarily mean the actor is a bad actor. It just means that something isn't clicking. Maybe the actor can't handle the constant and sometimes on-the-spot rewriting that goes on in a sitcom. Another actor may simply not be funny. To be able to apply funny rhythms and rules and still be naturalistic in a scene is a special acting gift. Not everyone gets that gift. Some less than funny actors have had the luxury of learning their craft on the job. If you watch their shows in syndication, you can tell the early episodes from the later ones by their comedic improvement. Remember, dying is easy, comedy is hard! The important thing is for an actor not to let getting fired destroy his confidence. With this major disappointment is also an upside. An actor that gets fired still gets paid!

If a massive rewrite is required, then all the writers go to the writers' room, order dinner[31] and get to work. Scripts will be delivered as soon as they have been rewritten, proofed, and copied. This probably will happen sometime when it's dark. This is the job of the night runner Production Assistant who comes in after the normal work day. His duties include copying and labeling the script for delivery... unless it's a green set and then everything gets delivered electronically. Actors should leave a light on for the PA delivering the script. The PA will not ring your doorbell unless he or she knows you have requested them to do so. Actors should get a good night's sleep, especially if they are going to be pre-shooting.

Sitcom Vocabulary Quick Review

Read these sentences. If the director gave you these notes, would you instantly know what he meant? If not, go back and review the explanation in this chapter.

We need a **blow** *for the* **act break.**

Replace the **button.**

The **callback** *is too far from the setup.*

Let's start with the **cold open.**

30 Not remembering lines is traditionally the actors' most common nightmare.

31 One of the perks of writing sitcoms is that you are well fed and not have to pay for it.

Keep it down at **craft service***!*

If we **cue bite***, we could knock a minute off the show.*

That's the **dichotomy***, the character doesn't get it either.*

The **double take** *is too big for this show.*

We'll be **doubling** *the shirt but not the pants.*

Dovetail *those two lines.*

It's an **echo***, so make it sound like the first one!*

Is the **gaffer** *done* **hanging***?*

Don't **give it away***!*

It's not funny if they don't understand the **irony***.*

The **mislead** *has to be more sincere.*

Make sure you are **off book** *for the run-thru.*

Pace up the **patter** *in that section.*

Pick up the cues*!*

Say it as written; the writers will **punch it up***.*

Save the **sight gag** *for the second take.*

The **slow burn** *can go a little faster.*

We'll do a **speed-thru** *before each scene.*

Don't do the **spit take** *until we're shooting.*

We have to rethink her **subtext***.*

We'll rehearse the **tag** *just before run thru.*

The **teaser** *is running too long.*

You're **telegraphing** *the joke.*

The smile is **tipping** *the blow.*

Did you notice, they always give your character a **topper** *for everything he says?*

Can you turn as you do the **turn***?*

That's a great **twist***!*

The humor will come from the **understatement***.*

The **wrinkle** *made the audience gasp.*

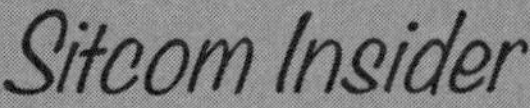

MY WRITERS' ROOM

A good writing room is about collaboration. A bad writing room is about competition. The worst thing that can happen in a writers' room is for someone to offer an idea and someone else to shoot it down with "that sucks." Cruelty and bad manners aside, ridiculing an idea only makes the room grind to a halt. Also, the person who offered the idea won't be heard from again for a long time. People who curtly dismiss others may claim they don't have time to listen to bad ideas, but I maintain there are no bad ideas. Any producer who runs an successful writers room knows that the end product (whether its a story, a line, or a joke) often comes from an idea that's 180 degrees opposite it,

By encouraging all ideas, you give writers the freedom to build on what each person says. In the best writing rooms, a good joke is like building a house. Once it's standing, no one cares who put in which nail and board. Everyone just enjoys living in it, and feels good they had a part in building it.

Matt Williams, my co-creator on Home Improvement *(along with Dave McFadzean) says, "There are infinite possibilities with the word 'yes', and very limiting ones with the word 'no'."*

Here are some tips for writers room etiquette:

- *Be on time. If someone says, "Let's take a 10 minute break," be back in ten minutes. Nothing is more draining than sitting around waiting for someone else. It also establishes a bad precedent. "He said 10 minutes, but he probably means 20." Soon you're wasting time trying to corral everyone.*
- *Don't veer off the track. I've seen writers rooms waste hours as people discuss "the trades", movies or TV they've seen, etc! Good producers nip these diversions in the bud. People may hate to write, but they'll hate it more if they're doing it at midnight. Also in bad writing rooms, people waste time criticizing the actors for ruining the jokes. (Bad writers don't know that actors can't play jokes, they can only play emotion and motivation. If you write that well, it will be funny) or "what idiots" they feel are running the studios and networks, and not giving them a chance to shine.*
- *If you disagree with an idea, don't dismiss it offer an alternative. Say something positive like, "that could work, but I was thinking..." or, "that's one way to go, but another way is..." Whenever you hear an idea you like, always, always, always acknowledge it, and compliment the person who said it. If you honestly can't think of an alternative to an idea you don't like, simply say you're not sure. Ask everyone else what they think. If it's a good writers' room, constructive criticism will be offered, or an alternative you can use.*
- *Last, but not least, when ordering a meal in, stay away from heavy food. Your eyes will be drooping, and you'll be no help to anyone.*

Carmen Finestra
Co-creator and Executive Producer, *Home Improvement*

Sitcom Career Profile

BRUCE FINN
DIRECTOR OF PHOTOGRAPHY

Bruce is a gregarious, focused, hard working, and creative guy. We first met him working on The Hughleys. *He not only designed but was published, and had developed innovative lighting equipment known as the Gambox, Topbox and Maxilight. Bruce always does more than you ask. It's very clear he loves what he's doing.*

What shows have you worked on?

My last few show include *8 Simple Rules for Dating My Teenage Daughter, The Hughleys, One on One, Style and Substance*, and *Leap of Faith.*

What are your responsibilities?

I design the lighting and supervise the electricians and grips during pre-lighting and shooting to achieve the best possible photographic look.

Did you have specific training in this field?

I was interested in photography from an early age. I studied at Antioch College and after dropping out struggled my way up the ladder starting as an intern. I always try to excel at whatever task I'm asked to perform, no matter how basic. I was a great PA. I made the best coffee!

How did you get your first job?

Michael Petok (a wonderful producer and person) vouched for me after working on single camera projects together.

What advice would you give someone who wants to do what you do?

Befriend and call huge volumes of business-potential clients. Persevere and shoot as much as possible. Develop your own style; learn from other's talents and flaws. Develop a positive attitude. Be helpful to others. Try to make every person on the set think you're happy, reasonable, responsible, hardworking, and a talented co-worker.

What do you like best about your job?

Performing my art and craft. Inventing and manufacturing innovative equipment that improves the selection of good tools cinematographers have to work with. Making money to support my family.

DIRECTORS OF PHOTOGRAPHY
Union: IATSE Local 600
Typical Weekly Salary: $3500-$5000
Hours Per Week: 31

Chapter 5 THURSDAY... CAMERA BLOCKING

In this chapter:

- What happens on stage before an actor arrives
- The steps in camera blocking
- Camera tips for actors
- The importance of the stand-in
- Why Lucy and Desi were trailblazers
- Preparing to record film style and tape style
- The responsibilities of a camera operator
- Career profile of a sitcom technical coordinator/associate director

Sometimes things must get worse before they get better. Thursday is the day that happens. After three days of refining both the writing and the performances, now things may seem a bit chaotic as we add the recording elements (cameras and sound) that make it a TV show. Lots of people have lots of questions or simply must talk aloud to do their job at the same time an actor is performing. Carmen Finestra describes Thursday in this chapter's SITCOM INSIDER.

> The camera persons and the regular crew work with the director and actors to 'camera block' the entire show. This requires a lot of work. There may be hundreds of camera shots to block and rehearse and the actors are pretty fried by the end of the day.

This phenomenon of the stage show getting worse is also common in the theatre. After weeks of just rehearsing the play, performances always suffer during "tech" when lighting and sound cues are added. In television, the challenges grow exponentially because of the myriad decisions involved in filming or taping with multiple cameras and microphones. However, with a great crew and a LOT of cooperation, the work gets accomplished.

SITCOM RULE

Say the line, then move. *Movement distracts from the important material. It causes the camera to widen, further distancing the viewer from the information.*

BEFORE REHEARSAL

As the actors arrive at their call time, there are many more people from the technical crew already on stage. They are setting up cameras and microphones often referred to, on a tape set, as **ESU**[1] or engineering set up. The art department is finishing some paint details and adding more artificial and potted greenery to the set. Additional wardrobe personnel are bringing clothing into some on-stage dressing rooms that have been constructed using plain black flats booked together behind one of the sets. The make-up room has been opened, waiting for makeup artists for any pre-shoots that will be done later that day.

Everyone seems to know each other and a guest actor may feel like a stranger in this extended family. The regular cast and crew are catching up with the technical crew on details of their week. You, as a guest, are left out. Everyone needs to study the newest edition of the script and see what changes have been made. Few rewrites for this show will be done on Thursday. Nancylee Myatt describes the writer's room today:

"Most of the time you'll be worrying about what you'll be eating for lunch or dinner - then after that is settled you'll spend a little time cutting the script for time and trying to replace jokes that were funny on Monday and now on Thursday aren't making you laugh anymore." All glibness aside, the writers are probably taking a pass at next week's episode in between all that eating. No matter what your job category, for questions about substantial script changes, you should quickly seek out the director. The day is already jammed full so there is no time set aside for re-blocking or reworking anything new.

DRY BLOCKING

When the stage is ready, guest actors might[2] finally be introduced to the tech crew. The director or AD will announce your name, or maybe only your character's name, to everyone. This is what the crew has been getting ready for. The camera department has prepped their cameras. The lighting crew is standing by to adjust levels. The audio team is setting up their microphones either on giant stands called **booms** or on the catwalk above.

Long-time boom operator Ed Valfre talks about camera blocking day from the sound department's point of view:

> By the day the actors are in front of the cameras, the sound department should have been notified of any unusual situations from sound effects and music playbacks to placement of an actor delivering dialogue in places that no microphone will go. In general, this notification is rare but it does give the job that fly by the seat of your pants kind of excitement.

1 Seeing ESU on the schedule for Thursday and Friday is usually a clue that the show is to be taped and not filmed.

2 Some shows (or stars) are better hosts than others!

Dry blocking begins with the crew watching the actors perform one scene at a time for its visual and audio content. The crew needs to see where the actors move and listen to what the actors say. The first scene to be blocked is not necessarily the teaser. Like every other day this week, the order of scene rehearsal is determined by many factors such as the star's and children's availabilities. One more scheduling factor is added on this day: the time it takes the cameras and booms to be positioned in front of each set. This makes it efficient to block every scene that takes place on one set before the crew moves the cameras and booms on to another.

SOME BACKGROUND

This is a good time to talk about the different kinds of recording mediums and what they mean to your process. One view is, that no matter how the images are recorded, they all end up being displayed on the TV screen in people's homes, so they all look like TV. Getting from the stage to the television screen in your home has taken many different routes. Sitcoms were one of the types of programs on early live television. Radio had these kinds of shows starting in 1929 with *The Goldbergs* and it was only natural for the form to make the jump to TV. *The Goldbergs* was the fourth sitcom to premiere on TV. The first sitcoms, like all other live shows, were displays of 30[3] frames per second of black-and-white electronic images. There were not very many camera shots and almost no special effects.

The only editing was the **live cutting**, and occasional **dissolve**, between cameras on the stage. Live cutting means editing on the fly. A dissolve is a specific kind of transition. Thirty-nine episodes made up the season's show order. The only way to have a repeat broadcast was to have a film shot off of a monitor at the time of broadcast. Because of their cost and poor quality, these kinescopes were not commonly made by the average weekly show. There would be a different summer series in that time slot for the other thirteen weeks and then the new season would begin.

As tape technology was developing, Hollywood with its rich film history had a more difficult time getting into the television arena because film is more expensive to produce. Re-use of "B" movies, movie shorts[4], and "serial" action series[5] was all that was in demand. In 1951, when television wanted to make a sitcom pilot[6] with Lucille Ball and Desi Arnaz, film came to sitcoms. Film actress Lucy did not want to move to New York to the live TV stages of 1950s television. Desi created Desilu Studios where they thought that they could approximate

3 It is technically a fraction less than 30 so that there is room for the sync signal which also contains things like captioning.

4 *Laurel and Hardy, Our Gang,* and *the Three Stooges* are still airing.

5 *Flash Gordon* and *Junior G-Men* are good examples.

6 At this time, called an audition.

the multiple camera techniques of live TV. With the help of innovator Al Simon, they placed sets side by side. They planned for a live audience. They used three film cameras and had to have the film processed, edited and then converted and transferred before it could be aired. This was a more expensive process but resulted in a product of such quality that episodes are still being aired to this day. Maybe the added input of an editor and the ability to repeat performance "takes" is partly responsible, but the biggest reason for the show's success was Lucy herself.

When tape came into usage as a recording medium in the 1960's, The networks had the ability to easily repeat episodes that had the technical quality of the original live telecast. By then, color cameras were being used. Video tape and film reruns resulted in reduced episode orders to number 25 or 26. Today, orders are even more reduced. A full season of 22 episodes is a major accomplishment for most shows. Many times shows will get a network order for 6 to 13 episodes until they are a rating's success.

In the early days, the economic savings from 39 shows to 26 allowed them to add a fourth camera. This meant a few more camera shots were possible during the visually "swinging 60s." There was not much postproduction editing done on those tapes because it required that the two-inch-wide video tape be sliced with a razor and sticky-taped back together.

Whenever feature motion pictures add a second camera for a setup, the cameras are referred to as the "A" and "B" cameras. Therefore, the film sitcoms started with "A" "B" and "C" rather than the video's cameras 1, 2 and 3 numbering system. In time, video added camera 4. It was so rare for film shows to be able to afford extra film stock that their occasional use of an "extra" camera was always called "X." Now, all sitcoms use four cameras regardless if they are shot using film or videotape. The cameras are lined up from right to left from the audience's perspective: A, B, C, X or 1,2,3,4. It is opposite from the actor's perspective.

It is much more difficult to break into comedy or dramatic television today than it was even 10 years ago. The learning curve is now much steeper and the latitude for error is much narrower. Typically, they still look for someone who is comfortable operating a camera and has the basic mechanical skills down already. These skills encompass the areas of framing and composition of shots, smooth zooming, panning and tilting skills along with the ability to work well with others. Confidence, the ability to collaborate, a good sense of humor and an ability to deliver the goods when necessary are all "must have" attributes for a successful multi-camera operator. An attitude that fits in with the team and isn't threatening or overbearing will get one farther along than all the talent in the world.

Once you manage to get on an actual set; watch, listen, soak up the atmosphere and learn as much as you can as fast as you can. An opportunity will eventually present itself and then it will be up to you to make what you will of it. I think everybody in the business has bluffed their way into a situation at least once in their career, the successful ones took the opportunity and made the most of it. The 2nd tier ones hadn't bothered to prepare themselves and the results usually showed.

Randy Baer, Camera Operator

TWO RECORDING STYLES: FILM-STYLE

There were two recording forms: film and tape. They both continue to evolve with some separate techniques and terminology, but both are now recorded digitally. Film-style cameras move on **dollies.** Think of a wagon with a mast for the camera...only much more sophisticated. This wagon is usually pushed but can also be pulled. It can operate on the floor or on tracks. The film camera operator is riding on the wagon. It can be levered up or down changing the camera's height from the ground.

The camera operator is framing the picture by looking through a telescope like portal. At the same time, he is using his right and left hands to turn little wheels with tiny handles to tilt the camera up or down and right or left. Since the camera operator is operating the camera, a dolly requires a dolly grip[7] to move it and a focus puller to adjust the lens. Film focus is calculated by running a measuring tape between the subject's eyes and the focal plane mark on the film camera. The focus puller also known as the first assistant camera makes this measurement and then pulls (sets) the focus during the performances. Precise marks need to be put on the stage floor to see that the distance between the actor and the lens is always consistent otherwise the image will be out of focus. This three-man team (camera operator, first assistant camera, and dolly grip) tries to blend shots from position to position so that as much footage as possible is usable by the editor. It's completely reliant on teamwork and trust. It is amazing to watch a good team to do their job well. That job is to tell the story by photographing the actors. This three-man team may work for years together as a unit. There is no reliance on shot numbers in this system. Depending of each show's routine, a technical coordinator[8] may, or may not, be on headset with the team reminding them of their moves. The dolly grips have put many marks on the floor marking the dolly's path.

Technical Coordinator Dan Fendel tells us about the origin of his position:

> When multi-camera filmed sitcom TV was born more or less with Desi and Lucy, somebody figured out that the show needed someone to coordinate the camera crews of operators, assistants and dolly grips and the job was originally known as "Camera Coordinator." This ended when, as the result of a jurisdictional dispute between the camera union and the DGA. The Director's Guild won the job and didn't want the word "camera" anywhere near it. Of course, the Director's didn't want their position diluted terminologically speaking by adding "Director" to it anywhere either, so this vague, complex, and obscure term "technical coordinator" was born in contract language as a compromise. When I was doing *Major Dad* and people would see my name go by VERY fast in the closing credits, what they THOUGHT they were seeing was "technical advisor" which led to some confusion that I was or had been a Marine.
>
> The way I usually describe the job is that I am the director's creative executive officer the way the First AD is his/her production one, that I am

7 Jobs with the term "grip" require the person to grip things whether it is a light, scenery or a camera dolly.

8 A Directors Guild position.

> the editor's advance scout and protector and, especially on shows which play "musical directors" week after week, a guarantee of continuity in shooting style for the producers, too. I'm also there to help the camera crews use their talents and, where possible, help make the actors' best work actually get transmitted to the audience--as such, the TC/Associate Director really bridges the ravine between the artistic and the technical and, in a pinch, also helps the AD/UPM staff get the practical side of things moving and happening efficiently, too. Of course, that's how --I-- do it, which some people LIKE and others are bothered by. If you want to play it safe, you take notes from the director and call cues, period. And the show isn't as good. Period. Smart producers, directors, AD's and UPM's and camera folks know this.

TWO RECORDING STYLES: TAPE-STYLE

Tape-style, the second form, developed from a video system. Video camera operators are a one-man band: a single operator pushes, focuses, and frames each shot. The **pedestal dolly** or ped for short is like nothing you've ever seen. Think of a heavy-duty microphone stand on wheels...only, in this case, the mic is a camera with extended arms to control the panning, tilting, focus and the zoom lens. This "ped" also has a pneumatic assist to raise or lower the camera's height and "wheels" to help it glide. Instead of the telescope like eyepiece of a film camera, the pedestal dolly's viewfinder looks like a little TV screen. It allows the operator to use his vision both for what's in the viewfinder and what he can see peripherally on stage. It is a complex piece of equipment that the operator must know intimately. Cameraman Martin Goldstein paints this picture:

> The camera and dolly is the operator's dance partner and the actors are the music. When it is otherwise, it's a walk uphill. Understanding and using the pedestal dolly is even more important than use of the camera. If one is clumsy with the dolly, it can slow down the operator and get the operator negative attention from others on the stage floor. Although the shot may be there for the director when needed, it may have been a painful chore getting it. If the pedestal is balanced and the camera head is balanced properly in the morning when the stage is cold, the dolly will remain in control. Struggling with the hardware on top of dealing with the "software" of the show can be exhausting. Remembering that the dolly is the operator's dance partner, one can look as though he is an accomplished ballet dancer with the Bolshoi or flail about like a hard core dancer at a punk rock concert.

Video camera operators rarely drop a mark on the floor because they have to concentrate on getting the image without the assistants. Because the video camera's viewfinder is actually a TV monitor, he can see the accurate results.

The camera operator frames a shot and then the **tally light**[9] comes on his camera when the shot is used live. When the light goes out, he goes to the next shot. Martin Goldstein advises:

> The operator should have his zoom and focus controls properly mounted in such a way that is second nature using them. If an operator has to think about which direction his controls work, it's already too late. The shot can be lost. Speed is equally important as accuracy.

The camera operator has an additional tool at his disposal. Goldstein describes it.

> The cameras are usually given an external feed showing the output of all four cameras. This is usually referred to as the **quad split**.[10] An operator should use it liberally. It's a great tool for matching an opposing camera's over the shoulder shot, avoiding duplicate coverage, or to find **iso coverage**[11] not given by the other cameras.

THE HYBRID

A third hybrid form was developed in the early 1980s and first used on a show called *Harry and the Hendersons*. This was a film camera on a tape pedestal. It had been continually refined because it gave the show the quality of film with some of the economy of tape: one tape operator is cheaper than the three-person film team.

24P–IS IT FILM OR TAPE?

In this period of digital innovation, new cameras have been developed that gather pictures electronically just as video cameras always have but are recorded at 24 individual frames per second, like film cameras. They are referred to as **24P** cameras. The recording can be on tape or on computer hard drives and recently on optical drives.

The fact that these new cameras take film's frame scanning technique but keeps the economic savings of recording digitally, accounts for their popularity.

So, does the use of **24P** cameras give filmlike quality? The element of film that remains superior to video is its ability to handle a wider range of light levels. Live

---

9 A light (usually red) on the camera that comes on when that camera is on-line.

10 The monitors on stage will be showing either the switched pattern of camera shots (**line feed**) or this simple four-way output showing each of the cameras.

11 The cameras, that are not on-line as the active camera of the switched feed, are also being recorded or "isolated" for use during postproduction.

television needed very bright lights at inception.[12] As the years have gone by, the tubes, and now chips, in the cameras have steadily improved and light levels have dropped. Today's video cameras are much closer to film in light handling ability. DP Bruce Finn discusses 24P.

> Being one of the first DP's to work with 24P for sitcoms has allowed me years of in depth experience to evaluate this fascinating new medium. 24P isn't instant film but it's getting close. For a sitcom that is being broadcast, the quality of the image is very compelling. The shooting advantages include a high quality picture from each camera on a monitor for purposes of lighting, framing, and aesthetic decisions. These decisions include production design, wardrobe, make up, playback to check technical or performance issues. Some very valuable attributes along with time and money saved.

All of the digital video cameras used in the 24P setup are new **Hi-def,** high definition TV format. Since most viewers, at this time, did not yet have Hi-def television sets, this was another challenge for camera operators. They had to frame for two separate and different formats at the same time. High definition TV has a different ratio for its wider shape. It is 16 units wide by 9 units tall. Normal TV is 4 by 3. The wide screen Hi-def image has more space on the sides. So, what does this mean for a cameraman framing? If he frames too tight, TV viewers might loose part of a face. If he frames too big, he might be **shooting off** the set or shooting where there is no set.

As these 24P cameras have come to the marketplace, video in general has improved. Adding the same frame rate as film causes most executives to marvel at the filmlike quality of the 24P cameras, especially when they see the cost savings of eliminating film stock and processing. Technology always changes but story telling stays the same.

WRITING SHOTS

Tape shows and film shows have different operating procedures on camera blocking day. In tape, The AD and director spend at least a couple of hours Wednesday night camera blocking (on paper) by waiting for the final draft of the script and then selecting and writing cameras shots in each of their scripts. After that session, the AD has to prepare another copy of the script for the technical director. The technical director is the person who physically switches between the cameras and acts as the crew chief of the camera and sound teams on a tape show.

As directors, we're big believers in the "Don't agonize" when it comes to these camera-blocking-on-paper sessions. You may be describing two hundred

12 At one time, every call sheet for Thursday had the admonishment "Do not wear white or yellow." It is still a good idea not to wear small stripes or checks because they interact with the electronic scanning to cause a distracting moiré or "worming" effect.

to three hundred sequential shots on paper.[13] The key is that the shots are written in pencil. They can always be changed. While sitting in an office or a near empty stage, it is a little abstract to envision the way that the actors were positioned and what the important focus should be. The next day on stage, it is easier to see if the selected shot is the angle and framing that, the director really wants to see in order to tell the story. If the original choice wasn't right, it takes less than a minute to change it. Actor/director Scott Baio was a seasoned performer from his years on *Happy Days* and his spinoff *Joanie Loves Chachi* before he came to direct many episodes of his next long running success *Charles in Charge*.[14] Baio described his challenge writing down the shots for the first time:

> I sat there for the longest time not knowing what to write down. I was completely dumbfounded. Then I pretended I was sitting there watching my show on TV. I just described what I was seeing shot to shot and it was easy.

The gospel of "Don't agonize" when doing camera blocking on paper was repeated to us by director Peter Baldwin (*The Andy Griffith Show, The Mary Tyler Moore Show, and The Bob Newhart Show*) and associate director Mikki Capparelli (*Living Single, 227*). They both had the wisdom to know that the shots were a preliminary blueprint. Since it's a visual medium, the choice becomes apparent once a director is looking at the show rather than *pretending* he is looking at the show.

GETTING SHOTS–TAPE STYLE

On tape shows, camera operators have an early meeting with the associate director where they are told the camera shot descriptions with sequential camera shot numbers. The number of shots depends on the story and the director's style, but usually number anywhere from 150-350. The operators know nothing of the new characters or the show's plot, but they know descriptions of fifty to one hundred shots that each of the four cameras are expected to compose today. They mark them on large index cards and keep them on their cameras. Martin Goldstein talks about taking shot notes.

> Operators write their notes to be read quickly and on the fly. Any note is a good note if it can be read fast. All sorts of shorthand have been used... Dick Harwood, the associate director who basically set the form for Tandem's[15] revival of sitcoms on tape, would use something like this for an

13 Paul Bogart would use as few as 70 shots while directing *All In The Family.*

14 Baio went on to star in other series as well as direct many shows in which he doesn't act.

15 Norman Lear and Bud Yorkin created the Tandem production company (1970-1982) for *All in the Family*. Norman went on to form T.A.T. (1975-1982) an abbreviation of a Yiddish phrase meaning "putting one's butt on the line." His other sitcom companies were P*I*T*S and TOY.

Sitcom is a purely television form. You can't see a sitcom anywhere else. You could take an episode of NYPD Blue *or* Law and Order *and show it in a movie theater. It's hard to watch a sitcom on a big screen. It's really a small screen creature. Part of that is that it is all auditory. It's the words more than the business. No one has ever looked at a sitcom and said, "This is the funniest 2-shot I have ever seen." You can close your eyes, listen to a sitcom, and get it. If you close your eyes during a film or* Law and Order, *you won't know what is going on.*

Television comedy owes a lot to theater. On a sitcom, the lenses of the cameras are the audience. Both the theater and television audience are outside the fourth wall. It is much more theatrical than a single camera style show where the lens is inside the fourth wall and the viewer has a sense of aloneness and intimacy.

Steve Zuckerman *Everybody Loves Raymond, Friends, Murphy Brown*, series director *Empty Nest*

over the shoulder shot (using a name or the initial of a name): ArchieX2Edith or AX2E. The first name is the character (Archie) the camera is looking at; the second (Edith) is whose shoulder it is over. The reason for the second name is that is not always readily apparent in a fast moving scene with multiple characters just how the shot should be built. So a little extra help, as to who to include or exclude in the shot, helps.

The associate director calls the shot numbers aloud on stage during the camera dry blocking. This is the guy talking during the actors' lines. First time sitcom actors may worry that the crew is not finding many jokes funny when actually they are missing the punchline while listening for their numbers. These same numbers are called on the headset system during every subsequent camera rehearsal and the taping.

GETTING SHOTS–FILM STYLE

It is completely different on film style shows. The film team receives no prior instruction before they watch each scene the first time, so no one is calling out numbers while the actors are performing. Possibly more distracting, though, are the extra people who join the scene. Varying people from the camera department, beginning with the second assistant camera operator[16] and loader,[17] follow every actor and put a tape mark down on the floor whenever that actor stops. Each character is assigned a different color tape. The secret for the actor is not to trip on the person laying down tape in front of him. Actors (**first team**) are replaced by the stand-ins (**second team**) for the camera blocking process. The film camera team marks their shots on index cards as they go. Rather than following one sequential number system, each camera operator keeps his own numbers. Shots change when actors move. Cameras consistently follow just one character or follow one character on a move to another.

GETTING SHOTS–24P

24P uses either tape or film style with many variations. On tape shows, operators used to move from shot to shot. If they weren't on-line, their camera was not being recorded. It wasn't until *All in the Family* was being taped at CBS in

16 This individual also claps the slate at the beginning of every scene when filming.

17 This individual used to load the film into the camera. Now he handles the digital recording.

Hollywood that a tape engineer named Marco Zappia[18] started doing sophisticated editing on videotape. Now tape, film, or 24P...all cameras are recording all the time.

DIRECTOR OPTIONS–CONTROL ROOM, VIDEO VILLAGE OR AMONGST THEM

During camera blocking, the director can be found in the control room, at a bank of TVs near the set or walking amongst the cameras directly in front of the set. Every director has his own style.

CONTROL ROOM

A director and his team in the control room or booth wear headsets to communicate with the stage manager, also wearing a headset on "the floor." The stage manager is the director's main line of communication to the actors. The director communicates with other crew members on different channels of the headset system. In the control room are TV screens called monitors showing what each camera is seeing as well as a screen showing the show as it is edited live. This is another difference between tape and film. A tape show will do a live edit called a **line cut** during an actual taping. It's like live TV with a backup because the individual cameras are independently recording what they are seeing. The editor gets 5 versions of the show. The line cut plus isos from cameras 1, 2, 3, and 4. This edit is switched by the technical director who is cued by a snap of the director or AD's fingers. They often save finger fatigue by using a small tin cricket toy to "click" during rehearsal. The booth is the hub. Newscasts, daytime dramas, game shows and sports broadcasts utilize the booth.

VIDEO VILLAGE

The hub on the stage floor is the bank of monitors where the director, TC, and script supervisor can sit with their rolling podiums and canvas director's chairs. This station, often nicknamed **video village**[19], can be moved around the stage to facilitate equipment placement as well as easy proximity to the set. Since 24P, this hub is used most often. How can film that requires developing be seen on video monitors? Film cameras have an electronic pickup off the viewfinder that will give a somewhat dim, but serviceable image of what is being exposed to the film. These video taps of film cameras are fed to monitors so that their shots can be monitored just like video cameras. Now, on almost all tape-style sitcoms, the director will choose to stay "on the floor" and let his associate director work with the technical director to cut between the cameras in the control room. On film shows, an audience switcher performs this same function. The reason for giving up the technical superiority and comfort of the booth is that

---

18 Marco was the award-winning editor on countless shows including *Roseanne, Home Improvement and 8 Simple Rules.*

19 We believe TC Tom Doak came up with this name.

the director likes to be in close range to give adjustments to the actors. When he is in a control room, his messages have to be relayed by the stage manager or via a booming speaker above the stage.[20]

AMONGST THEM

Some directors choose not to look at any monitors while camera blocking. If they want to see exactly what a film camera will be recording, they will simply climb on the camera and take a look through the eye piece. With a tape camera a director looks at the small viewfinder on each individual camera. The advantage to being amongst them is the proximity to the cameramen for direct communication.

CAMERA BLOCKING

Each scene of the sitcom teleplay may take up to one hour for dry blocking, working out each camera's exact framing on every shot, and a final camera rehearsal to see if everything works. Lighting adjustments and the planning of how each microphone will be deployed during the scene is happening simultaneously. Soundman Ed Valfre explains:

> Traditionally, in the sitcom world, dialogue is picked up by two boom microphones on pedestals from the floor or a series of booms hanging above the lighting grid in what is called, a **green bed**. When the actors go through their blocking with dialogue for the first time, the sound mixer and boom operators watch and take copious notes on how the booms will divide the scene. These notes will most likely change many times before the scene is recorded causing their scripts to resemble the abstract expressionist work of Jackson Pollack. Division of which microphone picks up what dialogue is based on several factors...distance between actors, pace of dialogue, lighting and at times, just laziness.

TIPS FOR ACTORS

The camera blocking process requires the director to review every shot as the scene is rehearsed. The action is stopped constantly for a slight camera or actor reposition or for a complete change of a shot pattern sequence. Actors don't ever get a chance to really play the scene because of the interruptions. On film sets, the actors will perform the dry blocking and then the second team or "B" team will come in to do the actual shot-by-shot blocking. The "B" team is the stand-ins who have watched the dry blocking or yesterday's run-thru, copied down the actors' physical positions, and then represents each character during this laborious process. Any blocking changes that affect their character must be noted and reported to the actor by their stand-in. Steve Zuckerman likes using the second team:

20 Some directors like the "God-like" quality to this studio address speaker. Others think it is impersonal.

> The actors go away. The second team is there and sometimes I have to move them. They might have to cross a little later. When the first team comes back, I don't have to tell them their changes. Their stand-ins do. What is amazing is that no one has ever objected. No one has said, "All week I have been doing it this way." They must appreciate their time off. They must say, "He had all this to do and I'm not going to bust his chops."

Videotaped sitcoms evolved without using the "B Team" concept. It is common, however, for there to be one stand-in available on tape sets to fill in for child actors who are in the schoolroom during a scene or when the extra curricular demands on the show's star are so great that relief is in order.

Camera blocking can be tedious for the actor. It is hard for the actor to appreciate all that is being done while repeating a section of the scene for the umpteenth time or standing still on his mark. Actual physical tape marks are rarely used for the actor's position on tape shows. Standing on a mark merely refers to stopping dialogue in position while cameras line up shots. On film shows, the marks are snipped so they are very tiny. There are also plenty of marks on stage for each piece of furniture that needs to be moved during the episode. Lighting sometimes lays actor's marks until the actors are familiar with them. The mark for the actor to hit will be left on stage only with an extremely critical position for a hard-to-get camera shot. Hitting that mark takes some skill in being able to see it from your peripheral vision.

This is a good time for the actor to make an impression on the director. Whether you are a stand-in, a guest actor, or a member of the regular cast, you can help make camera blocking easier. When you notice that you are casting a shadow on another actor that a slight lean or physical adjustment will correct, you are saving the director time and money.[21] Actors will often hear a director say, "Get me two eyes." When a camera has run out of room trying to get a view of you that sees both of your eyes, you can again make some slight adjustments to help.

An actor should keep these important things in mind on camera blocking day. Try to be consistent. If you haven't locked into your blocking or the way that you will handle a prop....NOW IS THE TIME TO DO SO! What you do now affects many other people. For example, if a camera is shooting an insert shot of a woman's hand holding a ring box, and the actress decides to switch hands, a different camera might be needed to get a better look at the ring. If that better angle is from a camera that has the previous shot, the director has to juggle all of his **coverage** in order to get that new shot. Coverage is all the camera shots. If

21 It is not the director's money, but his reputation is partially based on getting the show done in the time allotted. Money-saving efficiency that does not come at the cost of quality has been the hallmark of many successful directors. This, of course, means more jobs and more m-o-n-e-y. Okay, so it kind-of is his money.

a show has many characters, the producers may want you to "cover" all the actors with close-ups. Even with four cameras, this is sometimes a challenge. Reverse angle walls or moving of set furniture might be needed. To minimize the length of time required or the number of times an audience would have to watch the same scene, a director may choose to pre-shoot the whole scene without the audience. If the choice of camera is switched, the boom operator may have to switch which boom is recording the actor's line. It's a huge domino effect.

Actress and USC Instructor Marilyn McIntryre believes, "An actor should know which camera(s) are on the 2-shots and/or group shots and which one is yours at any given time. And ask the cameraperson what the shot sizes are. This will all become second-nature and give you the freedom as an actor and also save a lot of time and energy on the set. By the way, this is the way so many actors learn about directing." [22]

Another actor choice that affects camera blocking is handling a **practical** prop. An example of this is a functioning appliance or a light switch. Do you really switch the light on or do you just put your hand on the switch and wait for the lighting board operator to switch on the new illumination? This choice will be made for you depending on how many lighting instruments are involved in this lighting effect. Faucets, stoves, vacuum cleaners, blenders are just a few of the props that may or may not be practical. In one episode of the *The Hughleys*, D.L. Hugley was using a practical leaf blower inside a kitchen. It became apparent that no dialogue could be heard over the blower especially when the baby in the scene heard the noise and began crying during the dialogue as well. Camera blocking is the time when all these matters get worked out. In the case of the leaf blower it was decided to have the baby leave the scene earlier and that the sound of the blower could be put in during post-production.

Here's another thing an actor should keep in mind: If you can't see a camera, it can't see you! Camera blocking is the perfect time for an actor to sneak out of character and peak at which camera is pointed at him at any given time. A camera operator noticing this effort from an actor will go that extra mile to make sure the actor is seen in the best possible manner. You are showing respect to him as part of the creative team to collaborate with him. At the same time, these "peaks" should be VERY BRIEF to just get your bearings because remember the director is looking at the overall picture in order to line up coverage and wants to see the actor looking at his scene partner not into a camera lens.

When playing a scene with another actor who then crosses to the other side of you, you should **counter** his move. This means to readjust your position so that you are still 50/50 with him if the conversation is to continue. This will allow the cameras which were set to get each close-up to just switch to the other person.

The director sees all of your adjustments and awareness. He is watching the monitors, sees the same shadows, and sees the same camera problems. If you

22 Ron Howard, Michael J. Fox, Tom Hanks, Robby Benson, Michael Lembeck, James Widdoes, Tim Matheson, Peter Bonerz, Scott Baio, Amanda Bearse, Dorothy Lyman, David Paymer...to name a few.

fix it before he has a chance to stop things, you are a hero. Moving a light or repositioning a wall to fix the problems takes a lot of time. If you are asked to hold your position, DO IT. Remain looking at the actor with whom you have your dialogue. There is a reason for this. It is likely that two cameras are simultaneously trying to line up or match opposing shots. Your positions are critical. Director Madeline Cripe remarks:

> It is always surprising to me that actors don't understand "upstage" from "downstage." I can understand not being camera savvy ("camera right" vs. "camera right") but understanding the stage and your position on it should be a priority. The most commonplace problem is "upstaging" a fellow actor. By pulling their look upstage you pull them away from the camera. Typically, as unnatural as it may feel, two actors will be asked to stay on a 50/50 plane so the camera can see both their faces.

It may not be said aloud, but the director is going to remember your helpfulness if you get a chance to audition for him on another episode or show. You will also gain the respect of your fellow technical artists, if they know you are camera savvy!

Depending on your job function, it is not necessary to be completely versed in the technical aspects of shooting a sitcom, but an awareness of the process is helpful. Audrey Meadows, famous for playing Alice on *The Honeymooners* was guest starring on a sitcom episode late in her career. She came to one of us just before a scene was to be camera blocked and asked if it was okay to take the gloves from her purse during a certain line of dialogue. It was obvious that she knew that we would be on a master shot rather than a close-up at that time and, thus, the action would be seen on camera. She only asked in order to defer to the director's position of authority. Her long career had taught her much and her attitude was a joy to be around.

The basics of camera angles and camera positions are not hard to learn. An actor can absorb volumes by just sitting in the audience and watching a monitor during the camera blocking of a scene he's not in.

Television has a much smaller screen than motion pictures, so big panoramic shots don't read as well. Therefore, those master shots are kept to a minimum[23]. Those shots are used only for "geography" at the beginning and end of scenes and to establish location and the physical relationship of the characters. Almost all of the set-ups and punch lines are delivered in close-up. Close-ups are the staple of the television visual language. When someone is entering or exiting a scene or moving across the room, this is a good time for more geography. As soon as the movement is over, it's back to close-ups or small group shots.

When you are aware of which of the two center cameras are on you during

23 The outside cameras have the best angles for close-ups. Therefore, cameras 1 and 4 have the most shots.

camera blocking, it is another chance to check if you and your scene partner are 50/50, to that camera. Remember the new proscenium that you are lining up with is the camera that is shooting your master. For a short exchange between two characters, it may be the only angle. The proscenium that was assumed to be the setline might be slightly different as the cameras vie for position. Again, a simple small position adjustment or shift of weight will help the camera operator frame the shot.

In chapter three, you learned **DON'T MOVE ON THE JOKE**. Now that the scene is on camera, the close-ups actually accentuate the setups and the jokes. The camera cuts between them helps give the structure and rhythmic precision to sitcom jokes. Everyone who works on sitcoms gets used to this. Now you must refine your movement even more. The rule from this chapter, **SAY THE LINE AND THEN MOVE,** asks you to feel the rhythm of the set ups and punchlines, and the audience's laugh. You have an indication from each run-thru of how big the laugh will be. A full audience will laugh even longer. As a performer, you now have to decide whether to deliver the joke and beat it *or* stay for the laugh and the ensuing reaction shots that will follow. There is no hard and fast rule here. Each choice is dependent on the character's point of view.

Take this example: Lisa Kudrow on *Friends* delivers a joke that her character doesn't know is funny but her scene partner (or the audience) does know is funny. If she went on about her business, the audience would not be able to see her face, especially her eyes, to know her character was oblivious to her funniness. This would rob the audience. We have to know what her character is thinking (or not thinking). In a case such as this, the actor should not move to his next position until all three elements (the set-up, punchline and laugh) are completed. The director will bounce between the close-ups of the person who delivered the punchline *and* the reaction of the person who delivered the setup until the anticipated laugh if finished.

Conversely, other jokes will work better if the character delivers the punchline and immediately high-tails it out of there. This leaves the camera with only one reaction shot: the person left standing still in the scene. This type of delivery is very effective when one character is knowingly zinging the unsuspecting scene partner with an insult. It leaves the insulted character mulling over the insult. In a case such as this, the actor delivering the punch line should move immediately after the punchline while the audience is laughing. The director can show enough geography that the audience will know that the insulter walked away. The "funny" will be the insulted person's reaction shot.

GETTING NOTES

Different people have differing opinions on what makes and sells funny. For example, many network executives are fond of close-ups: the more, the better. They have been known to even ask for close-ups as characters enter at the beginning of a scene. Directors struggle with this kind of note. The director wants to be true to telling the audience the story and use a master shot to have the audience know what kind of room and where the character has just entered but must also service the requests of the network executives.

It is important for everyone to realize that any note from the producers or the network comes from a desire by that person to see the story slightly different from the way the actor is playing it or the way the director is directing it. Getting to the root of that need is what can help your work relationships and ultimately help the show. The director, using a shorter time on the master shot or slightly different framing, might satisfy the network's note for an entry close-up. Actors can try performance adjustments as they respond to notes. Don't write off a challenge as "just another stupid note."

Sitcom Exercise:

Choose a 2-character scene from the appendix. With a partner, stage (or block) yourselves as if four cameras were filming you. Remember to stay 50/50 with your scene partner when you are standing or sitting in close proximity. Try opening up to camera. Remember that if you can't see your imaginary cameras, they can't see you. Be very specific how you handle props, especially practical ones. Practice countering your partner when he crosses in front of you. Remember to lean on your upstage leg if you are casting a shadow on your partner's face. And of course, say the line, then move making your choices on what serves the joke better from your character's point of view.

AFTER CAMERA BLOCKING

When all of the scenes have been camera blocked, three things can happen: the actors and most of the crew can go home, everyone gets ready for a run-thru, or pre-shooting will begin.

CAMERA RUN-THRU

Carmen Finestra explains the second scenario.

> At day's end, a camera rehearsal is held for the producers and writers. Obviously, everyone is just looking to give notes on the camera work, knowing the actors won't be at peak performing levels. Any tweaks to the scripts hopefully will happen now.

This camera run-thru is the first time the episode will look like a television show and not a theatrical experience. It usually takes a minimum of fifteen minutes for the stage to be readied for the run-thru. The camera and sound equipment is positioned in front of the first scene because the show will be run in order.

Actors are studying the scripts because no one should be **carrying**.[24] The very occasional actor that still has a script in his hand during the camera blocking tends to make the script supervisor and director nervous that they won't have a solid grasp of the lines when the audience comes in tomorrow. This actor is robbing himself and his fellow actors of a valuable chance to see how the material plays.

The writers have been in **the room** all day working on the next script. The show runner might have taken a break from this to watch closed circuit views of the camera blocking on a scene that was shaky at last night's rehearsal. He might even be called down to the stage to watch the dry blocking of a scene that had a major rewrite last night.

All the writers are called down for the camera run thru. Actors are in wardrobe and all working props and effects are "live." For this run thru, the writers and other office personnel will watch the switched feed monitors from the audience bleachers. The show runner and network executives will watch from a viewing booth often located above the last row of the audience area. On sets where the director is working at a video village, the show runner will usually be next to the director giving notes as they go along. The bulk of these notes will address camera work and not performance.

Now is when the play finally looks better. There might be a few camera or actor missteps, but it is now close to a real television show. As directors, we always like to make a copy of this run-thru to review at home this evening. Without the need to pay attention to every camera move and cue, it is easier to see if the story is being told clearly and if all of the acting subtleties and camera coverage is working.

PRE-SHOOTING

After, or in lieu of a run-thru, if any scenes need to be pre-shot everyone involved prepares for that. Actors not involved in the pre-shoot scenes are released for the day. It is becoming common practice to pre-shoot some scenes on camera-blocking day; some shows do more than others depending on each individual script. Some examples of scenes that may be pre-shot are exterior scenes that need to be shot on location, scenes with special effects, scenes that eliminate lengthy waits for the audience during complicated make-up or costume changes, scenes that may require a lot of extra coverage, or scenes that are playing in a swing set so far away from the audience that it's easier to pre-shoot and replay them the next day.

Those actor staying for pre-shoots get into hair, make-up, and wardrobe and get ready to perform. Network and studio executives may or may not be around for pre-shooting. The editor may show up to see what he has to quickly edit for the audience playback the next day. The script supervisor is recording every piece of information imaginable from keeping the takes straight to continuity and time code to find the takes later. The show runner and director do multiple

24 Most actors have the scripts out of their hands by Wednesday. Now everyone must.

takes until they are satisfied with both performance and cameras.

Pre-shooting is challenging: everyone is tired from camera blocking, but this is the *only* opportunity to tape or film these scenes. To compound the difficulties, the actors don't have the benefit of a full audience. The crew may be so tired that they aren't the willing audience they were at the beginning of the day. Everyone has to rise to the occasion and find that extra energy. The sooner the pre-shoots are completed, the sooner everyone gets to go home and rest up for show day!

FINAL PREPARATIONS FOR SHOW DAY

After any pre-shoots, the rest of the cast is released and the crew will push the equipment aside for the set dressers and painters to put any final touches on the set for tomorrow. Lighting may stay and tweak a few instruments. Wardrobe may have to do some last minute alterations.

Tonight is the last time that the writing staff will have hours to work on changes to fine-tune the script. Ideally, the script won't need major changes or restructuring. Just like when the script was first read at the table by the actors, seeing it on camera for the first time makes the story more alive. This day was important for that reason. Reading a script takes some imagination to envision the show itself. Watching the actors rehearse makes it easier. Seeing it on a monitor is the closest thing yet to a real television show. For all the interruptions and time that the actors have spent working on technical considerations rather than concentrating on the script, everyone can tell that all the elements are starting to come together. The only thing missing, now, is the audience. Everyone feels a great anticipation for tomorrow!

Sitcom Vocabulary Quick Review

Read these sentences. If the director gave you these notes, would you instantly know what he meant? If not, go back and review the explanation in this chapter.

Cameras are in place we're waiting on the **booms**.

The network is pow-wowing in the **booth**.

No one should be **carrying** *during network run-thru.*

You need to **counter** *her move.*

We can't get the **coverage**.

We'll do a **dissolve** *there rather than a cut.*

We'll start **dry blocking** *with "A".*

The **dolly's** *coming your way.*

We'll start as soon as **ESU** *is done.*
We'll get **first team** *into wardrobe while we dry block with* **second team.**
Say good morning to the guys dripping coffee on you from the **green bed**.
Take a step closer so we can frame for **hi-def**.
We're on you with the **iso.**
We'll show the audience the **line feed.**
The **live cutting** *will be tricky until we get a feel for the audience reaction.*
Keep the **monitors** *turned away from the actors.*
The **ped** *can't get in there.*
Is the stove **practical?**
Look at the **quad split***!*
Please take a step upstage because we're **shooting off.**
Who knows what goes on in **the room!**
We're shooting on **24P.**
Look for the **tally light.**
Video village *is moving.*

Script Supervisor's Thursday Tasks

- ✓ *Read new shooting draft*
- ✓ *Repeat Tuesday/Wednesday duties*
- ✓ *Create Scene/Page Count Breakdown and give to the 1st AD*
- ✓ *Create Daily Progress Report for any preshoots.*
- ✓ *Mark script for take numbers*
- ✓ *Log time code, audio loads, film loads, takes, camera descriptions in script*
- ✓ *Log any notes for specific takes, mistakes, wardrobe, prop, lighting, boom shadows, etc.*

Sitcom Insider

RESPONSIBILITIES OF A CAMERA OPERATOR

The responsibilities of a camera operator come in varying degrees and in all shades of colors depending on the producing company, the director, the associate director, or camera coordinator of the episode. That said, however, I think they fall into three main categories. First, is the ability to work well with others, i.e. the relationship with the other operators on the set, the craft people, and the production staff. Secondly, technical/mechanical i.e. knowing one's equipment well.

Thirdly, the application of the operator's own talents, physical ability, intuition, and patience.

There is a short learning curve to understand how each director likes to work; in effect finding his/her shooting "style." The "style" or manner of photographing the show can be quite different between directors. For example, some directors like close-ups while others prefer to shoot their actors loosely at the hip. Some use the zoom lens liberally and like to make dolly moves on air, others not. Some prefer extensive coverage options offered to them while others prefer to adhere to their existing schedule of shots.

Today, in film and now in digital tape, each camera is recording its own coverage continuously. The responsibility for a camera operator has grown enormously since decisions are now generally deferred to the editing room. Consequently, difficulties lie with the producer's expectation of a usable shot during the entire length of the scene when that is not always possible. Moreover, the director may not make it known to the operator when he expects the operator's camera to be on the air, or the director's staging may be at cross purposes to the operator's need for a usable angle. In today's production environment, if it is not clear, it is the operator's responsibility to "speak up" and elicit from the director or camera coordinator what shot is expected and when during the course of the scene.

On the other hand, with the production staff working mainly from the stage floor rather than a control room, the operator can get directions from all sorts of sources. The director, the associate director, camera coordinators, even producers have whispered in my ear in the heat of battle. It can be unclear which master to serve. So it's a responsibility (as simple as it seems) to remain relaxed and patient (accepting of eccentric personalities) yet, in the end, listen only to the director. That can keep the operator's career from getting bruised.

From an operator's perspective, goodness flows from the top. At any given camera angle, if the director has staged the scene well, it will make sense and it will be extremely easy to shoot. It is very easy to pick up on the rhythm of the scene, and the operator's shots, numbered or not, seem to flow into another.

It's a camera operator's responsibility to not only pay attention to his own work, but to the needs of his fellow operators (camera and boom) on the floor. It can, at times, get very crowded when the cameras and sound booms are competing for floor space in a busy scene. In today's production environment, operators tend to use shorter lenses to protect their depth of field. Consequently, they work more closely to the proscenium line. When operating a center camera, one can play back farther, for example, in order to let the other cameras cross shoot more easily. So, an operator, while watching his finder, is peering along side the camera to see where others are positioned.

Martin Goldstein, Camera Operator

Sitcom Career Profile

DAN FENDEL

TECHNICAL COORDINATOR/ASSOCIATE DIRECTOR

Dan is the kind of guy who does his job... and more. He is probably one of the most interesting individuals you'll ever meet because he always has three careers going at once...and he's passionate about all of them.

What shows have you worked on?

I've done about 2,000 episodes of many, many series. The longest runs have been *Family Matters* and *Major Dad* but I've done the famous (*Seinfeld, Friends, Fraiser*) and the relatively unknown (*Pig Sty, The Marshall Chronicles*) and everything in-between.

What are your responsibilities?

The Technical Coordinator assists the director in planning and executing camera coverage.

Did you have specific training in this field?

I attended USC's School of Cinema but got too busy working in the 'biz' to formally graduate.

How did you get your first job?

As for getting into being a TC, a good friend from USC was doing it, had a schedule conflict and needed someone to take over a show he was doing and could no longer do. He helped me get the gig and let me sit in with him for a few weeks to see how the routine went before he departed for his other show. They hired me for one week, more or less on probation, and that was many years and shows ago.

What advice would you give someone who would like to do what you do someday?

No matter what other experience you have (and certainly some camera and directing and production work is essential) you really need to try to do some hands-on editing if you can.

What do you like best about your job?

The variety--the three days are totally different, the creative rewards of doing the various tasks are wide-ranging, and it's just plain fun to "watch TV" (at least on the booth monitors) for a living.

TECHNICAL COORDINATOR/ASSOCIATE DIRECTORS
Union: DGA
Typical Weekly Salary: $3000
Hours Per Week: Until it's done

Chapter 6 FRIDAY...SHOW DAY

In this chapter:

- Overcoming nerves
- How show days differ on each series
- Where to get tickets to be the live audience at a sitcom
- Advice to an aspiring camera operator
- The role of the warm-up guy
- Pickups and why they are necessary
- The importance of the audience
- Career profile of a camera operator

Today is the day that we all get to the finish line. Finally, we are going to reap the reward that we have been working toward all week...the audience's laughs. Certain calmness is evident on stage as you arrive on show day. There is no mystery to what needs to be done today. To be sure, there is a set of changed pages waiting for you. Most of the changes are small things like a different **handle** at the beginning of some lines. A handle is one or more incidental words that lead in a sentence. It gives dialogue a conversational tone.[1] In addition, there might be yet another punchline to a joke that has changed every day this week.

Unless the episode is the pilot for a series, the personality and operating style of the regular characters have long been worked out. Because the lead character has the most lines, they usually have the most small changes. Guest actors might have only one change, but it can be a major adjustment for their character. In some instances, there might be a complete change of attitude and purpose for some characters that are in only one or two scenes. It is always a challenge for guest actors. The characters that have been created just for this episode are there only to serve the plot and to present challenges to the regular characters.

> **SITCOM RULE**
> ***Make sure you set it up.*** *The audience will not laugh if they don't clearly understand the premise or set-up of the joke.*

Sometimes rewrites happen during the filming of the show if the scene does not get the expected audience response. Character actor, Charlie Dougherty tells about a rewrite when he was guesting on *The Drew Carey Show*.

1 The most famous handle is the Valley Girl expression "Like, you know..."

> I had been playing this strict, officious supervisor all week. There had been minor rewrites every day. Come show night, we did two takes of the scene in front of the audience and the actors were told to standby while the writers huddled in front of the set. After a few minutes, I was handed the rewrites that we would shoot immediately. After reading the hand-written page, I walked up to the show runner and said, 'So I'm gay now, right?' I wasn't joking. The character's dialogue had been altered so much that the character was completely changed.

The show runner just laughed at Dougherty's question, but that was the confirmation of the new direction.[2]

Years earlier, legendary show runner Mort Lachman (*All in the Family, Gimme a Break, Kate and Allie*) was approached by an actor, who said, "My character wouldn't say this." Mort, showing all the toughness of his many years of writing for Bob Hope, replied, "Yes he would. The script has your character's name right above those very words." The actor would have certainly gotten more help with a less challenging approach.

SHOW DAY REHEARSAL

A few different things can happen on show day. Rehearsal can be just a few hours, then actors will get into hair and makeup before doing the audience show. Other shows prefer blocking and taping the entire show prior to the audience's arrival. Still others will rehearse and do a run-thru.

In all these cases, the director may have changes before any work begins. He may have taken home a quad split tape of the scenes that were camera blocked yesterday to review and come in with a list of shot changes for the technical coordinator or associate director. These notes are usually given to the camera crew before you go "on camera."

Carmen Finestra explains the block and shoot option.

> On *Home Improvement* we blocked and taped all day without an audience, to make sure we had the scenes right and in the can. Certain producers sat in the booth with the director to make sure everyone agreed on how a scene should look... Having the security of the scenes in the can from the afternoon helps make the taping pressure-free, and allows the actors "to run with the material" i.e. perform at a high level.

In both rehearsal cases, every scene that wasn't pre-shot yesterday is reviewed on camera with the attention going to any changes that require new blocking or new shots. Before moving on to the next scene, it is run again just to sharpen the pace and energy. The cast gets used to cue biting. Make-up and hair can

2 Finally, the actor decided that character was actually not gay but flamboyant. That take was never used in the version that aired.

be scheduled around each scene. 2nd ADs or 2nd stage managers are adding **background artists.**[3] Lighting is **tweaking** or adjusting the lights. This can be many things: moving a black flag in rectangular frame that purposely partially shadows the light, opening or closing the barn doors that fit unto the front of the lighting instruments, adjusting the focus of the light, or adding or deleting an instrument.

If the show runner wants to see a run-thru, it happens immediately after the scene rehearsal. The show will be performed from top to bottom (in show order) with cameras. The emphasis is on finding the performance energy again. By now, the cameras and sound should be fully integrated so there should be no stopping or adjusting for them. Notes will either be given after each scene or at the end of the whole show. The secret is now to build up everyone's confidence for the audience.

Rehearsal often ends with a full script speed-thru of lines. After all, louder and faster is funnier.

Sitcom Exercise:

Record an episode of two different sitcoms. Watch the first one. Turn off the sound. Watch it again while you stop and start as needed so that you can write down a description of the shots used. Start simple. Use the following notation:

E: *Establishing shot that sets up location*

M: *Master shot that tells geography*

G: *Group shot with three or more characters featured*

T: *Two shot with two characters featured or one character featured over the shoulder of another*

S: *Single shot with one person in the frame*

Note the patterns of shots. Compare the shooting style of one show to the other.

DRESS SHOW

Traditional videotaped shows would break after the rehearsal and get everyone into make-up and wardrobe while they brought the first audience in for the **dress show.** This name came from live television's final dress rehearsal.[4] This show would be taped and serve as the first of at least two performance choices for the editor. The Dress Show would be performed in about one hour. There

3 Extras.

4 Red Skelton was known for his off color dress rehearsals of his CBS variety show.

would be no **retakes**[5] because things that went wrong could be fixed at the next performance. The decision whether to have a dress show (or not) lies with the show runner. Carmen Finestra explains:

> Some sitcoms tape two shows on Friday, one early (around 4 or 4:30) and one late (around 7 or 7:30). They then edit the best of both versions. Generally though, the early shows lacks energy and much of it never gets used. Sitcom actors come alive at night. That's when it feels like real theater.

GETTING READY

Everyone who works on a sitcom has a special routine for the hour before show time. The audience is being loaded into their seats, so it has to be quiet on stage. Department heads are going over their pre-show setup checklist, and reviewing with their crew the assignments for each scene, or catching up on paperwork. Some wardrobe is being given last minute pressing or steaming.

On a tape show, the AD is running shot numbers with the TD and camera crew. Since there have been two days of changes, he is making sure everyone has eliminated the same shot numbers and added the same A and B sub-numbers between other shots. On film shows, the camera operators may be reviewing notes they scribbled and may approach the director for clarification. As directors, we like to give a last minute check with the show runner, and then pay a quick visit to each department to see if there are any unanswered questions. Finally, a visit to the make-up room and a moment to stand behind the last row to observe the audience really gets the adrenaline pumping because we know this is show time!

Actors each have their own final preparation routine. Some like to run their lines, one last time, with the stage manager, stand-in, dialogue coach, or another actor. Others walk through all of their positions on the set, if the set is screened from audience view. Some use a meditative quiet time in their dressing room. Others smoke a cigar. A few like to hang out backstage amidst all of the pre-show activity.

THE AUDIENCE

Getting an audience for the dress show is somewhat of a challenge. One reason is the 4 or 5 o'clock in the afternoon start time. The audience is asked to arrive and wait in line more than an hour before. Most of the hard-core fans of the series would not be available this early. The show contracts[6] with a service such as Audiences Unlimited or Audience Associates which guarantees filling the approximately two hundred seats of the audience bleachers. These services give away "free" show tickets. According to Steve Sheets of Audiences Unlim-

5 Doing a scene over.

6 For a negotiated fee.

ited, "We are hired by producers. We currently have about 30-40 shows that we are presently servicing that cover all of the networks. Our group department books tour groups, seniors groups and school and college groups. We also have a website[7] where individual tickets can be ordered online." This website gives *very* detailed information about their service as well as fun information about current TV shows.

Other audience service groups hand out hundreds of ticket at popular Hollywood tourist locations. At one memorable taping, we were stunned when most of the jokes did not get any laughs. When we noticed that the audience was predominately foreign speaking tourists, the mystery was solved. Even if they speak English, the audience starts getting hungry and thinking about dinner just as we are starting the second act.

THE WARM-UP GUY

A stand-up comic is hired to be the official host for the audience. Sometimes one of the show's writers fits neatly into this added job. Director Alan Rafkin[8] used to warm-up his audience before putting on his director's hat. The **warm-up** performer serves two very important functions: keeping the audience pumped and at the same time keeping them focused.

First, he gets the audience in a comfortable and joyous mood. Remember, there are approximately 200 seats. The reason for that is the hope that someone will always find every joke funny enough to start laughing and the group then follows without thinking. Group dynamics dictates that a happy crowd will laugh out loud at things that they might only smile about at home. Often a previous episode is shown to the audience to familiarize them with the show. There are no lights flashing "laugh," but there are microphones over the audiences' heads specifically recording their responses.

The second important function for the warm-up performer is to keep the audience keyed into the show's storyline. Between scenes, the equipment needs to reposition to the next set and the actors might need to change their wardrobe for any scene that is not played as continuous action. Warm-up guy Mark Maxwell Smith would play challenging guessing games with the audience to keep them alert. Some shows have been known to have a live musical combo to play light jazz during longer **resets**[9]. Others use a DJ. Blas Lorenzo of Klassic ProDukShuns and DJ Interactive Entertainment explains:

---

7 www.tvtickets.com

8 Alan Rafkin was a droll witted director of hundreds of sitcoms including *Coach*. He was a curmudgeon with a heart of gold! His contributions reached beyond Hollywood to his alma mater, the University of Syracuse where he gave his time and financial support to mentor students interested in sitcoms.

9 Stopping a scene at a certain point, moving props, walls or cameras and then starting from that point. This can also refer to going BACK to a certain point and starting again.

> Music is a big factor in raising the enthusiasm level for any sit-com. Desi Arnaz utilized music like ammunition to a soldier. He had so much talent, that he could entertain an audience as long as it took to finish shooting an entire episode. Music helps in uplifting the environment of a set into something memorable. Music communicates in every language. A good DJ can be a key part in celebrating the accomplishment of weeks of work.

In addition to being a DJ, Lorenzo is a warm up guy. He is an actor that comes from an improv background. Lorenzo describes the job the way he sees it:

> Warming up an audience is fun! If you're not having fun, how do you expect the audience to have fun? The cast and crew have worked all week long to put together the best possible show. The warm-up should create an environment that celebrates their talent and effort, and makes the audience members feel like they're a part of the party...which they are. Without them, there is no party.

During the ten to fifteen minutes or longer for costume changes, the audience might forget an important plot point. They are sure not to remember the last line of a scene that serves as a set-up for the punchline that starts the next scene. The last thing that the warm-up performer says before the scene starts is a reminder of what is happening in the show. During a short **hiccup,**[10] the warm-up always has to repeat the last line for the audience. Sometimes the director will ask the actors to **overlap** the last lines as the scene starts again.

Great warm-up guys can make all the difference in the flow of the show. Some go on to much greater fame and fortune. Actor Bob Saget worked as a warm-up guy early in his career, but he went on to star in the hit series *Full House* and to host the popular *America's Funniest Home Videos.* Saget continues to perform live as a stand-up. He has had his own HBO Comedy Hour and directed both television and feature films.

There have been many very funny comics who have not been invited back to warm-up more episodes because they forgot the most important part of the job: keeping the audience aware of what's happening in the show. Others don't understand that they should use all of their "A" material before the show starts and then just be a good host during the taping. It is not good when the audience wants the scenes to end so that they can go back to enjoying the warm-up person.

---

10 A reset of 30 seconds or less in the middle of a scene. The cameras continue to roll and the delay is edited out later.

ELIMINATING THE DRESS SHOW

These days, even with digital film, the dress show has become almost nonexistent. Film shows could never afford the amount of film stock necessary to shoot two full audience performances. 24P is scheduled just like film at many studios. Even with this savings, most show runners make the decision NOT to do a dress show. Some believe that the air show is always better so, the dress is a waste of time.

What is missed by the lack of a dress, is the chance to remind the actors where all of the laughs are in the show. Four days ago, at the table, the show was very funny. Each day after that, the comedy was improved by the staging and the performance tuning. It came even more alive and funny once on camera. Don't forget the sitcom rule. **MAKE SURE YOU SET IT UP.** The audience will not laugh if they don't clearly understand the premise or set-up of the joke. It is common that one character may set up a joke and someone else **pays it off** (delivers the punchline). A considerate actor is aware of this fact. He makes sure that he doesn't bury the feed.

THE CATERED MEAL AND NOTES

Today we were working on pace and energy. We have been working so hard on the pace, that there are a dozen jokes that we forgot are funny. The audience tells us where. During the catered meal between the dress and **air shows**, reminders of jumped laughs dominate the acting notes. Jumping a laugh is continuing with dialogue when the audience wants to laugh. Jumping causes a problem by shortening the laugh and causes the audience not to hear dialogue that follows. In effect, it kills two jokes with one misstep. Both the actors and whoever is cutting the cameras can be guilty of a jumped laugh. If the camera is prematurely switched to a shot of someone who was not involved in the joke, the audience will stop laughing to get some new information. This is because the audience came to experience a live show, but their eyes immediately look up at the monitors above them as the scene starts. We found this to be true even if the actors are right in front of them. The flickering images of television are that appealing.

If there has been a dress show, the meal break gives the writers an hour to come up with alternate punch lines for the jokes that were heard properly, but were not appreciated by the audience. The catered meal for the cast and crew is either between shows, if there is a dress performance, or it is after rehearsal when there is only one show. The meal is often called "lunch" even though it is served closer to dinner hour. Actors are touched-up for hair and makeup after the meal, while the air show audience is loaded into their seats. The director will often meet with the cast to give final notes, do a speed-thru or simply to remind them to "hold for laughs."

> *On a bad sitcom, massive rewrites are done Friday between the first and second show. No actor can possibly gives his best if he's having new material flung at him (or her) at the very last minute. These shows tend to be written "joke to joke" instead of "moment to moment," so they don't engage you when you watch then on the air, no matter how the great the jokes are.*
>
> Carmen Finestra, Co-creator and Executive Producer *Home Improvement*

THE REASON FOR AN AUDIENCE

The air show is scheduled at about 7pm. It is a lot of work to load-in, entertain, and present the filming or taping as a polished total performance. Then why do shows bother? The laughs are that important! Situation comedy uses the laughs as a main ingredient of its mix. When every element is clicking, there is a rhythm (of three, of course). Set-up. Punchline. Laugh. Set-up. Punchline. Laugh. Set-up. Punchline. Laugh.

The radio comedies of decades ago like *The Burns and Allen Show, Fred Allen*, and *The Jack Benny Show* always had live audiences. Television kept that tradition. There has always been a fear that if you tried comedy without the audience, it would sound as if nothing was funny. This is especially true now with the way society has more things going on in the room than just the TV. Families no longer gather around the set with rapt attention. Now, the TV is more likely to be on in the background as dinner is being prepared. Hearing laughs might actually cue someone to look up at the screen.

Larry Gelbart (*Danny Kaye Show, Your Show of Shows*) always thought it strange that the network insisted on adding laughs to *M*A*S*H* since it was set in the battlegrounds of Korea.[11] He was allowed to make only a few episodes without the laughs. About the same time, Jay Tarses (*The Bob Newhart Show, Mary, Buffalo Bill*) was successful at making *The Days and Nights of Molly Dodd* without an audience or canned laughs. It was so unusual for newspaper critics not to hear laughs, that this show was described as a **dramedy**. *Ally McBeal* followed this tradition with an hour-long show. Although the line was now blurred, we don't think that *Ally* was a sitcom. It was a drama with many comedic scenes.

In recent years, some true half hour sitcoms have used a single camera movie style and not used an audience. *Malcolm in the Middle, Scrubs*, and *The Bernie Mac Show* are good examples. These single-camera shows follow an entirely different rehearsal schedule: often there is *none*. This type of show is more reliant on its film style and the taste of the individual director's single point of view to convey the timing of the comedy. Even though it is animated, we consider *The Simpsons* one of our favorite sitcoms. It has no laugh track.[12]

Whether a show needs a laugh track or not, the harsh reality is that audiences are used to the track and usually miss it when it's not there. There are two examples of shows where lack of a laugh track was thought critical by their networks. *Police Squad*, a fast paced gag and non-sequitur oriented show, lasted only six episodes. It went on to become a very successful movie series as *The Naked Gun*. In the movie theaters, the group dynamic took effect and there were many laughs. Before the recent *Watching Ellie* series was invited back by NBC, a laugh track was added.

---

11 Filmed in Malibu Canyon State Park.

12 *The Flintstones*, the first prime time animated sitcom, did use a laugh track.

THE AIR SHOW

The air show often begins with cast introductions. Only the regular cast is introduced with the star coming on last. Often the star (especially if he is a stand up comic) will take the warm up microphone to thank everyone for coming, then tell a few jokes.

The audience for the air show has many fans of the show that wrote in for tickets. Also in the audience are friends of the cast and staff. The fans are always good laughers. Agents and managers of actors on the show are not considered the best audience. They have been known to only nod to each other and mouth "that's funny" rather than actually laughing out loud. This kind of silence does not help the actor's performance.

The air show is really energy charged. It can be nerve racking for an actor. The late John Ritter (*8 Simple Rules for Dating My Teenage Daughter, Three's Company*) told James Brady from *Parade Magazine*, "We tape before a live audience. And I still get butterflies. I'm nervous for about the first five minutes, then I'll make some little mistake, and after that I can relax." Actress and USC Instructor Marilyn McIntyre talks about her first sitcom experience:

> I was a theatre person, accustomed to performing in front of a live audience but there was insanity on the floor-- the studio audience, the warm up guy! It was somewhere between a carnival and being thrown to the lions at the Coliseum. I was one of four women guest stars that week...all theatre people. We played a woman's therapy group that Tony Danza had to join. I sat and watched Tony in the scene before ours. He did something that was so brilliant: he went out and made the first mistake. I'd seen him do this scene all week. He knew it cold. I knew that his flub was a fake. He did this to lift the load from everybody else. How smart was that? Our scene came off flawlessly!

Emmy winning director Will Mackenzie (*Reba, Scrubs, Moonlighting*) loves the energy that only an audience can bring:

> My attitude towards a single camera sitcom like *Scrubs* and a four-camera sitcom in front of an audience is the same. What the single camera show doesn't get is the fever pitch that two hours in front of an audience gives. At times, it borders on too silly and the actor's can get carried away. Sometimes I have to keep the lid on, but the audience's influence is mostly good.
> Shooting single camera for twelve to fourteen hours a day over a five-day week means that the actors can't keep up that kind of hyper pace they have in front an audience. The shots look better, but you can't get the same comedy. As a result, the comedy tends to be more sophisticated.
> I love them both. The four-camera lifestyle is great. You can have a life and can even go to the theater at night. When I look at the final product

> though, nothing looks as good as the single camera show. But the people who watch don't care about a great moving dolly or steadycam shot. The viewers only care about what happens to the characters, the situations they get in, and the humor.
>
> Directing single camera makes your multi-camera stuff look better because you get used to taking the extra effort with each shot. I don't want to settle for not seeing the actors. I'll cut a hole or open a door to get the camera in for a better shot, especially if the star is new and can't cheat for camera well. After doing a single camera show and going back to 4-camera, I end up moving the cameras up into the set more.

Each scene begins with a loud bell or buzzer going off. This is a traditional signal, on studio lots, that film is rolling and everyone needs to be quiet. It is the Pavlovian signal to tell the audience to settle down. Tape shows then roll videotape and sound backup tape. When both are running at speed, the stage manager loudly counts down beginning with "5" and ending with a silent "1." The cast begins speaking off the countdown. On a film show, the procedure is a little different. Sound tape is rolled. Every individual cameraman turns on his own camera. When sound is up to speed, the second camera assistant will slate the scene. He will turn to each camera so that the letter of the scene and take number is clearly photographed. Then he claps his slate. The clap is a visual and sound cue that helps to synchronize film and audiotape in editing. At this point, the director calls "Action" and the actors begin.

Actress Nancy Travis (*Becker, Three Men and A Baby*) who is equally accomplished on stage, screen, or television gives her insight into working in front of four cameras:

> I have been on three sitcoms thus far in my career and I have found that perhaps the greatest misconception about acting on a sitcom is that one needs to try harder or "push" to be funny and sell the jokes. It is important to be relaxed and remember that even though an audience is present, there are also four cameras to capture your every nuance. "Bigger is not better". Concentrate on your relationship with the other actor and your objective in the scene. The jokes will either work or they won't. Ted Danson is a master to watch. He seems as though he is barely working - his acting looks effortless - but in the finished product his performance if fully realized, detailed and every joke works. I have had a great time working with him on "Becker."

After the scene is over the director calls "cut" or "clear." The cast waits for notes. The show runner, network, studio, and director are now extremely critical about getting every beat[13] and every laugh "just right." They keep a running

13 "Beat" came from famous method-acting teacher Constantin Stanislavsky's pronunciation of the word "bit." Actors kept the term because it suggested that performances are like music.

tabulation of what "worked" in each scene. After the scene is finished, they quickly confer and decide what notes need to be given before it is done again. This resembles a huddle.

These decisions made in the huddle are critical. The audience can get worn out by the end of the night if everything is done more than two times. In that case, the quality of the laughs will not match from the first act to the second act. If the shooting runs too long, the audience may simply leave giving the cast NO RESPONSE to their work.

If a certain joke was delivered well and still received a less than anticipated audience reaction, the actor will probably be given a new punchline just before starting the scene again. Most show runners will have anticipated a few of these situations and had the writing staff prepare several alternative lines. If not, they will come up with one on the spot.

The director gives all acting notes. The script supervisor is standing by to go over the exact words of the rewrite. Actors have to be loose enough to be able to remember and deliver new lines with no rehearsal. This acting challenge is NORMAL for a sitcom. The ability to adjust will result in more jobs but the immediate reward is that the actor does not have to go through the scene again with egg on his face because of a failed joke. Most of the audience thinks that the actor ad-libbed this funnier line and will laugh even louder. Again, surprise is the key ingredient that causes laughs.

The prop crew resets the scene, makeup and hair people run in to give a quick check to make sure everyone looks the same as in the first **take** and the scene is redone. Each time a scene is done, it is assigned a take number for keeping things straight during editing.

It is of utmost importance that each actor matches all of his actions exactly with the first take. This allows for the editing to be able to use the best of both scenes. This matching will be second nature to the actor, if he has been using his rehearsal time effectively. Teenage actress Ashley Monique Clark who played Sydney on *The Hughleys* had to match in this department store scene:

```
                    SYDNEY
Why don't you go, I just need a belt and some
socks...(OFF DARRYL'S LOOK) C'mon, Dad, you can
trust me.

                    DARRYL
Okay, here's my credit card. Daddy needs to get out
of here before he has to pay the two drink minimum.

DARRYL EXITS. WHEN SHE'S SURE HE'S GONE, SYDNEY BEGINS GRABBING
CLOTHING OFF THE RACKS AND TURNS TO THE SALESGIRL.
```

SYDNEY

```
Okay, I want this, but tighter, I want this but
shorter. Oh, and I want this with the matching
thong.[14]
```

Clark repeatedly rehearsed the order in which she pulled clothes off the rack. She knew she had to maintain continuity. Although her actions seemed random, they were actually carefully planned.

If any of the changes requires new action or positions, actors must confirm this with the director who can then make the decision to accept the mismatch. In the interest of not wearing out the audience, the director will usually yell out to the crew "Moving on!" after the second take. However, the scene may not be done, just done for now. The director should take a minute now to ask the script supervisor to circle his selection of the better take for each part of the scene. This saves many hours of viewing each scene later in editing.

Moving through the entire show in this manner takes two to three hours[15]. The scenes that were pre-shot yesterday are shown to the audience on the monitors that hang above the bleachers. This way they do not miss any crucial scenes that move the story along. The editor has made a preliminary edit in order to show the audience these scenes.

> *After working on your standup craft, one knows when to move on while the audience is laughing and when not to. Acting is a whole other universe. Obviously, in TV, in front of a live audience it's sort of similar to standup as you must hold for the laughs before continuing----not too unlike the stage--and yet I don't believe in hard fast rules but for sure, in film acting, with no feedback in a comedy, it's easier to play the reality--the moment to moment, and although you know it will get laughs in the cinema, you have a choice to take a beat and realize that if you move on too swiftly they (the audience) won't hear the next line--or not. Eventually--the great ones find a great combo of all these variables that works for them. The most important thing though is the believability--be it as a comedian, a TV or film actor--and the laughs --if they come, should come from a truthful place.*
>
> Richard Lewis, Actor/writer/comedian and author of *The Other Great Depression*

CURTAIN CALL AND PICK-UPS

When the show is completed for the audience, the warm-up performer will reintroduce each cast member for curtain call applause. Make sure you check with the AD or stage manager to find out what the etiquette is for this show. It might be, for example, that guest actors always come out from the wings beside the set and the star makes an entrance from an upstage door.

The audience now leaves, but we're not done...**pick-ups**! During the evening, as each scene was evaluated, the moments that still weren't performed as well as expected were marked. Now the show runner and director compare their notes and decide which scenes or portions of scenes need to be done again.

14 *The Hughleys* © 2001 Twentieth Century Fox Film Corporation. All Rights Reserved.

15 Sometimes four or five. We've both worked on a few episodes that work past midnight.

This time it will be without an audience. The AD is given the list and he informs the crew and the actors the order of the pickup scenes.

This is when the crew goes into hyper-drive. Remember that the show was filmed in order so that the audience would understand the story. The pickups are scheduled out of order for many different reasons. The first concern is getting the minors who are guarded by child labor laws to be through by the legal hour. The second is convenience. Wardrobe, hair, set, set dressing, and makeup changes take a LOT of time. The AD may suggest the most efficient order to get the pickups done in the least amount of time.

To be successful, actors need to know two things about pickups. The first is that it is easy to match the physical position they were in at that point in the scene that is picked up. The script supervisor has taken extensive notes logging time code, takes, camera descriptions, and any incorrect lines. The script supervisor is the authority on matching blocking, wardrobe, hair, makeup, and everything else. At any given time during a scene a script supervisor can tell an actor which hand was holding which prop while noting what shoulder an actress' hair was or was not draped over. Trust a good script supervisor. Continuity is their specialty!

Perhaps the harder part for an actor is matching the energy level he had in front of the audience. It is the end of a long day and everyone is tired. The kind of focus that an actor unconsciously gives to work an audience for a laugh is difficult to duplicate.

That is another good reason why it was important to shoot sitcoms in front of an audience. There is something in almost every actor that makes him make that extra effort when an audience is present. That extra effort, whether conscious or not, gives the scene just enough to make it even funnier. Comedy is all about levels of loud and fast. A pickup energy level that might seem "too big for the room" is usually slightly less than what was given during the air show.

If the AD and director decide that you won't be needed for a pickup of a small portion of a scene you were in, they will release you to go home. Here's our tip: stick around! It has happened more than once that, as the pickup is being done, there was a decision to change something in the scene that required an unplanned expansion of the moment. If you are still there, you may save the day. This tip will work for directors and ADs as well. Never release any actor that was in a scene that is not finished.

There is also another reason to stay after being released after a show. Crew and actors share a special camaraderie after a successful week of work together. Everyone generally lets his hair down and the stage is released from the tension of "getting it right." Carmen Finestra told us, "After the taping, everyone usually goes to a designated restaurant to party. You've earned it." The sad part of this is that certain crew members are still working. The cameras are being put away, film is being labeled and sent to the lab. On a show that is starting a new episode the next morning, sets are being struck for the next morning's load in.

Pickups are done and, except for the crew that needs to strike equipment and swing sets, now everyone is finished. The AD or stage manager calls in a loud voice for everyone to hear "That's a wrap!" We have a good feeling about all the hard work we did this week. We hope that as we get this show into postproduction, it will be as funny and look as sharp as it seemed tonight.

Sitcom Vocabulary Quick Review

Read these sentences. If the director gave you these notes, would you instantly know what he meant? If not, go back and review the explanation in this chapter.

We're saving the stunt for the **air show**.

The **background artists** *are upstaging the principals.*

This isn't a **dramedy.** *Punch the joke!*

The **dress show** *came in five minutes long so we need to pace it up.*

Don't put a **handle** *on that line. It hurts the joke.*

Come through the door again after the **hiccup**.

We had too many **jumped laughs** *in that scene.*

Set it up so we can **pay it off**.

There are no **pickups**!

Roll **playback**!

Keep the energy going after the **reset**.

We'll need to do a **retake**.

Match the action of the first **take**.

Let's take a five while they're **tweaking** *the lights.*

The **warm-up** *guy is really great!*

Overlap *the setup when we restart the scene.*

Script Supervisor's Friday Tasks

- ✓ *Read revised shooting script (or revised pages only)*
- ✓ *Transfer blocking notes. Stay on book in order to prompt actors*
- ✓ *Advise actors of dialogue if they are having difficulty*
- ✓ *Do scene/page count breakdown and give it to the 1st AD.*

- ✓ *Prepare for show*
- ✓ *Mark script for take numbers, etc.*
- ✓ *Log time code*
- ✓ *Log information regarding audio loads and film loads*
- ✓ *Log all takes, camera descriptions, etc. in script.*
- ✓ *Log any and all notes given that pertain to that take.*
- ✓ *Log any mistakes, i.e. incorrect line reading, wardrobe, prop, lighting, boom shadows, etc.*
- ✓ *Turn in completed, neat script to production office. Have copy made for yourself. The original goes to editing.*
- ✓ *Do Daily Progress Report. Turn it into 1st AD.*

Sitcom Insider

ADVICE TO AN ASPIRING CAMERA OPERATOR

I can't think of anything better than the timeless advice that still stands strong-"Get Experience!" Any type of experience that involves photography, video production and working collaboratively will be of benefit for the rest of your career. The type of experience you obtain really doesn't matter in the long run. What does matter is that you are working on projects from which you can learn. Small scale productions such as wedding videos, demo/audition tapes, home grown music videos all give you hands on experience that give you a foundation to build on. In fact, I feel that the larger variety of experience one has the better they end up being in their final area of expertise. Experience gives you empathy with all of the fields that make up production and experience gives you a broader range of contacts to network with as you move through your career.

A secondary, yet silent partner to this advice is to "Listen"! Listen to what others are doing while they are working and learn through osmosis. Listen to actors, listen to directors, and listen to writers, editors and producers. There is a wealth of experience to be gained through observation and it is free for the taking. All you have to do is be aware enough to take advantage of the situation and learn from it. A day in which you do not learn at least one thing new is a day that has been wasted!

The best piece of advice I can give is to take any opportunity that presents itself to observe or participate and go for it! The more familiar you are and the more comfortable you are with a given situation the better you will be able to perform when your opportunity arises. Everybody has butterflies in their stomach when their turn comes but those that rise up to the occasion are the ones that are able to use those feelings to their best advantage.

Randy Baer, Camera Operator

Sitcom Career Profile

RANDY BAER
CAMERA OPERATOR

Randy is a camera operator who has never wanted for a job. He is a great craftsman! We think that the secret to Randy's success is in addition to being a great guy, he is also no maintenance. Randy is a problem solver who is experienced enough to figure out a solution without drawing attention to himself.

What are your responsibilities?

At its most basic level my key responsibility is to be the human interface between the director's vision of how a shot should be composed and the mechanical operation of the camera itself. Realistically though, I feel that I am an integral part of the visually creative side of the production since so much of the job depends on my judgment and interpretation of events. There are dozens if not hundreds of small decisions that have to be made during the filming of even a short, three minute scene.

Did you have specific training in this field?

I started my professional career at local TV stations in Tucson, Arizona working as a general crew member. It was there that I had the opportunity to work in nearly all of the areas of television production. I learned set construction, lighting, audio, camera, stage managing, makeup, editing and graphics. After moving to Los Angeles, I started to focus my career more on camera operating and worked for ABC Network and various sporting event producers before moving full time into freelance camerawork (meaning no specific affiliation with any one production entity). Each time the opportunity arose to try something new I took it, feeling somewhat assured that my experience and behind-the-scene observation skills would give me the confidence to rise to the occasion.

How did you get your first job?

When I first started working in sitcoms there were still the remnants of the old studio apprentice system which allowed you to observe, learn, and then eventually move into being a full time sitcom operator. Even though I was already an experienced camera operator with hundreds of hours behind the camera, I was still required to "observe" sitcoms and prove my skills before I was I allowed to be a member of the team. Fortunately it didn't take much more than a week or two to learn the idiosyncrasies of situation comedy which led to me being an often requested "observer" by several experienced camera operators. The win-win situation being that I would do the work and gain some more experience while they would get paid for having little else to do besides hanging around and having fun (and maybe having a drink or two at the dinner break).

What do you like best about your job?

Truthfully, I have got to have one of the best jobs in the world! In what other line of work do you get to judge the quality of your day by how much fun you have had? I love working with actors and I love working with the type of "show biz" people that make up my professional life.

CAMERA OPERATOR
Union: IATSE Local 600
NABET Local 53/57, IBEW
Typical Weekly Salary: $800-$4000
Hours Per Week: Varies whether you work one or two shows. 10- to 14-hour days

Chapter 7 POSTPRODUCTION, GETTING THE NEXT JOB (AND ANYTHING ELSE WE FORGOT)

In this chapter:

- Why actors get a hiatus but writers don't
- The editing process
- The importance of matching
- Sweetening the sitcom
- The reel as a selling tool
- How to contact the authors
- Advice and inspiration from sitcom pros
- Career profile of a sitcom editor

The episode is filmed or taped, but it is far from finished. In fact, some members of the team are now just getting into the game. In the first chapter, we talked about all the preparation that comprises pre-production including the audition, the script evolution and putting a staff and crew together. In this chapter, we will discuss the one-to-three week process that completes the episode. For those of you who are not going to be working on the next episode, we will cover how to parlay your experience into more sitcom work.

Sitcoms usually shoot three weeks in a row and then take a hiatus week. Clever scheduling will make sure that the hiatus weeks fall on weeks that have holidays[1] and avoid scheduling conflicts that would otherwise interfere with the time needed to produce each episode. Scheduling conflicts may include the show's star having a personal appearance on talk shows during a rating's sweeps week, giving birth, guest starring on another sitcom or television movie, or a comedy club date. A television movie commitment with the series star benefits both the actor and the network that airs this series. It broadens that star's audience. If he or she is the lead in the movie, a longer hiatus is necessary. An important comedy club booking, Las Vegas performance, or

SITCOM RULE
Gotta be clean for comedy. *There is a rhythm and subliminal signals that an actor gives an audience that indicates the end of the joke. Any extraneous word or movements that distracts from this, hurts the comedy.*

1 Most crews work under union contracts that guarantee higher pay for holidays. Producers try to avoid working on holidays to avoid that added cost.

talk show appearance more neatly falls into these single weeks off. When a star appears on another show (sometimes playing his character from his show) it is called a crossover. Kelsey Grammer played Ted Danson's old friend (not Frasier) in that very funny episode of *Becker.* This is an example of stunt casting but not a crossover. Either way, this is done to boost the ratings. Grammer probably shot *Becker* during a hiatus week from *Frasier.*

NO HIATUS FOR THE WRITERS

For the writers, the hiatus week gives them time to catch up on scripts. Although the season started with about a six-week lead-time on scripts, by the end of the 20 to 22-episode season, some shows barely get to each table reading with a complete script[2]. Television is so voracious in its appetite for product, those that can meet the demand get the power. The incredible amount of work and hours spent on each episode is used up in one half hour of the television schedule. This is why the head writer becomes the person in power. No one else can go to work without the scripts.

Executive Producer-writer Al Burton (*Charles in Charge, All in the Family*) participated in writing every episode but was not the head writer. He exemplifies the former system of a producer-show runner rather than a writer creator-show runner. He said,

> That change in power came about because of economic reasons. Warner Bros. and the other studios started paying big money for new scripts. When they reached the money limit, they had to start offering a bump up in credit to reward these writers. The cost of the pilot scripts had to be amortized over the entire series. They couldn't justify also paying a separate executive producer who wasn't the creator. Norman Lear and Grant Tinker knew how to make shows really good without being the head writers. They have a 360 degree eye and know all facets of the show including casting. Some head writers can do this well but not all of them. Some know how to write funny stuff but can't execute well. It is helpful if the producer-show runner can get along well with the head writer. I think that it's an error not to have a separate executive producer but that error is one that no bookkeeper would agree with.

Ambitious writers who want to get their own pilot produced, or are moonlighting writing a feature film, have to find some spare time to write. Hiatus weeks may be the only time they leave the studio a little earlier and have time to write on their own. This is quite a challenge for any writer who has already spent the day writing "on staff." Nancylee Myatt has been in the sitcom trenches for 15 years—where she was often the ONLY woman on the writing staff. Myatt had to leave primetime and go to animation to finally get her Emmy. She has a very

2 The writers' brains are tired from dealing with notes!

realistic view of the sitcom world. She echoes Writer Michael Kaplan's view (see SITCOM INSIDER, Chapter 3) that writing for a sitcom can be frustrating. She advises:

> If there's anything that you love doing and are good at other than writing for television, do it. Go, have a normal life. Don't sell your soul or get your heart broken by show business. Creating a hit, or even working on one is like winning the lottery. Everyone thinks they can write, and the market is flooded with the talented and untalented. And these days, even the film community is coming to the small screen and taking the television jobs. The competition is fierce. But it pays better than just about every job in America. So if you decide to throw your hat or spec script into the ring and get lucky enough to get hired, SAVE YOUR MONEY.

We have to concur with Nancy's opinion. Of course, we wouldn't have written this book and you wouldn't be reading it if there was no hope for employment. Veteran sitcom writer Ian Praiser offers a different piece of advice:

> When things aren't happening the way you want, it's easy to sink into a hole. Just know it only takes ones "yes" to change your life. Look for the "yes." If you're going to give up because you haven't heard the "yes" maybe you haven't worked hard enough.

There are many sitcom jobs and the sitcom form will always exist. New people are getting their start on sitcoms constantly. Ignore the odds of how many people are seeking the same jobs. The main frustration will be that talent is not the final arbiter of getting the next job.[3] Especially in the wake of reality TV's popularity, we have seen SO MANY exceptionally talented (previously working) writers unemployed. Likewise, we see this waste of great talent in the acting and directing fields as well!

Touchstone Televsion's Steve McPherson purposely plans his "end of the season wrap party" before the next season in announced. He laments the reality of television, "Things that you love, don't get picked up; things that you don't like get made." He wants every individual involved on a sitcom to celebrate "just being part of the process" where they can say, "I created that, I was a part of that."

But back to the lucky employed sitcom writer's routine. Monday morning of a hiatus week means the writing staff can work hard on completing the scripts in progress. Writer/producer Jamie Wooten (*Half and Half*) describes what happens in his writers room.

> The day starts with about an hour of pop culture discussion: what we watched on TV the night before, what movie we just saw, what restau-

3 Did someone say nepotism?

> rant we ate at, and if it's Monday morning we read through the tabloids, especially the Star. Then it's plunging into the rewrite for the day, the story breaking, or the notes. No breaks, no phone calls, working through lunch. Writers come and go when they need to, but mostly the focus is on the task at hand. Some producers say they don't feel creative until after the sun sets. I say that's bullshit. They just don't have a home life they enjoy and want to get back to. There is no excuse on having insane hours. If you're organized and use your time to get the work done, then go home. How can you reflect life if you never take the time to live it? My responsibility as the person who runs the writer's room is to get the job done, but also to treat my writers as human beings and to respect that they have a life that is not sitcom only. I don't trust anyone who wants to work all the time. Repeat after me: IT'S JUST TELEVISION.

All writers rooms have a different tone. Michael Langworthy (*8 Simple Rules*) who was both a lawyer and standup comic before his sitcom-writing career, quips about the advantage of sitcom writing, "you get to swap jokes and not have to entertain drunk people."[4] Writer Keith Josef Adkins paints a great picture:

> The writers room is a very sacred place. Ten to twelve writers spend 9 hours a day, five days a week, 44 weeks out of the year, with each other. Whew! That's a lot time, yes, but it's what helps build the bond that creates the comfort that allows writers to feel free to be funny. We share our fears, lunacy, secrets, and our joys... we share everything. AND IT NEVER LEAVES THE ROOM. Well, except when it shows up in a script. In a nutshell, the writer's room is the family room. Lots of eating, arguing, politics, teasing, sibling rivalry, and sometimes a little discipline from Ma and Pa. And every now and then, the youngest sibling has to scream to be heard. And that's just family. There's a real special bond that happens in the writer's room. And the better the bond, the better the show.

Some shows habitually work VERY long hours. It is not unusual for a **page 1 rewrite** to take until 2 or 3 AM during a production week. Usually hiatus weeks are not as gruesome.

BEFORE EDITING

Like the writers, the postproduction team does not get a hiatus. Over the weekend, or overnight after the show is shot, the footage is transferred as digital computer information. For shows that are filmed, this means that the negative needs to be processed and then transferred to electronic form.

---

4 We hope Michael is talking about the drunks being from his standup experience not the time he spent as a lawyer.

For 24P digital tape or conventional tape, the process is easier. All of the material is digitized onto an array of computer hard drives. This is done by the assistant editor who logs all the information. Gone are the days of physically cutting film from work print copies or assembling rough cuts of videotapes from cassette copies. We live in an age of nonlinear editing; the times of linear editing are long gone. Linear editing meant the show was assembled from teaser to tag without going back. Each subsequent change to an edited assembly had to wait until the next complete cut of the show. There was usually time for only about three or four versions before the show had to be finalized for airing. The post-production supervisor makes sure the material is transferred and that the editor is ready to begin assembling the first cut of the episode.

Here is what new sitcom actors have to face up to:

1. *It is fast.*
2. *Be prepared each day.*
3. *Come to work with some conclusions drawn about the scene and particularly about your character.*
4. *Be prepared to change as the script is re-written every day; frequently between shows on the day of filming.*
5. *Bring a pencil or two and write the blocking in the margins in order that you may keep going in run-through.*
6. *Learn your lines as quickly as possible.*
7. *Be prepared to drop lines and learn new ones.*
8. *Be completely off the script when it is time for run-through.*
9. *Timing is everything – In the delivery of a line and playing the scene overall.*
10. *Take criticism and use it to your advantage.*

Katherine Helmond Actress,
Who's the Boss, Coach, Soap

ASSEMBLING THE FIRST CUT

On a videotaped show, the camera's output was recorded as well as the switched feed dictated by the director that serves as the basis of this first cut. A technical director or an audience switcher who chooses among the four camera feeds generated a switched cut manually. He operates a machine called a switcher that edits instantly. It looks like live TV for the studio audience watching the filming or taping.

On filmed shows and film-style digital shows, the editor may only have some notes from the director as to how the shots fit together. Many editors and directors prefer to let the editor make a rough assembly of the shots before the director gets involved with the process. Some directors, in the interest of time (and probably control), want to work with the editor from the beginning.

MAKING THE ACTOR LOOK GOOD

Getting to the best take of each line of dialogue is the main objective of this first cut. This is where it is easy to see how technically proficient an actor is. If the actor matched his physical movement and even more importantly his energy level from take to take, it is easy for the editor to navigate between performances. It is common to hear cuss-words used in an edit bay when an attempt to get to a good performance is stymied by non-**matching action**.[5] We like to occasionally invite an actor into the process for a couple of hours[6] for them to see how easy or hard this is. After a short time, some actors have been known to swear at their own images when they realize their best performance cannot be used because of a mismatch.

Mismatching and energy level are not the editors' only concerns. Editor Mike Cole (*One World*) once compiled a tape for an actress on a series he was editing, showing her a consistent clicking sound she unconsciously made with her tongue. So many takes had been unusable because of this nervous habit. Seeing-was-believing for that actress. There was never a problem again.

Editors also run into problems when actors have not held for jokes. If an actor is speaking while the audience is laughing, there is a chance that the editor can get that line clean by moving the audience track covering the line. Just as the cameras are isolated, the audience's mics and the booms are recorded separately on spare audio tracks. But often, the laugh is so loud that it bleeds into the actor's mic so it renders a piece of dialogue unusable. Cameraman Martin Goldstein acknowledges the importance of audience awareness. "Operators need to pay attention to the audience behind them. If the writers are lucky enough to get a great laugh on a joke, don't forget to hold long enough to give the editor some footage to work with."

In postproduction, the editor is limited to what has been already committed to tape. The better the actual the performance, the easier the edit. *Home Improvement's* Carmen Finestra tells us "90 percent of the show you see on the air comes from the evening performance." Certainly, a show can be cleaned up in editing, but a marginal performance can never be made great. During a show, a producer might say, "We will fix it in post." That solution only goes so far. Sometimes a small movement or pause made a good joke not score a big response from the audience. They were distracted slightly. This is where the sitcom rule **GOTTA BE CLEAN FOR COMEDY**

> *I often refer to show biz people as circus people because we all seem to be the one's that don't particularly fit into the ordinary 9-5 life. All of us have egos and most of us seem to be the only members of our families that broke away from our childhood homes. We're thick skinned, self-deprecating professionals that do our jobs well and take pride in doing our individual part to make someone else look good.*
>
> *But to me, the best part of the day is the laughter. We laugh at the writers' jokes, we laugh at each other and we laugh at ourselves. If I've been caught in an embarrassing position I have been know to say, "If I can do just one thing to make somebody laugh today then I have served my purpose."*
>
> *At this point in my career, it is taken for granted that I do my job well and done my part to make the production better because of my participation in it. These are my base level expectations that aren't even considered a variable any more. I work hard, I have a good time doing it and I get a great sense of satisfaction out of my contribution to the end product. I enjoy being a member of the circus family and find it hard to visualize another field that would offer half the rewards this one does.*
>
> Randy Baer, Camera Operator

5 Starting in chapter three, we warned that you have to be able to reproduce the same performance and action each time. Once it is recorded on tape, it becomes very critical.

6 Danger! The length of time to complete an edit is proportional to the number of people in the room.

applies. Any extraneous word or movements that distracts, hurts the comedy. One crisp gesture is better than a muddy movement. Director Bonnie Franklin[7] would demonstrate a useful technique to young actors who tended to wander around on stage. She would begin at Point A and walk with purpose to Point B. The moment she arrived at Point B, she would ground herself by touching a piece of the set. For example, she would firmly put a hand on the back of a chair. It was a clean movement. It had no extraneous, distracting gestures. We have passed on this technique. If a musician were trying to illustrate our **GOTTA BE CLEAN FOR COMEDY** rule, he would say staccato is better than legato. Remember that comedy has innate rhythm to it. It is a sharp rhythm not a smooth one. That's why people are instructed to punch a joke, as opposed to stroking it. We gave a good example earlier of *Girlfriends* Tracee Ellis Ross breaking the spaghetti over the boiling pasta pot.[8] Ross wisely chose one clean sharp movement to punctuate the joke.

Editing can help performance timing. The audience is an impartial judge of what is funny. The editor and director are using their experience to second-guess some of this. If the performers didn't make it clean, they might get some help after the fact. A producer may instruct an editor to "tighten up the jokes." Tenths of seconds are removed between lines[9] to help increase the pace. As much as one minute of time is removed from the show at this time. This is without cutting out any dialogue. It is ideal for most shows to come in about two minutes long as shot. By the time the **director's cut**[10] is complete, it might be less than one minute long.

Sitcom Exercise:

Without watching, record a scene from two different sitcoms. Turn off the sound. Play back the first one. See if you can tell what the scene is about just from the visual storytelling. Write down the plot it in a sentence. Watch and listen to the scene. See how accurate you were.

Next, turn on the sound. Playback the scene from the second episode. This time, turn away from the TV. See if you can tell what the scene is about just from the audio storytelling. Write down the plot in a sentence. Watch and listen to the scene. See how accurate you were.

7 Franklin is even better known as an actress from starring on the long running hit comedy series *One Day at a Time.*

8 Kudos also to the prop department who had the pot steaming (for many takes) on a non-practical stove!

9 Time is never removed from the laughs.

10 The DGA contract stipulates that directors get to edit their show first...or at least give notes on the first assembly.

Besides cutting together the **first assembly**[11] of a show, postproduction is going concurrently on *many* episodes. Editor Timothy Mozer describes a normal editing week:

> Our show (*Girlfriends*) shoots in front of a live audience on Tuesday night. So, on the preceding Monday, the producers pre-shoot some scenes. I get the dailies on Tuesday morning and edit the scenes for playback in front of the audience when they film the remainder of the episode that night. My assistant digitizes the dailies on Wednesday morning. I edit the new episode beginning that afternoon, and finish it by Friday night. At that time, I make a VHS tape of the show and send it to the director. I get notes back from the director on Monday morning and make those changes. I run the show with the producers on Monday afternoon and they give me more change notes. On Tuesday, we shoot another episode, so I am tied up with another pre-shoot. On Wednesday, I show the producers their changes on episode #1 and the show then goes out to the studio and network for even more notes. While we wait for those notes, I continue editing episode #2. After we address studio notes on Thursday and network notes on Friday, episode #1 is locked and I hand it off to my assistant and jump back to episode #2. And so it continues, all the way to episode #22.

The director's contractual control and obligation to the episode is complete after he does his cut. If he is working on the next episode already, he has worked with the editor during lunch hours or after rehearsal during Monday and Tuesday of the week after filming or viewed a copy of the assembly and given notes to the editor. The show runner now gets to make his changes. He might go back and look at some other performance options, but mostly he is cutting out the jokes that didn't work as well as others. The trick always is to remove them without hurting the story continuity.

THE PRODUCER AND NETWORK CUTS

With a strong show, that got even longer laughs than expected, it becomes a problem to get the program down to time. This is the time that network is allowing for this program including opening titles and end credits. It does not include commercial time. Opening titles are the opening of the show, sometimes accompanied by the theme song. It always gives the name of the show, the names of the lead actors and often the name of the show creators. End credits are the end of the show where the names of the crew spin by (so fast that you can hardly read them.)

As we said in an earlier chapter, sitcoms usually run about 22 minutes. . The easiest scene to cut is the tag. The tag of the "No Fat" episode of *Everybody*

11 The director's cut.

Loves Raymond, as we say in the business, "landed on the cutting room floor." Sometimes it is necessary to cut out another entire sub plot rather than butcher the "A" story through heavy handed cutting. This is why actors who have been involved in a successful cameo length performance, will view the show on the air with friends and family only to find that they were eliminated from the episode. It is not necessarily their fault. It might have been the only option. Then again, it might have been the least humorous part of a very funny episode.

The **producer's cut** is now within a couple of seconds of the length required by the time slot. The network executives view this. Knowing their target audience for this show's slot, they may ask about a performance of a joke they think plays better from another take. Understanding that the show is now on time and needs to be delivered very soon, their notes are less than at any other stage of the project. The editor now works with the show runner to make any of these last changes, finds the frames[12] necessary to bring the show in at exactly the right time and transfers the show to an edited master.

THE ON-LINE ASSEMBLY AND SWEETENING

Although the show is now edited, postproduction is still far from over. The master must now be assembled[13] using the final edit decision list that was created during these last couple of days. Years ago, all the work cuts were made using ¾ inch videocassettes. The time code from this edit decision list was then replicated using the master tapes. Similarly, in film, the original negative was conformed to the edge numbers from the work prints. Computerized editing has not only made the rough cuts easier with no loss of generation with each subsequent copy, the final "on-line" assembly is now just making sure that each source is properly setup as the master is rendered by the computer. Film no longer needs to be touched.

Work on the soundtrack is now the focus of getting the show ready to deliver. The editor did his best to smooth out the sound track at each edit point. Every editor knows that you can trick the eye of a viewer with a cut that happens on action. If the action is similar, the viewer might not be able to see

> *When things aren't happening for you the way you want, you can't seem to get anyone to read your stuff, you've done all you can, it's easy to sink into a hole. Been there, done that. Just know that "no, you haven't done all you can," you only think you have.—I know this is true because it has happened to me three times (once when I was just making a call to borrow money from my mother). It only takes ones "yes" to change your life. You can't predict when (which is the bitch). Somebody once said "If you give up, then what the fuck did you do all that work for?" Actually, I just said it, but it's true, isn't it? You either want it or you don't. I say, "Want it."*
>
> Ian Praiser, Writer, *Tracey Ullman, Suddenly Susan, Caroline in the City*

12 Each frame is 1/30th of a second regardless of whether it was shot originally on 24 frames per second film, 24P digital tape or 30 FPS videotape. These small last minute cuts or extensions can always be found in the transitions between scenes.

13 The assistant editor will make the "on-line" final assembly of the episode to be sent to audio postproduction.

"Messing with Their Minds"

As an Editor, I like to mess with peoples' minds by telling them "I do my job best when you don't know I was even there." "Then why are you needed?" they ask.

With the exception of effects-heavy programs, an editor does his job well when the cuts seem natural and the flow of the program is smooth. My cuts should not call attention to themselves nor should they interrupt the natural arc of the story.

Cutting time elements from a program that is longer than the allotted time is where the compromises are most often made. Often the material that needs to be cut is accompanied by changes in position of the major characters, an exit of another character, or an important piece of story material that is needed to move the plot along. This is most often where we have to grit our teeth and try to make it work. Surprisingly, we can do that very often, which is good because most shows are shot fairly long and cut in editing.

Being an Editor is not for everyone... it requires attention to detail, an organizational leaning, the ability to deal with computers but not seem like a "techie" and there is a need to think quickly with others waiting to see your solution. It can be and is very rewarding and you can make or break a show in post.

Mark West, Emmy winning editor,
Dave's World The Hughley's, One on One

slight mismatching. However, the moment that there is a mismatch in the sound, every person that watches the show will think that there is something wrong with an edit. This is regardless of their technical expertise because television pictures are flickering images with a change of angle at every camera cut. Sound is continuous. You can't fool the ear.

The music composer or coordinator has viewed the final cut to see what music cues are needed. The cut is also pre-laid on a multi-channel audio recorder with any necessary sound effects. It is typical to add a light track of birds chirping for outdoor scenes that were shot on stage. Crickets replace birds for a faux outdoor night scene. If there was a lot of background action in some scenes, the "walla"[14] tracks are added. Room tone is pre-laid for scenes with no background actors. Room tone is the sounds that go on in an empty room with no one moving. It may appear silent to the naked ear, but actually there is ambient sound. During pickups, it is common to record 45 seconds of room tone in a swing set used only on that episode. These things are needed to make the scene sound as if there were no edits.

All of this is mixed together in a final session that lasts an hour or two. Any off-stage dialogue or lines that need to be looped[15] are done at this time. More room tone needs to be added with any of this replacement dialogue. The biggest job at the final audio "sweetening" mix is smoothing out the laughs. Some of the jokes were edited from a pre-taped performance with no audience. Others were from the second or third take in front of an audience and got a smaller laugh than the first time they saw it. If a show was taped in front of two different audiences, the quality of the laughs will be different. The editor

14 Before leaving the set, the background actors were asked to recite thirty seconds of soft "walla, walla, walla" which sounds just like nondescript conversations when mixed in the sound track.

15 Unlike location filming, very little dialogue that is recorded on stage needs replacement. Location film footage used to be made into loops that would repeat constantly until an actor could recreate the line perfectly while watching.

tried to make this unnoticeable, but there is an insurance policy: the "laugh man."

There are a very few highly specialized people that "laugh" a show. Most viewers are aware that this is a process but usually for the wrong reason. They complain often about the "phony" laughs in some shows. The "laugh man's" job is not to put in bigger laughs but to smooth out the laughs that are already there. Two hundred people who attend the recording of a show laugh more often, much louder and much harder than people in their living rooms. They were entertained before and during the event and might be attending because it is their favorite show. They are also well mic-ed.

Charlie Douglass was a technical director when *I Love Lucy* was the first multi-camera sitcom being filmed. Since that filmed show was trying to emulate a live television studio audience with their edited film studio audience, Charlie recognized a need. He developed a small box that had a series of laughs on tape. Using this tool like a typists uses a typewriter, he was able to select an appropriate laugh that would cover an edited laugh that needed smoothing. He could skillfully play the machine like a keyboard instrument. He was very protective of this invention and worked hard at getting cleanly recorded laughs from each subsequent show he **sweetened.**[16] When asked if the people inside his box "were still alive?" he would just raise an eyebrow.

Charlie's son Bobby followed in the same career and was in much demand as were the small crew of "laugh men" assembled by John and Carol Pratt. Their work is valuable because of their technical skill but more for their ability to know exactly how an audience would react to any joke. The begin-

Soap operas were a good place to learn multiple cameras. You are shooting 80 pages a day. I did one for NBC and one for CBS. For NBC, you had to block the whole show in your head and write and number all the camera shots before any rehearsal. You would then get there at 6 o'clock in the morning and the actors would say "No!" When you don't know how to adjust, it is so hard. You have to turn your script into a scene. The good news was that, my first show, I was snapping my fingers away and the TD was taking it where it was right. All I could say was, "Thank you." At CBS, it was so much easier because it was a half hour show and I could rehearse and then hand my shots to the AD.

The transition from theater to television was a two-step process. I had a show Off-Broadway that got great reviews. The executive producer of Another World *asked if I would like to do an episode of his show. He said, "Come and observe." I knew people had observed for years and never gotten a shot. At that time, I had enough power, that I asked my agent to get me half of the directing fee upfront and the other half whenever I did the episode. I observed for six months, but not every day since I was still doing plays. I ended up doing only two episodes.*

John Whitesell ended up hiring me on Search For Tomorrow. *I actually hated soaps but would be their fill-in director for about two years That was a great job. Then I wanted to move to L.A. and test the waters. I knew Chip Keyes, a producer of* Valerie's Family. *So again, I went to observe. Peter Baldwin was directing a lot of episodes and was very gracious to me. I met all the executives and was still going back to New York and doing plays, which gave me some cache. Beth Uffner was their agent and decided she would represent me, which was the best thing that ever happened.*

continued next page

16 This can refer to adding laughs or to the entire process of audio postproduction.

> *Observing is helpful if you don't know how to do it. However, observing just to be seen is not helpful. You have to know somebody. Chip got me to Beth. Beth knew everybody in the business and was very good at starting people out. She said that I had to be here during pilot season. Barnett Kellman directed the pilot for* Murphy Brown *and it sold. I was able to get an episode of* Throb *which he now could not do. That got me started.*
>
> Steve Zuckerman
> *Everybody Loves Raymond, Friends, Murphy Brown,*
> series director *Empty Nest*

ning, middle and ends of each laugh are very different depending on the joke. These skilled artists can duplicate the natural sound of a studio audience.

Sure, some producers want to use this process to bolster their weaker material. Very few producers will try to give a joke a bigger laugh than it deserves. The entire week of production was spent making sure each joke was properly written and properly delivered. If something still ended up not working, it should have been edited out of the final show. Now is not the time to betray all of this work. The final mix is done and the show is now complete. It is delivered to the network for airing. Sometimes the entire process finished so close to deadline that it has to be fed to the New York network transmission center by satellite, but this is frowned upon.

GETTING THE NEXT JOB: THE ACTOR'S REEL

While all of this post-production is being completed, the actors and director might be involved in another episode or trying to get a job on another show. Each of them should use their work on this episode as a tool in getting that next job. It is often joked, "You are only as good as your last job in Hollywood." This means that you should get a copy of this work. The director is given a copy as part of his contract. The actor needs to fend for himself.

You want the best quality possible so a dub of the master would be preferable. If you were the primary guest star of the episode, it might be possible for you to get the producer to make you a copy when the show if finished with postproduction. If this fails, knowing when the show will air means that you can tell you friends to watch and you can tape it at home or have a professional record it for you off the air.

Just how do you know the air schedule? The best way is if you became friendly with the line producer during the week. This person knows about the schedule better than anyone. It might be as simple as a call to him to get the right information. Sometimes the newspaper TV section will have a wrong listing or there could be a last-minute preemption. Networks have their own individual websites as well. There are a couple of companies, such as EditPlus, that specialize in recording shows off the air. They do what they call an **air check**[17]. This term comes from radio, when advertisers wanted to be sure that they were getting the airtime they were paying for. These same companies, like EditPlus,

17 Recording a show off the air for purposes of archiving it or checking its content.

help actors put their demo tapes together. Dave Manship's EditPlus calls this "a necessary tool just like pictures and résumés." This copy of the episode (or scenes from the episode) needs to be on your reel. Just as you constantly need to update your headshot, you should also update you acting reel. Because casting directors and producers don't have the time or patience to watch an entire episode of your work, actors should only provide one short scene to show them of this latest effort.

A few independent editors specialize in making slick presentation reels. They understand that less is more. The entire reel should be well under ten minutes long. Five to seven minutes is ideal. You want to show the best moments of your work. You also want to show yourself in any scenes that you are working with major stars on popular shows. It is only natural for the person seeing it to think that if you were good enough to work in that company, then you might be good enough to work with them.

Editing this type of reel is painstaking and time consuming. Be clear about how much the editor will charge you for making your reel. Don't cut corners on this. A poorly designed or executed reel will reflect badly on you.

Directors are guaranteed a copy of the episodes they direct as part of the Director's Guild contract. Often a producer who is considering hiring a director will request a sample episode of that director's work. Director Steve Zuckerman comments:

> If you put together a reel or show someone an episode, it doesn't show too much about you. It looks the same as the other episodes of that show. What it doesn't show is how the week went. Did you do it on time? Did you do the shots or did the TD or AD do them? By the time it is edited, all sitcoms look the same. But my agent said I had to give them a reel so you try to give them something that they are looking for. They might be looking for a lot of physical comedy. That will help. If you are looking for a single camera show, you might have an episode with some single camera elements.

WRAPPING IT UP

We have tried to cover a broad spectrum of jobs in the sitcom world. We hope you will have an appreciation for the number of talented people who collaborate to make a sitcom. Since writing this book, we have a greater knowledge and appreciation of the intricacies and day-to-day details that every crewmember attends to in order to do their job with ease and finesse. Just like there are great actors, who "make it look easy", there are great network and studio executives, writers, designers, set decorators, costumers, editors, script supervisors, propmasters, boom operators, cameramen, grips, gaffers, TCs, ADs, and

SMs[18] who amaze us with their vast knowledge and expertise. We hope we have represented everyone as accurately as possible and would be receptive to any corrections and comments, or your favorite sitcom stories. Contact us at www.sitcomcareer.com.

Director Linda Day was typical in that she didn't start with the sitcom job she has today,

> I went from office jobs in radio, television news, and talk shows, to 10 years on and off as a script supervisor. I spent 5 of those years as a script supervisor on various projects with Jay Sandrich. I was watching one of the best and getting paid for it, too. This was heaven.
>
> During one of my heavenly lulls, I took another office job, organizing the *Mary Hartman, Mary Hartman* headquarters. I had one stipulation: NO SECRETARIAL DUTIES. The first day, they sat me down with a Dictaphone to transcribe a writers' meeting. The second day, Norman Lear rightfully had me fired. The third day, Jay called with a pilot project: *Soap*. That was the last office job I had.
>
> A year later, I did the pilot of *WKRP*, again with Jay. When Jay went back to do *Soap*, Ted Kaye (the associate producer) asked me to stay with *WKRP* as their associate director. Big break!
>
> The end of the second season, Hugh Wilson gave me an offer I truly couldn't refuse; I got my first shot at directing. The particular script I directed happened to get special recognition for its content In 1981, I was nominated for an Emmy for an episode of *Archie Bunker's Place*, a Norman Lear show. I didn't win. I think I was mainly disappointed because I didn't get the chance to get up and publicly and personally thank Norman Lear for firing me back on *Mary Hartman, Mary Hartman*![19]

The people we interviewed agreed on two things. First, a sitcom career IS fun. Second, a sitcom career IS NOT glamorous. Camera Operator Randy Bear shares:

> My friends and I all laugh at the realization that at one time or another all of us thought that being a camera operator was a glamorous position. The thought of being right there in the action, working directly with actors and directors was just about as good as it could get. The reality of the situation though is that if you are good at what you do then you end up being intimately involved with everything that is happening on the stage. Every single element of production is geared to one thing and that is making an actor look good and appear funny on camera. It is my job to make that happen. Production days are often long and the mental

---

18 Notice we ended with a run of three.

19 Linda, consider Norman thanked.

> concentration is constant– not to mention the physical toll it all can take on your body standing all day. Cameras need to be moved, set and prop changes need to be double-checked, dialogue changes need to be processed and worked into the pattern of camera shots. None of this is especially glamorous at 2 in the morning after you have been up since 6 a.m. then driven cross-town for an hour so you could be at work by 8.

Some of our contributors praised the income and opportunity to have time with their families.[20] Director of Photography Bruce Finn tells us "the hours are much less demanding than a single camera episodic schedule." He says that one of the things he likes best about his job is "making money to support my family." Martin Goldstein agrees. "Sitcoms are attractive because they generally provide for a good base income. Additionally, and maybe more importantly, they tend to keep regular hours leaving room for a family life and free weekends."

Writer Michael Langworthy (*8 Simple Rules*) reminds aspiring sitcom writers "a career is a long term process rather than a sprint." We think this is true of any sitcom career. We hope that this book will give everyone who reads it a greater respect for this very specialized form of television and the artists who toil every day[21] to bring it to the viewing public. Our basic philosophy when we began teaching a sitcom technique class, was the more you understand the style and structure and technical requirements of this medium, the better you will be at it. We believe that knowledge is power.

We also think that luck or good fortune plays a part in a successful career. In the Emmy nominee issue of *Daily Variety*, Sarah Jessica Parker and Jennifer Aniston both mention it. Parker is quoted, "The only time I ponder the good fortune that we've experienced is when interviewers ask what the ingredients are. I think it is just good fortune, really good writing, and smart producing." Aniston said, "Someone is watching out for me, or something. I wish I could say that I had all these options mapped out and that I made these smart choices. But I was really just lucky." Luck aside, there is no doubt that these women are gifted, dedicated artists who know their craft!

We hope that the information contained in these chapters will help you get a job, do it well, and enjoy it while it's going on. We know that working in sitcoms is a great job. Maybe you'll agree!

When interviewing people for this book, we asked industry professionals "What advice would you give someone who would like to do what you do someday." Richard Lewis had some thoughts on his route.

> I'm in the class of Leno, Boosler and Kaufman from the early seventies. There were few comedians then and we worked from sheer passion. Any-

20 This is in comparison to working on other forms of film and hour long television, which work MUCH longer hours.

21 Except during weekends... and hiatus.

> one should work from that place regardless of what part of the arts you strive for. Sadly, many comedians in the 80's and 90's just used standup to be seen by casting directors. That's cool but to me, a half-assed attempt at standup is a waste for an actor. If you want to act then study, do plays, and be seen as an actor, not a comedian. It's that simple. Figure out what you want, go for it, be true to yourself and surround yourself with winners and people who believe in you and be able to trust their criticism and guidance.

Writer Ian Praiser advises:

> To find out the qualities that make you unique, first you have to find out who you are. Listen to the way you talk to people, how they talk to you, what things get you going and how does that lead into other things, your feelings on people, things, events, politics, your family, anything. Try to remember all emotional things, not the things in the middle, but the things in the extreme. Tragic, sad, ironic, funny, awkward. And try to remember the time in September... sorry, I love that song. Remember how all these things have changed in you over the years, because that gives you more perspective, objectivity, distance, maturity and also puts you back to the little person inside you, you know, the honest one. The more you know who you are and how you react to things, the more you bring to the table. Each actor, writer, owns a treasure of life experience like the locket in *TITANIC*. Don't throw it in the ocean like that stupid old woman, where it's no good to anybody.

This final piece of advice comes from script supervisor Ellen Deutsch:

> Look within. First and foremost, there must be passion deep within your soul. If you don't go within, you'll go without. You will not be successful in this industry. It is hard work, long hours, with very few "atta girls' along the way. You learn quickly that Hollywood and Show Business are NOT synonymous with "glamorous." But, if you love it. Really, really love it, and can't imagine doing anything else but this, then yes, most definitely do it. As the lyrics go: 'THERE'S NO BUSINESS LIKE SHOW BUSINESS.' In my thirty years of being in this business, I have never once dreaded a Monday morning. Not many people can say that. There is a lot I have gone without in my life, but loving what I do every day leaves my soul at peace.

If there is anything that you wish we would have included or a question you'd like to ask us, again, go to our website sitcomcareer.com and we'll try to get you an answer.

Sitcom Vocabulary Quick Review

Read these sentences. If the director gave you these notes, would you instantly know what he meant? If not, go back and review the explanation in this chapter.

You can edit it from the **air check**.

I swear it was in the **director's cut**.

We had to cut the scene to get **down to time**.

The editor should be done with the **first assembly** *this afternoon.*

It needs a **page 1 rewrite.**

The **producer's cut** *is still 10 seconds long.*

We have to get **room tone** *before we move on.*

We'll **sweeten** *it in post.*

We need some **walla** *from that scene.*

I couldn't use that take because he didn't **match action**.

Sitcom Insider

When I ask my students, as I inevitably do at the beginning of any sitcom writing class I teach, why they want to write a sitcom spec script, I get answers like, "It's fun." Well, that won't get you to the end of your sitcom script because a lot about writing isn't so much fun. Or I hear, "To tell a story," or, "To make people laugh." I've even heard, "Because I really, really, really want to." All of those are good reasons to write something, but not a sitcom spec script. The only reason to write a sitcom spec script is: **$$$.**

Let me explain. Every other format has a range of outlets, some of which you can actually control. If you write a play, it doesn't have to be done on Broadway for people to see it. A screenplay can be done low budget, you can even raise the funds and do it yourself as an independent. If you write a novel -- even if it doesn't get published -- you can self-publish and it's still legitimately a novel. Same with short stories and poetry. Everything else has a reason of its own to exist. And you can write it just the way you want to write it, even if nobody wants to buy it. But not a sitcom. You have to do a sitcom on commercial television. There's no other place for it.

What this means is you have to follow the rules. There is not a formula -- formula is what leads to predictable dull scripts that nobody wants to read past page fifteen. However, there is form -- quite a different thing. There is a very specific form and you must follow it. And it doesn't matter if you know how to do it better or funnier or fresher. That's not your job when you're writing a spec script. You're job is to do it exactly the way it's done and still be original.

So, how do you keep your original voice within the confines of a very rigid form? By finding stories that have something emotionally meaningful to you (that's your original voice) and then translating that passion into the established sitcom character in the world of his show (and there's the form).

For example, when I was writing for Everybody Loves Raymond, I was looking for family relationship stories because that's what the show is about, and I thought about my relationship with my Dad. I loved painting and drawing, and my Dad, who was a salesman, could only relate to my artistic interest by having me decorate the windows of his store. I remembered how much I hated that the only way my father could see any value in my talent was if it was "useful" for his business. I still get upset just thinking about it.

So, I connected with that emotional current and translated it into the characters of Ray and Frank in the world of the show. The result was the script for "You Bet," an episode about Frank taking a surprising interested in Ray's sports writing. Ray cautiously starts to feel gratified and respected until he discovers that his father's interest in his work is only to get inside information so he can place sure-thing bets on sporting events. Ray's sense of betrayal and anger at his father's using him like this made for a strong emotional narrative and a script that I really wanted to write. Even though "You Bet" had no connection to the actual details of my life, the whole concept came from my personal connection to the emotional content, and that connection informed every decision I made in writing that script.

In order to bring your personal connection to a story, you need to find out why you want to tell that story. You already know why you want to sell the story, (see **$$$** *above) but that's quite different than why you want to tell the story. Why you want to tell it is where "you" are in the story. Getting you into the story is what makes the difference between an okay script that follows the rules but doesn't seem special, and a great script that excites agents and makes producers want to meet you.*

The best stories come from your own emotional life. Things you care about passionately. Things you hate, things that make you angry, things you're afraid of. They come from pain, humiliation, jealousy, embarrassment. Comedy gold mines, all.

And when you do find a story with a personal emotional connection, please do NOT give the story to an outside character. Find a way to tell the story through the character whose name is in the title of the show. If you're writing for Bernie Mac then the story starts on Bernie, it develops around what Bernie does, and it ends on Bernie. Bernie has the problem, the emotional current that drives the story, and he gets the big face-off. In addition, the conflict ought to be with another regular character, not a new character you've invented.

That is how you get your personal creativity inside the form. If you do that, you are well on your way to a fresh and original story that shows you have imagination and still know how to serve the needs of the show. That's on the money! About $17,000 an episode. Now tell me that's not why you want to write for sitcoms.

Ellen Sandler, Emmy nominated writer and writing consultant–
http://www.sandlerink.com Services/Resources

Sitcom Career Profile

TIMOTHY MOZER
EDITOR

Tim has two essential skills needed in this profession. He knows funny and works fast. Also, Tim is incredibly easy-going and a great guy. His reputation preceded him and he lived up to the hype!

What shows have you worked on?

I have worked as an editor on *Wings, Frasier, Men Behaving Badly, Jenny* (Jenny McCarthy's short-lived sitcom), *Encore, Encore* (Nathan Lane's even shorter-lived sitcom), *Stark Raving Mad, Girlfriends,* and *So Little Time.*

What are your responsibilities?

The editor has only one responsibility: Make it funny. If a bit didn't work in front of the audience, fix it. If you have to change the timing on a joke, do it. If you have to steal a reaction shot from another scene, or even another episode, do it. Just make it funny.

Did you have specific training in this field?

My only training for being a sitcom editor was spending 5 years as an assistant on *Wings. Wings* was a family. A generous family. The people there turned to me and said that I should make sure I didn't leave the show in the same capacity in which I began. In year 3, the executive producers let me edit an episode. By the end of my fifth year, in addition to all my assistant editor responsibilities, I had edited 17 episodes of *Wings*, two episodes of *Frasier* (which was produced by the same team as *Wings*) and had received Emmy and ACE Eddy nominations for one of the *Frasier* episodes. At that point, I was able to get hired as an editor on *Men Behaving Badly*.

How did you get your first job?

LaserEdit was being used on 99% of the sitcoms in Hollywood. And almost immediately after I got trained on it, I got called from Paramount Studios for the job on *Wings*.

What advice would you give someone who wants to do what you do?

Think it over carefully. I love what I do and am thankful for having the opportunity to do it. But, I know many people who are out of work and some who have been forced to sell their homes. The business is changing. More and more film work is leaving the country. And more and more students are graduating film school and moving to Los Angeles. Today, we have fewer jobs combined with more people looking to fill the ones that remain. That is not a situation to be entered into lightly.

What do you like best about your job?

If I am working on a good show, I get to laugh all day.

EDITORS
Union: IASTE local 700 (Editors Guild) and the DGA
Typical Weekly Salary: $2500
Hours Per Week: 40 to 50

Chapter 8 CHANGES ON MULTI-CAM SITCOMS...(IN WITH THE NEW!)

In this chapter:

Why downward inflections land jokes

The difference in tape and film style shooting

Who watches, where, and why?

The reasons the TV image is better

The importance of reaction shots

There has been a tremendous amount of changes to the multi-cam sitcom since we wrote the first edition, so many of them for the better. Many of the good changes can be credited to the progress in technology. Sitcoms still rely on funny performances of quality material. And some would argue, that is the only thing that matters. If that is so, then it is a wonderful luxury that sitcoms have never looked better.

The better visual quality is for two reasons. The high definition pictures on the screen are shot and lit in a more sophisticated manner. And the delivery system is better.

COVERAGE

We talked about the difference in tape and film recording in Chapter 5 of this book. Tape, being the original medium of television, had its tradition in live editing. There was only one version of a show[1], the one that was cut live. That rarely occurs now. **Tape style shooting,** getting the one version of the story, hardly exists anymore. The director no longer thinks shot to shot. He doesn't need to cut the show as he goes. In tape style shooting, the cameraman's shot only had to be good when the tally light was on. Not so anymore.

With the sophisticated and easier ways to edit film, a production company wants more than one choice for every moment of the teleplay. In fact they want as many choices as possible. The way to get this is **film style shooting**, which is done by making all the coverage **usable** all the time. This

SITCOM RULE

Jokes have to land! *In order for an audience to know when it's time to laugh, the delivery of the line must have an ending. A sure way to get a laugh is to make sure that the actor has a downward inflection at the end of the punchline so it is clear that the idea is finished.*

1 Eventually one or two and finally all four cameras were also recorded (iso'ed) for some adjusting of precise cut points in post production.

means that nearly all angle and size changes as well as all movement followed by the cameras is motivated and therefore looks good whenever the camera is recording.

The director is the mastermind[2] who coordinates camera moves with character movement to create as many **on air[3] moves** as possible. Nevertheless, all four cameras want to offer a choice of every moment of every scene. The director tries to have as few **off air moves** as possible. Meaning that he only makes a camera's coverage no good when he is changing size, framing, or the character being shot to make the total shooting of the scene efficient. The goal is still Desi's original goal to record the scene as efficiently as possible while the audience[4] is still fresh. With film style shooting, there is often a **first pass** and **second pass**...sometimes even a third. The cameras are shooting different coverage with each consecutive pass. Are you now seeing the plethora of choices that will exist to tell the story? It makes editing more of a challenge or perhaps an embarrassment of riches.

The director's script will reflect whether it is a film or tape style show. You already know that the director designs the shots or plans the coverage for every scene. A tape style show will have the director's master plan, his shots, marked to the right of the dialogue on his script.[5] A straight line will begin immediately after the word of dialogue when a shot begins and continue horizontally to the right edge of the script page. On top off that line or immediately below that line, there will be 3 pieces of information: a description of the shot, the camera number[6], and the number of that shot sequentially. On a film show, the director's plan may also be charted but without lines emanating from a specific word of dialogue. Instead, many directors make columns for each camera (A,B,C,X or X,A,B,C). Then in each column the director will describe what he wants to see from that camera and then indicate when that changes or morphs into something else. As we said in Chapter 5, cameras consistently follow one character or follow one character on a move to another. When the latter happens, it is called a **dump**.[7]

---

2 Especially on shows that were previously filmed, the Director of Photography is a great ally and highly involved in this aspect.

3 Notice the irony that the "air" doesn't really exist anymore because that word refers to live broadcast TV.

4 And actors.

5 Also known as "marking his script."

6 Or camera letter. We have explained where 1,2,3, and 4 are sometimes A,B,C, and X.

7 This method of switching to another character is sometimes used in the final edit, so the camera operator must make this a smooth move.

SOME EXCEPTIONS

In some smaller or remote markets,[8] as well as some educational institutions, the older tape-style method is still often used. Why would a college teach something that is obsolete? Because it is a great way to learn how to tell a funny story. There is a huge amount of knowledge that comes from the immediacy of seeing how the live editing plays to or against the humor. For example, a student can learn immediately that cutting to a **reaction shot**[9] can extend a laugh. This is how it works. A character delivers a punchline. The audience laughs, then, just as the laugh peaks, the director cuts to the character that is reacting to that line. This character has a point of view about what he just heard. Observing that POV makes the audience laugh longer, creating a second peak in the laugh.[10] Conversely, it becomes clear that cutting away from a funny line too quickly can kill a laugh. It is vital for students of comedy to get a feel for what will enhance the audience's enjoyment of a punchline.

Another reason that many schools still teach tape style recording is that the schools don't differentiate between types of shows that are shot multi-cam (news, daytime drama, etc.). Since so many of the support jobs involved remain the same, there is still a great number of reasons to teach the tape style process.[11]

DIRECTOR OF THE FLOOR

Another great change due to technology is that the sitcom director is nearly always on the floor during camera blocking and shooting. Since no live cutting is going on, his proximity to the actor and immediacy to everything that's going on benefits the show in countless ways. It is not a big deal to program a television monitor to show a quad split, or to set up 4 different monitors that corresponded to the cameras. All it takes is pressing a button on a remote. Also, the technology that exists makes it easier and easier to do a video assist on film cameras; or just show the image of a digital camera on the monitors.

A director is more effective[12] (and faster) giving his own notes rather than having a go-between deliver his notes to either the crew or cast. Also there is nothing like a director feeling the energy of both the stage and audience live. In the booth, a director would only hear the audience unless a cameraman panned

8 More about this in Chapter 10.

9 This planned reaction shot can be hung off the original straight line on the director's script.

10 In Chapter 5, we mentioned that Asaad Kelada had as many as 400 shots. He usually cut back to the joke teller and again to the other person trying to get a, high degree of difficulty, four-peaked laugh.

11 Until you understand exactly how the final product will look, it is hard to work just off the quad split. So, spend time practicing this and spend time in editing.

12 And faster, since the Director's skillset includes being able to speak in the actor's (and every other department) language.

the bleachers with his camera.[13] It may be an apocryphal story, but it is said that the first director who insisted that the director not be in a booth but **on the floor** was an actor who became a director: Robby Benson. Perhaps he sensed, having been an actor, that other actors would prefer that one-on-one face time with their director.

THE SWITCHER

A new job was created when shows went from tape style to film style. This job now comes under the jurisdiction of the Directors Guild of America and the position is called the switcher. We briefly mentioned this in Chapter 5. The switcher performs a very important job. He does a live cut from the four cameras recording so that the audience can see it on the TV screens above their heads in the bleachers. So the switcher is the storyteller using the choices from that particular pass being recorded. He has to have the physical dexterity of a TD and the story sense of a director. His choices will influence whether the audience laughs or not and for how long. The director may or may not give a plan for a line cut to the switcher. Often, the director will guide the switcher to his vision, especially on tricky sequences, so that the audience will see close to the same edit that the director will eventually assemble in his cut of the show. No matter who decides on the live cut, getting it right is important because the reactions and laughs of the audience are important to the actors performing.[14]

THROW AWAY THE CUT

In the years since we wrote *The Sitcom Career Book*, post production has become even more fully used. Especially with the speed of modern non-linear editing systems, almost all shows rebuild the edit rather than just fixing some late camera cuts, tightening up the pauses where there is no laugh, and cutting for time.

This software has multi-camera functions that allow all the cameras to be lined up and in sync with each other in the computer like they were in real time.

> As we shoot our show in front of a live audience, we have an "Audience Switcher" who switches the video feed of the four cameras being displayed on monitors above the audience. It is important to note that this individual plays a key role in their reaction; namely, their laughter. And even though most of the scenes play out right in front of them, audience members usually train their eyes onto the television screens, so the Audience Switcher can dramatically affect the rhythms of laughter and the actor's pace of performance. Yet, as key as this position is, we don't use the switched ("line") feed in editing. And seldom as reference, if at all. We only use the four cameras grouped together as a quad for our source

13 And even then, the director can't see much, because the audience is not lit.

14 As well the audience that will view it on TV.

material. Typically, the switched cameras in a live broadcast setting are marginally late, so if we used the line feed, we would constantly be grabbing the source camera to fix the edit in post. Also, crossing takes (using an alternative performance) is problematic, for the same reasons. Using only the grouped source cameras simplifies and expedites the cutting process.

Tim Ryder, Co-Producer, *3rd Rock From The Sun*
Associate Producer/Editor, *That '70s Show*
Editor, *Anger Management*

LANDING THE JOKE

The relationship with an actor playing a role and his audience is a partnership where the character says something funny and the audience laughs. The audience needs that clear indication that it's their turn to do their job. That job is based on listening and watching for the clues the actor gives off. This is where the sitcom rule: **JOKES HAVE TO LAND!** becomes important. In our spoken language, an upward inflection is a clue that we've either asked a question or "I'm going to say something more" and I want you to continue listening[15]. This is evident and we recite a list where all the items in the list have an upward inflection until we get to the end of the list and we go down. That downward inflection is the clue that we are done.[16] And in comedy that downward inflection is the audience signal that the last thing we said was funny and it's your turn to laugh.

Remember the sitcom rule: **COMEDY COMES IN THREES** that we discussed in Chapters 1 and 4? These rules play hand in hand. This new sitcom rule: **JOKES HAVE TO LAND!** doesn't just apply to runs of three. Any and all punchlines are more likely to get a laugh if they end down. This will make them land! Now, there are exceptions. We must also tell you that you CAN land a joke without a downward inflection. Actors do it all the time, especially when their ending inflection is a character based choice. No matter the inflection, a well-delivered punchline that lands gives a clear indication to the audience when to laugh. It is also makes it easier for the switcher to do the line cut when he's clear that the joke is over.

FILM STYLE LIGHTING ON MULTI-CAMERA SHOWS

TV shows are lit differently than they used to be. Once single camera comedies became popular, it became glaringly evident that a single camera show had a better "look" than a multi-camera show. This was no great surprise to cinematographers of multi-camera shows who knew that you can create a more refined look when you are only designing the lights for one shot at a time, in one

15 Valley girls just talk all the time with upward inflections but that is a character affectation.

16 It puts a button on the joke.

direction rather than **cross shooting**, or shooting in many directions at once, which is what the multi-camera system does by design.

Many cinematographers, especially those who shot both single camera and multi-camera shows, or came from the single camera world of episodic television or features, met the challenge and began lighting multi-camera sitcoms differently. The first thing they did was take down the light levels in general. Everything wasn't so bright. Next, they did more directional lighting, employing a key and fill lights, that resulted in both light and shadows. Since audiences were getting used to single camera shows looking like movies, the look of multi-cams became more textured. Simply, they looked better.

This better look was enhanced by the cameras getting better. The depth of field was sharper in even lower light settings. And on the other end, people own flat screen TVs that provide great sound and crystal clear pictures. The sharpness of digital TV screens that viewers watch (and even computer screens) make the finished product that the consumer watch look great. As a result, the TV audience's visual taste is more sophisticated.

MOVING THE SUITS

Once video village became the director's place to view the audience show, this hub began to get more crowded and more crowded. Makes sense. Everybody wanted to be where the decisions were being made. It is now a general practice to have three[17] separate viewing areas to watch the show while it is being recorded in front of the studio audience. The first, and most important, is video village. The director, associate director, script supervisor, and show runner gather here. Sometimes the writing staff is here as well. It often moves so that it is close to the standing set or swing set in which the scene is taking place offering fast, easy access for the director and script supervisor to the actors and the associate director to the camera crew.

The next important viewing area is where the DP sits. Its location is determined by where the DP can get the best view of his monitor. And his monitor is of better quality and receiving the most accurate depiction of the image being recorded.[18] The third area is for the suits. The network may or may not be on the floor, their choice.[19] They may be coming from the studio and be dining while viewing[20] in a room adjacent to the stage. If this is the case and they are not close to video village, there will be a phone with which they can talk to the show

17 Sometimes even four.

18 Plus all the bells and whistles that chart that image.

19 Or sometimes a slick UPM placing them as far away as possible when there is contentious relation between them and show runner.

20 Often with a great bottle of wine.

runner. And there is always the exception where the suits are in video village[21]. The final area is for VIPs. It can include parents of child actors and their guests, agents and managers of talent on the show,[22] and anyone else that is important enough to be on the floor.

Sitcom Vocabulary Quick Review

Read these sentences. If the director gave you these notes, would you instantly know what he meant? If not, go back and review the explanation in this chapter.

The director likes **cross shooting** *because the performances match.*

Camera A will carry Mike to the kitchen and **dump** *on Molly when Mike passes her.*

The director is so young that he only knows **film style shooting**.

Let's make sure we get her close-up in the **first pass** *and the two shot in the* **second pass.**

She has blocked the scene so beautifully that there are nearly no **off air moves.**

We will do an **on air move** *when Selena crosses right; A and C follow her.*

Suits are **on the floor**.

Let's do a second pass just for **reaction shots**.

A director who learns **tape style shooting** *has a clear understanding of comedy editing.*

The editor loves the director's coverage because everything is **usable**.

21 Does that large make it become Video City?

22 Unless they are schmoozing with the suits.

Sitcom Insider

RESPONSIBILITIES OF A CAMERA SWITCHER

The switcher's position is definitely a hot seat. You can kill a joke. You can cut too soon or too late. You can milk a joke, take reaction shots that extend the laugh. You are a storyteller who can deliver laughs. You mark your script. You have a game plan. You know you want to take the cut from camera "A" to camera "C" on a specific line. If this is a laugh line you have to sense the timing of the time to cut. As soon as the laugh starts to fade you can make your move. Go too fast and the audience goes silent or they miss the next joke. It's like playing a piano. Do you want the tune to be like jazz, or slower and bluesy, or rock and roll MTV cut/cut/cut as rapid as you can get another character in focus.

A good switcher checks out the equipment, any playback, and attempts to secure a logo of the show to use on the monitors in downtime. He determines a 'cut' of the show during blocking and rehearsal. In some instances the director provides me with a marked script as to how he or she would like it cut. Ideally there is a final producers' run thru prior to the audience being seated to give me the opportunity to show the producers and director the cut I have planned.

Switching a show is a very subjective job. Some directors want reaction shots, some want to hold on a character with no cut aways if another character doesn't have a line. In some instances there will be more than two takes of a scene. When this happens I often take the liberty to show the audience a few of the other camera options to try and keep it fresh. If the audience is repeating the lines with the cast you've got a problem.

It is important to set geography for a scene. This usually happens with the master. However, there are times when a joke plays better with a pull out or reveal as they intend to show on the air. Often the floor decides to make changes on the fly. A new joke, a new exit or entrance, or a character moves to make a joke play better. Many times the booth where I am is left out of the loop... time is such a mistress when the audience is in their seats. All you can do is to watch and anticipate. The booth does have the opportunity to hear line changes from the script supervisor, but any camera changes often happen while the scene is underway.

There are usually 4 cameras but I've have worked up to six (four on dollies, one on a jib arm, and a steadicam). Optimally you want to be 'off book' that is having memorized a lot of the script so you can watch the quad and 'punch' the proper camera. If a script is good, the jokes organic and flow, it makes the job all the easier. It seems natural. If the jokes are forced you really have to work at recalling the joke insert.

This job of switching did not exist until the 1990s. Technology was not around that would allow you to see the picture from a film camera until the film was developed. Technology today brings HD to the mix. The picture quality now is as though you were in your living room with HD TV for both the audience who is watching the filming of the live show and the switcher who is looking at a quad split.

I try hard to make it a show for the audience. I think cable access because that is the budget we have. I put a test pattern up when the audience is loading in. It looks professional but means nothing to the system. Once we are starting to get underway I put up the show logo. This draws attention to the screens and gets the audience used to where they will see the close up of the cameras. When the cameras are slated I try to match the clap of the slate to cutting to black. Then I listen very hard for the director to inhale just before they call action. A half second before action is called I put the live picture up...usually but not always the master. If I have any doubt I always ask the director what camera they would like me to open on. But usually it is obvious, especially if a camera makes a move during the opening shot.

Every show is different. Every production has their way to do their thing.

At the end of the day the plane lands, no one dies, and hopefully we get to do it again next week.

David Reid, *Mike and Molly, Pair of Kings, Becker, 8 Simple Rules*

Sitcom Insider

I didn't know how blessed I was when my first job in television turned out to be assistant to the Executive Producer of Maude, Rod Parker. And, of course, we were all under the guidance of Norman Lear.

It was there I learned it is never "good enough" and watching pros like director, Hal Cooper, taught me how much more there is to directing than just getting it in the can. It was an education in and of itself.

Starting out as an actor, Hal had an uncanny ability to not only "read" actors and guess what they were going to do, but he knew how to communicate with them – and when to shut up and let the actor prevail. One such example was on one of the episodes of Maude that was a 5-part storyline when Maude decides to run for political office and her husband, Walter, finally gets fed up with the whole process and leaves her.

When Walter moves into a swinging singles apartment complex, Maude's neighbor and best friend, played by Rue McClanahan, nags and nudges Maude to go get her husband back. "You have to tell him you miss him, you love him, and you want him to come home, Maude."

Maude reluctantly acquiesces and they both go to see Walter at the apartment complex.

Maude knocks on the door and turns away from it, facing the audience. As she hears it open she delivers the rehearsed speech: "I miss you. I love you. Come home." She has no idea the door has been opened by a short, chubby, black actor, who promptly responds: "Honey, you ain't young enough! You ain't short enough! And you ain't black enough!" as he vehemently slams the door.

The audience roars as Bea just stands there with the infamous glare on her face. Finally she does a slow double-take to the closed door and the audience roars even louder.

In the booth, Hal Cooper is sitting in total silence with his hand in the air ready to snap his finger for the TD to switch to the next camera shot. Rod Parker, Norman Lear, and all of us in the booth are holding our breaths. Softly Hal says: "She's going to do it again." Sure enough – just as the audience laughter is subsiding, Bea starts to do another slow take to the door.

The audience is laughing hysterically. In the booth, Hal still has his hand in the air. Now we're all incredulous as Hal nods "She's going to do it again! And sure enough – Bea's impeccable timing has her do a third slow take and now the audience is rolling in the aisles. They're bringing down the house. And that's what happens when you have actors who can play their audiences like a violin, and they have a director who can read them like a book.

Fern Field, *Maude, Monk, Counterstrike*

Sitcom Career Profile

PATRICIA EYERMAN
SWITCHER

Mary Lou has worked with Pat and also had the pleasure of teaching with her. She is knowledgeable, generous, and articulate. She has great sense of story. Her affection, sense of history, and enthusiasm for what she does and show business in general makes every moment you spend with her a great pleasure

What shows have you worked on?

I have had many jobs. As a switcher I have worked 10 seasons on *Two and a Half Men* and 5 seasons on *Dharma & Greg*. I directed *Bob Hope Specials* and served as the Associated Director on various musical variety, sitcom, game, and awards shows.

What are your responsibilities?

First, I learn the script, observe the staging, and make note of the director's camera layout, including distinguishing between the 1st and 2nd pass camera coverage and various line cues for coverage changes. I take these notes and block out a line cut making note of all reaction shots, cuts for movement, and dialogue. Then, I make sure that the line cut tells the story of the play and carries the plot forward, as well as develops the characters involved. During the air show, I play back via DVD or DV cam various scenes that have been pre-shot and edit playback to the audience to capture their reactions. I also supplement my pre-planned cut with additions based on the audience reaction and actor performance while keeping the comedic pace alive.

Did you have specific training in this field?

Yes, I have a Masters degree in Theatre. I have been working as an Associate Director since 1973 in the Los Angeles area in a variety of formats; both live and pre-taped, mostly for network prime time. That work involved camera blocking, editing, cueing various production elements, multi-tasking during live programming. It trained me to know cameras, how shots are put together, timing, to think on my feet, to think ahead and to anticipate. It also taught me how to tell a story thru camera cutting, tempo, and reaction shots. That training led to being offered programs to direct.

How did you get your first job?

I was a multi format Associate Director/ Director and attended a Networking Mixer at the Directors Guild of America. There I met a producer who shared a common background at a local television station. A few days later he called me and asked me if I knew how to audience switch for Situation comedies and would I like to work for him. I took the job; that job led to others.

What do you like best about your job?

I like that switching is a creative job. Through my line cut, I can tell the story of the comedy, I can create laughs thru reaction shots and pacing, which helps the producers and director know what is working and what needs to be adjusted both to the script and camera coverage. My cut also aids the actors by supplying them with Audience reactions to their work, which can amplify their performances and let them find additional nuances in the script. I like that it happens Live and is reminiscent of the enjoyment I got from directing for television.

What advice would you give someone who would like to do what you do someday?

Pay attention to how sitcoms are put together, study how they are cut, how the shots are organized in the final edit. Learn the craft. Observe other switchers during a taping, watch how they organize their script, keep notes, interact with the director, layout the cut. Line your own script and see how it compares to the switchers who are cutting the show. Learn to work fast, be flexible, think ahead, and be pleasant. Finally, Network! Network! Network! Make as may contacts in the sitcom world as possible and let them know your career goals. And make sure that when the opportunity arises you have completely trained yourself to do the job.

SWITCHER

Union: Directors Guild of America, IATSE or non-union

Typical Weekly Salary: Varies

Hours per week: Typically the job is a two-day hire. The goal is to be hired on two shows per season....a show that works Monday/ Tuesday and Thursday/Friday

Chapter 9 SINGLE CAMERA SITCOMS...MORE EXPENSIVE BUT WORTH IT!

In this chapter:

Why they became popular

The three aspects of production

How it is different for writers

Adjusting as an actor who doesn't hear laughs

The difference in directing responsibilities

The pros and cons of single vs. multi camera

Single camera sitcoms have been around for 50 years. We are thrilled that in *The NEW Sitcom Career Book*, we can devote a whole chapter[1] to talk about this different method of filming the same type of material, in an entirely different way. To the viewer, the end result is the same; you watch a 20-minute[2] show and hopefully laugh your butt off. The experience of creating these 20 minutes is radically different.

LIKE A MOVIE OR EPISODIC

Shooting a single camera sitcom is similar to shooting a movie or one-hour episode of a dramatic material...only it's funny. There is a sizable amount more work done by the director and most other departments in **prep** and during **the shoot**; **post** is basically the same. The easiest way to explain these three aspects of film production is to quote from *Directors Tell the Story (*Focal Press, 2011), Mary Lou's third book co-written with director Bethany Rooney.

> **SITCOM RULE**
> ***Match Action****. For continuity, and especially when different angles are being shot sequentially not simultaneously, it is essential that actors' delivery, physical business, and blocking are similar take to take.*

PREP

Since their book is written for directors and the director leads the whole production through prep, Mary Lou and Bethany explain everything from the director's perspective:

---

1 Let's be honest, it really should be a whole book, and we have one we recommend!

2 Network total length is closer to 22 minutes (shorter if syndicated) minus the show open and closing credits.

> Prep is the critical week to ten days before principal photography begins when a director prepares for the upcoming shoot. It happens during the film or television show's pre-production period. What does a director do during prep?
>
> The director interprets the script and selects every element that will appear in the frame...Specifically, during prep the director reads the script and breaks it down for story, character, style, and color. The director casts, or chooses, the actors who will appear in this episode along with the series' regulars. It is a time to discuss tone with the episode writer and have countless meetings with department heads to answer their questions so that they (and their crews) can have everything ready that you will need. The director scouts and chooses locations during prep and finally, and probably most important, plans how to shoot the episode and generates shot lists or storyboards (or both) that will be his or her roadmap during the shoot.

The prep time on a single camera sitcom (by DGA rules) may not be shorter than 3 days, and often is as long as 5 days. The abbreviated schedule is due to the shorter page count. Writers write the script in the same way and actors audition in the same way. The difference for performers is that they will have no rehearsal days before the shoot, unless they do a read-thru. The writers will not get a chance to watch run-thrus and rewrite.

ACTOR'S PREP

Because an actor will get less rehearsal time on single camera sitcom, it makes the audition and work he does on his own before the shoot, all that more important. There are three books that have been published since *The Sitcom Career Book* came out that we think should be on your radar and clearly can give you some insight into how an actor prepares. The first is the fun *8 Characters of Comedy*[3] (Atides Publishing, 2006) by Scott Sedita. The second is written by the accomplished actor Basil Hoffman (*The Artist, My Favorite Year*) and is entitled *Acting and how to be good at it* (Ingenuity Press, 2006). The last one is *The Science & Art of Film Acting* (16 Coaches Long, 2012) by John Howard Swain. Scott's book outlines eight archetypes that he has identified. He explains that the book is a teaching guide is his intro:

> ...the main focus is on characters and the funny actors who play them. It is a very specific character analysis, complete with personality traits, character histories, physicalities and anything else an actor needs to play a sitcom character.

3 We know a writer who says there are infinitely more, but we think this approach is helpful.

In addition to the way we have shown how to identify jokes and how to deliver them, Sedita shows you how the character you are auditioning or playing might be like other sitcom characters who have come before. This is not to say, that a character is a caricature, but rather that their specific traits might give you insight into creating the character before you audition or before you reach the set to film.

The great director Sydney Pollack writes in the Foreword to Basil's book:

> Basil Hoffman writes about acting from the inside of the craft in a practical, clear way without mumbo-jumbo or mystique. He knows what he's writing about, and you can feel his years of experience on the pages of this book.

Basil's approach begins with the actor finding out everything he can (from the script) about the character he is playing and identifying his "essence." He then goes on to explain how an actor must live "in the moment" as that character.[4] John's book is a clear step-by-step technique that teaches actors how to do their homework thoroughly.

Regardless of the actor's approach, the actor on a single camera show is going to get less time to play around or try things and most of that has to do with how it is shot.

THE SHOOT

Instead of a live show, in the sequential order of the script, in front of an audience, the shoot on a single camera show is over many days and usually **boarded**[5] to accomplish the most efficient use of time. It is the AD who boards or schedules (often many times, many ways) for the director and producer to approve. The workdays are generally much longer, and there are few if any rewrites.

From *Directors Tell the Story*, here is summary of the shoot.

> The shoot is the critical length of time it takes to complete principal photography. A primetime network episode usually shoots between 7 to 10 days. It is also known as the production period.
> What does a director do during the shoot?
> During the shoot the director shapes the actors' performances and runs the set while those performances are being recorded on tape, film, or some other digital medium [...] In addition to that, the director oversees all aspects of telling the story with the camera and sound recording

4 As well as a whole lot more...he did after all write a whole book to explain his approach.

5 Scheduled. Notes what specifics are needed for each eighth of a page in a script.

equipment on the sets or within the locations selected so that the filming of the script is done in an orderly and efficient way so as to stay on time and within budget.

THE ACTOR'S TYPICAL SHOOT DAY

An actor will show up at his call time which can be as early as 6 am (earlier for woman or those getting special effects makeup). He reports to the AD or Second who hands him the sides[6] for the day and tells him to report to set for rehearsal, go to lunch, go to make-up, or go to his dressing room and chill.

If he goes to set, he will do a quick blocking rehearsal, hopefully without too many people watching. Once the scene is worked out, the crew comes in and the actors do the scene one more time for **marks**, or for the purpose of placing tape marking precisely where the actors stand as we described in Chapter 5. Like a multi-cam film style sitcom, second team replaces the actors and the camera team gets to work.

THE MISNOMER OF SINGLE CAM

Single cam might imply that only one camera is shooting. That's not true much of the time. There is often an "A" and "B" and sometimes even a "C" camera shooting simultaneously on a single cam sitcom. So why aren't they called multi-cam shows? The big difference between multi-cam and single cam shows is that they don't cross shoot, meaning that, no matter how many cameras, they don't shoot in many directions at the same time. Instead, they shoot in one direction, **turn around**, and shoot in the other direction. This is done for the purposes of lighting. Turning around requires relighting.

Multi camera lighting is very clever in using one character's key light as the other's backlight. All of those keys lights are on the upstage side[7] of the actors. The multiple hard shadows created will fall on the floor by the cameras instead of on the walls of the set. The fill light comes from down stage.[8] However, the ability to set lights for each setup during single cam is much more precise and, of course, more time consuming.

THE ORDER OF SHOOTING

Shooting order is determined by the director and usually moves from the widest shot, or the **master**, to the closer coverage. There might be an even wider establishing shot. Again, the director determines when this gets done especially if it involves cranes, airplanes, or other special equipment. Often the master is shot with only one camera rolling especially when that shot requires a lot

6 This term comes from the cost savings by giving an actor just the portion of the script that includes his part. For a 150 page play, this could be a photocopy of just one "side" of a double sided printed script. Sitcom scripts are always single sided. Actor' sides are shrunk 50% to carry on set.

7 Opposite of the audiences view.

8 There is a bank of large soft lights or white board reflectors just above the audience's view.

of movement and different angles. Other times, for the sake of efficiency, a closer shot such as a two shot or medium shot might be done simultaneously, hence the need for the "B" camera. When that happens, the "A" and "B" cameras might be sitting right next to each other shooting with different lenses.

> *An actor has to stay focused on the real intention of the character at every moment. What's the action, the motivation, the "verb" behind the scene? In comedy, the actor takes that motivation and "raises the stakes," in actor-speak, to make it even more important. That's where the humor is. That's what makes jokes work.*
>
> *Sometimes, though, the story disappears in the joke parade which is why actors always hope they're working with writers who like to collaborate, who will listen when you point out that the story is lost and who will want to figure out a way to get it back.*
>
> Patricia Richardson
> *Strong Medicine, Home Improvement, Ulee's Gold*

Once the master is shot, the direction of the key light has been established, so the only changes to lighting will be to beautify the shot as the camera moves in, especially on the close-ups. And to repeat, once everything is done in one direction, you turn around and do it the opposite direction. This is where the sitcom rule: **MATCH ACTION!** becomes important. For continuity, an actor must duplicate the same performance in order that these separately filmed pieces can be edited together. There is nothing more frustrating to an editor than not being able to use a great piece of footage because it glaringly doesn't match. The script supervisor is the actor's friend and guide to making sure this does not happen. An actor should always ask if he is not sure what hand he used to pick up the coffee cup, or when he put it down. The director should be making sure the energy, pace and emotional content of the scene will cut together. One great method of curing an actor who habitually mismatches his action is to invite him to watch editing one day. Within an hour the actor will start yelling at his own image on the monitor since his best performance wasn't used because there was no match.

Throw in a **steadicam** and even more variations come into play. This is because the steadicam is a camera designed for moving easily and fluidly without the use of a dolly or track because it is held in place by a harness worn by one person. The camera can go wherever the steadicam operator has enough room to walk. Its use and the use of other handheld cameras have become common. Traditional coverage -master, medium, MCU, CU -has changed as a result. For example, a single cam show such as *Modern Family*, has a definite visual look that deviates radically from traditional coverage, and tosses in a breaking the fourth wall look to camera to give it a documentary style. They film with at least two cameras every take. Also, the show uses long lenses. One of its directors, Jason Winer describes why in the *DGA Quarterly*:

> ...I want to create foreground-background separation...I like to tell jokes in three dimension. I like to use the focal length of the lens to be able to

shift your attention from something happening deeper or shallower. Not a lot of comedies on television tell jokes in that third dimension."[9]

NO LAUGHING PLEASE!

While shooting a single camera show, no one can laugh. This is essential because the pieces of coverage that will be edited sequentially (for the most part) have not been shot simultaneously even if both the "A" and "B" camera are shooting at the same time. If someone (or hopefully everyone) on the crew was laughing, there wouldn't be any way to either separate or match the laughter on set from the dialogue. Remember, on a multi-cam show, the audience laughs are being recorded live are mic-ed separately and become part of the fabric of the show since the laughs are actually used in the final product.

One essential job of the director on the single camera show, as well as any comedy, film is being the arbitrator of taste. He must determine what is funny. There is no audience laughing to tell him something worked or if the jokes landed. Similarly, the actors don't have the instant feedback from the audience. They must deliver without benefit of laughter. They must trust that the director knows funny and will announce when something is by saying, "Print it[10]; moving on."

CAN'T HELP IT

There is a magic moment that often happens on single camera comedies when the director calls "Cut" and the stage explodes with laughter that everyone has been holding in. Nearly always, this happens the first time they see a scene or when someone has made a mistake.[11] Occasionally, there will be that moment while shooting when the director, crew, or even the actors crack up while shooting because it is so funny. The tragedy of this style of shooting is that that laughter will ruin a very funny take.

THE CREW

A single sitcom show usually shoots in 5 days. That means that the whole crew has to be there every day. Remember on a multi-cam show, the full crew is only there two days: camera blocking day and show day. If no preshoots are being done, you need the hair, makeup and running crew of the wardrobe departments only on show day. This makes single camera shooting more expensive.

WHY SHOOT SINGLE CAM?

So single camera shows take longer to shoot, are more expensive to produce, the actors don't get to gauge their performance because someone is laughing

9 Kronke, David. "Family Planning" DGA Quarterly, Spring 2012, p36.

10 "Print it" is an old film term, like "rolling" and "cut." It wouldn't sound right to say "Digitize it!"

11 Remember we learned from Desi, that things lose their spontaneous funny without the surprise of hearing it fresh.

in the moment, and the performances don't match perfectly because they are not shot simultaneously. So "Why shoot single cam?'

There are many benefits from shooting this way. It nearly always looks better to a discerning eye. A multi-cam show does not have the benefit of having the subjective POV. It may always appear that it is a theatrical play being filmed. That makes the experience of the story feel more objective. Single camera shows, on the other hand, feel more like you are inside the actors thoughts because the closer the actors eyeline gets to the true eyeline of the characters looking at each other, the more intimate the performance might feel. That is not possible in multi-cam shows, because the closer that eyeline is, the better the chance you will see another camera in the background shooting from the opposite direction. Single camera is shot more "inside" and multi-cam more "outside, looking in."

Of course, the argument for those who feel that the multi-cam format is superior, will say, "We don't care how they feel, we want them to laugh! Spontaneous laughter is our goal!" And there are single camera shows or hybrids (more in next chapter on those) who value the funny. *Modern Family* Executive Producer and Creator,[12] Steven Levitan, is quoted in the *DGA Quarterly*:

> No one ever says, "Oh *Modern Family* is great but the lighting looked a little crappy." I will gladly sacrifice a little beauty of the shot for the freshness of the comic moment. We talk a lot about cameras, about the specs, and what it does for lighting or whatever. I say, "Does it make it any funnier?" A camera that makes it funnier is the one I want.[13]

There are other benefits as well. Single camera shooting allows for varied use of standing sets as well as use of more and different kinds of locations. Instead of using standing sets in the same way over and over again, a single camera set can be designed to have 4 walls and those walls can be **pulled**, or removed. It makes shooting in every part of the room possible. It also may take more lighting equipment or the moving of existing lighting equipment. Going on location is normal. A DP gets to shoot real exteriors using natural light or real places that lend authenticity to the production.

The sound crew uses different equipment on a single camera show. There is no giant rolling boom stand. Instead, the soundman is more often holding a mic attached to a fish pole[14] when he is standing on or above the set. There are more places he can be since shooting is only happening in one direction.

There is a huge difference for a writer on a multi-cam show. Instead of hearing jokes during run-thrus, and determining whether to punch or replace them,

---

12 Along with Christopher Lloyd (*Frasier, Wings*), the son of David Lloyd (*Taxi, Cheers*).

13 Kronke, David. "Family Planning" *DGA Quarterly, Spring 2012, p37.*

14 Not literally; it's just called that.

the single camera comedy writer has to get it "right" out of the gate. If it is not on the page, it won't be on the screen. The writers' room is not a place where you gather as a group to do rewrites night after night. Single camera writers are more solitary than multi-cam writers. This may be not as much fun; or might relieve the pressure and competition of pitching jokes in the room. A single camera show, nearly always has a writer on set, present during every minute of filming.

There have been articles in the press that single camera shows are more popular with the network executives and the people who make them but that audiences like the live feel of multi camera shows more. Then shows like *Modern Family* come along and disprove that with high ratings. Jason Winer, who directed the pilot and many episodes of *Modern Family* told a group of other directors that he worries that when he runs some scenes for the creators, that they lose faith in a some jokes since he can't show them any close ups of the punchlines with his two cameras. Now, he says, that "I have those two cameras moving around like they are choreographed to look like a multi-camera show."

Again, we want to emphasize that the subject of the single camera half hour comedy could fill up another entire volume. Iconic shows such as *M*A*S*H**, *Get Smart, Gilligan's Island, Hogan's Heroes, I Dream of Jeannie, Beverly Hillbillies, Bewitched, Brady Bunch, Leave it to Beaver, Wonder Years,* and *The Andy Griffith Show* blazed the path. *Dream On, Days and Nights of Molly Dodd, Sports Night, Action, The Larry Sanders Show,* and *Frank's Place* added their own unique and superlative flavor to the mix. Nickelodeon, Disney Channel, TV Land and ABC Family keep the voracious taste for sitcoms alive no matter what the networks decide to do with such hits as *Zooey 101, JONAS,* and *10 Things I Hate About You*. Finally, *The Office. Community, Cougartown, Weeds, Entourage, Sex and the City, Everybody Hates Chris, Flight of the Conchords, 30 Rock, Malcolm in the Middle,* and *Modern Family* continue to show how vital (AND FUNNY!!!) the single camera format can be.

Sitcom Vocabulary Quick Review

Read these sentences. If the director gave you these notes, would you instantly know what he meant? If not, go back and review the explanation in this chapter.

The First AD **boarded** *that scene for Monday after the move.*

The actors have to hit the **marks** *or their singles will be out of focus.*

We'll shoot the **master** *first, and then go in for the coverage.*

What do you mean we only get a day to **prep**?

It is wrong to think that everything can be fixed in **post**.

After we get the master, the wall needs to be **pulled**.

We have two sizes of **sides**.

The **shoot** *will last 5 days, with 10 hour days.*

The **steadicam** *will allow us to get into the bathroom stall.*

One more shot and we **turn around.**

Script Supervisor's Tasks

A script supervisor's duties on a single camera sitcom are the same but for the fact there is no rehearsal, so everyday is a "shoot day." And well, actually there is a difference. The form (facing page) is different. And there is no time code and each camera shot is written out from the beginning of the shot to end. Example: Mstr. Dolly in to med 2/s (initial of character name put in a circle), see (initial) x out, hold (initial) single folo biz, push in to tite single. Hold.

Or something like that...with a bit of hieroglyphics in there. That's about the only thing different. In multi-cam I just write 4 cams or show marks unless it is a particular camera doing a particular insert shot or something; then I write the specific shot.

Ellen Deutsch

Sitcom Career Profile

DENISE DOWSE

DIALOGUE COACH

We were familiar with Denise's stunning acting work in both TV and film before Mary Lou was lucky enough to work with her as a dialogue coach on Girlfriends. *Denise's contribution ranged from simply running lines to the insightful coaching she did which contributed to the truthful, detailed, moment to moment work that all the actors did on the show. Her acting and directing career prohibits her from coaching full time, but Mary Lou got the opportunity to work with her again years later on BET's* Reed Between the Lines.

What shows have you worked on?

I do more audition coaching these days but started out on *Girlfriends* for 5 seasons, *The Game* a few episodes, *Reed Between the Lines* for two seasons, and a few pilots.

What are your responsibilities?

It varies from show to show. Simply, I listen to delivery & interpretation of lines/scenes - become the actors' external eyes & ears. I talk with them about the arc of scenes and story. Since I work on sitcoms, I help actors find the funny... And come tape day, I help them with lines.

Did you have specific training in this field?

No, I had no specific training - I was a theatre major in college and ran and directed a theatre for 6 years in Germany. I've been working in Hollywood for 20 years as an actor and director (primarily theatre). But I dig actors and love working with them as they discover their character's journey.

How did you get your first job?

I had been coaching actors for auditions and several of them had read for Eileen Mack Knight. During a commercial strike she called me and asked if I'd be interested in coaching on *Girlfriends* (as she was casting at the time). So, I jumped at a new opportunity!

What do you like best about your job?

Actors - without them, I wouldn't have a job! But seriously that is my favorite part I smile on my way to work–I love affording the actor with an environment where they feel comfortable enough to give themselves permission to "play," explore and create as I become their audience and offer feedback and perhaps raise the stakes.

DIALOGUE COACH
Union: None, independent contractor
Typical Weekly Salary: $100 day to $2,500 a week
Hours per week: 40-50 hours a week full time, varies when coaching guest stars.

Chapter 10 MORE MARKETS (MORE JOBS!!!!)

In this chapter:

What's being done in foreign markets

The wonderful alternatives to TV

Why live action cartoons are really sitcoms

All about the money

Phil in Moscow

Mary Lou directs on spec

Successful web series

There has never been a more exciting time to be in the comedy world. In addition to network sitcoms–some traditional, some not, some multi-camera, some not–there are sitcoms being produced in foreign countries, for interstitial fillers between other broadcast shows and as cartoons. Others are being made directly for the internet called **web series**. Viewers are watching comedians perform in comedy specials, comedy competitions, on late night talk shows,. And still brilliantly on the iconic *Saturday Night Live*. Comedy movies are even being nominated for Academy Awards.

It is no wonder that as we write *The NEW Sitcom Career Book*, sitcoms are hot again!

A LITTLE BACKGROUND

Sitcom certainly predates television. Besides the similarities with centuries-old comedic forms including Punch and Judy puppet shows, there were actual sitcoms on radio in the United States in the 1920s through the 1940s. Television was invented not much after radio, but it did not come into use until the late 1940s.[1]

When we researched the complete list of American sitcoms on television for Appendix Three, we found that many of the early television sitcoms were the most successful of the radio sitcoms. They moved to television, often with the same actors. Some were recast for TV. *The Life of Riley* was recast for

SITCOM RULE

Think Yiddish. Talk British. *Jokes no matter in what language they are delivered, have particular rhythms that lend to the humor. To deviate from these rhythms often takes away from the audience's experience of funny. American sitcoms, because of their roots in the Yiddish theatre and then vaudeville, have a particular rhythm.*

---

1 And even then, not many people had television sets.

one season with Jackie Gleason, but then reverted back to William Bendix who played Chester A. Riley on the radio version and in a 1949 feature film.

Lucille Ball was in a radio sitcom *My Favorite Husband*, but it was changed substantially, when she wanted her real life husband Desi Arnaz to play the part in the reworked *I Love Lucy. Amos 'N Andy* was recast, since the black characters were played by white actors on radio. Other radio shows like *The Goldbergs, The Jack Benny Program*, and *The Adventures of Ozzie and Harriet* made easy transitions to the new medium of television. The biggest change in making those programs was, of course, adding pictures to the telling of the stories. The second big change was that the stories had to be written using only a few sets as locations. Radio, with just a few sound effects, could go anywhere.

IT'S ALL ABOUT THE MONEY

Television is an advertising medium. If enough people watch a show, advertisers are willing to cover the production costs. Production costs for sitcoms are moderate for television networks. The scale escalates from reality shows (which are the least expensive) to game shows and then variety shows. Classic variety shows were each hosted by a singing and dancing star of the day with other show business stars as weekly guests on the episodes. This has gone away. Currently, variety has celebrity judges for amateur[2] singers and dancers or celeb guests.

Sitcom is next up on the production budget list. Far more expensive to produce than sitcoms are hour-long dramatic programs. The introduction[3] of primetime animated sitcoms is probably worth its own book; they capture a huge[4] part of the comedy watching audience--And with that viewership, a part of the advertising revenue. Part of the natural ebb and flow of the popularity of sitcom is when one of the lower cost types of television program is intriguing enough and unique enough to grab audience attention for a few years. From *Who Wants to Be a Millionaire* to *American Idol*, at the height of their popularity, they get aired several times a week and push sitcoms aside. As those shows start to fade, sitcoms regain more popularity with both the audience and the network executives. As we write *The NEW Sitcom Career Book*, sitcoms are again on the rise. Sixteen of the thirty six new network scripted shows are sitcoms.

NETWORK SITCOMS

New media can also have an effect on the number of and production budgets of sitcoms. Early television was primarily three networks: NBC, CBS, and

---

2 Since we see the casting notices for all of these shows, they are mostly beginning or wannabe professionals.

3 Starting with *The Flintstones*, which has been the incorrect answer to "Which is the first TV show that showed a married couple sharing one bed?" The correct answer is the very first sitcom: *Mary Kay and Johnny*.

4 And loyal.

Dumont. The decline of Dumont was at about the same time as the ascension of ABC. Three networks remained the primary market for sitcoms until the late 1980s. That's when the second big change happened to sitcom.

By that time, the typical budget was about one half million dollars an episode. Then, two things happened. FOX network started broadcasting. At first, it was only for a late night talk show, but soon they added a Sunday night sitcom, *Married With Children*. Soon, they were adding shows on several nights a week and now are one of the strongest networks, especially for sitcoms. Their early programs were produced for about half the costs of the other three networks. Salaries of everyone working on those early fourth network sitcoms were proportionately lower.

At the same time, studios like Warner Brothers, Universal and MGM who all produced sitcoms for the big three networks decided to also try something new, but similar to what Fox had done. Competition for airtime on ABC, CBS, and NBC was fierce. The top rated shows were picked up for new episodes and the lower ones were cancelled. A few shows like the drama *Fame*, the CBS first year sitcom *Charles in Charge*, and the ABC third year sitcom *Too Close for Comfort* were all cancelled because of low ratings. The studios who produced these shows decided that the rating were far higher than what new network FOX was getting and they all independently decided to keep producing episodes and sell them as first run **syndicated** programming on a station by station and station group basis. Production budgets were cut to the same as FOX was spending. The sitcom syndication market flourished. As the years passed, many studios started their own ad-hoc networks, the big four now have a dozen or more competitors.

We may be at another big transition for sitcoms. Fewer people are now watching network television than in previous years. Many weeks, the current top rated television show has a lower rating number than the numbers that got *Charles in Charge* and *Too Close for Comfort* cancelled by their networks at that time. Audiences still have an appetite for sitcom, as well as many other forms of programs.

In a recent interview with Josef Adalain of Vulture.com, FX president John Landgraf told him that their model is different than the big networks in that they keep costs down by giving show creators and actors less money up front and more through re-runs. He also said that producing their own shows, rather than buying them from big studios, allows then to keep costs down and keep more money from the syndication of reruns. Audiences and show runners like that FX and their ilk keep further away from interfering in the production than does the traditional networks.

The invention of the remote control and the advent of cable television have allowed audiences to easily surf across many channels of programs. The Big Four networks are seemingly equal stops on the "What Shall We Watch" trip. And with the larger audience share, other program suppliers have been increasingly adding sitcoms to their own mix of programs!

THE STABLE STAPLES

A huge amount of comedy content, both new and original is being programmed by three cable channels: Nickelodeon, The Disney Channel, and TV Land. The first two cater to a younger generation; the last attracts an older crowd. We are thrilled that Nick and Disney Channel found that kids love to laugh! When Mary Lou teaches younger actors, she finds that those who grew up watching these channels have excellent comedy instincts. The timing, rhythm, and music of the dialogue has imprinted on their brains. These networks have also created mega stars out of Miley Cyrus, Nick Jonas, Mitchel Musso, and Selena Gomez. Often, these artists and groups such as the talented singers from *Big Time Rush* will tour when the show is not shooting-- adding to the popularity of the shows. These networks also provided a huge amount of online content for their viewers as well as sometimes rerunning old network shows.

Nickelodeon, rebranded as Nick Jr. and TeenNick, are on the MTV children's cable networks. Disney Channel has tweens shows and also younger content under their Disney Junior banner. Some are single camera style, some multi-camera that shoot with an audience and others are **block and shoot**[5]. Their schedule usually includes shooting during more than one day of the week. This is a result of a style common to many kid oriented sitcoms. They are akin to live action cartoons. There are usually many special effects that would be difficult to shoot in front of an audience because of computer graphics including green screen replacement of backgrounds. A choice has to be made to select which scenes will be shot in front of the audience and which will usually be played back as a rough cut from the shooting the previous day and the afternoon before the audience is seated. *Pair of Kings* and *Wizards of Waverly Place* are particularly ambitious in their use of special effects.

A Disney-style show, *Mr. Young*, is produced for Canada, but now is being run on Disney XD. On one particularly ambitious special effect episode, one of the actors had to projectile vomit as a result of his character's milk allergy. A choice was made to shoot that scene pre-audience, because it is hard to hide all the special effect pumps and tubing necessary for such a **gag**.[6] Time ran short and the scene had to be performed with the audience present. It is always important to have black screens or curtains in front of any set when a joke will be given away if the audience can see things being set up. This was done so well that the audience didn't notice all of the paraphernalia when the screens were pulled and the scene started. The plan was for one long blast of milk to come from the upstage side of the actor's mouth. The audience laughed and screamed so long that the effects crew continued with an immediate second blast, which extended probably the longest laugh in the history of that series. These are the

---

5 Multi-camera that shoots with no audience. It is very common now; not just an occasional pre-shoot.

6 Not just a shorthand for a "joke." On many sets, especially feature film sets, stunts and other special physical effects are also called gags.

intangibles that a live audience can give a sitcom. When the laughs don't stop it makes the effort and careful planning worth it!

TV Land started by rerunning some of the classic sitcoms from the early days of television. They have broadened their reach in the last few years to air new ones created just for them like *Happily Divorced* and *Hot in Cleveland* and its spinoff , *The Soul Man.* These shows work on the normal 5 day schedule we describe in our book.

Hot in Cleveland is especially notable for taking established sitcom talents such as Betty White (*Golden Girls*), Jane Leeves (*Frasier*), Wendie Malick (*Just Shoot Me!*), and Valerie Bertinelli (*One Day at a Time*) and casting this power-house of talent in show created by Suzanne Martin that shows them all off!

AND EVEN MORE

ABC Family's programming is similar to a traditional network who offers a mixed bag of both dramas and comedies. Their sitcoms include *Melissa and Joey* and *Baby Daddy* and reruns of *That 70s Show.* TNT tends to re-run recent sitcom series and develops other than sitcom styles for their new production. CW was a merging of WB and UPN. This put a slight dent into the great number many black oriented sitcoms that made UPN famous.[7] USA had made its reputation on quirkyy drama like *Monk* and *Burn Notice* is now diving deep in the original sitcom pool while also rerunning the ABC hit sitcom *Modern Family.* FX has edgy fare, including comedian Louie C.K.'s *Louie.* This is a groundbreaking sitcom style that is so thought provoking, that some episodes might technically not even be sitcom. They gave a home to Charlie Sheen after his split with *Two And a Half Men.* Also notable is their show *It's Always Sunny in Philadelphia*[8] which reruns on Comedy Central.

WHEN 5 DAYS BECOME 3, 2, OR 1

Tyler Perry shoots his sitcoms for TBS in one day. Daytime dramas have been using this schedule for years. Perry applied this workload to comedy. BET (Black Entertainment Television) rehearses and shoots in 3 days. One day for rehearsal and two for camera block and shoot. These shows shoot, like Perry's-- multi-cam style but without the benefit of an audience. The great challenge in not rehearsing for the traditional three days is that the script does not get to go through the constant refinement and actors get to rehearse less. And without a camera blocking day, you do not have the similar time to perfect the shot pattern. Without the show day you don't seat an audience and present a well-rehearsed stage play. You have to rely on your knowledge of the writing, shooting patterns, and the performance precision needed in single camera sitcom.

7 Along with Wrestling! But some could argue that the WWF *is* comedy programming.

8 Which began life as an internet pilot.

The audience is always an independent judge of this, but the small budget of this style does not allow for that.

WATCH OR REWATCH ON INTERNET

You can watch or re-watch episodes of televised sitcoms online on Hulu, Veoh, TV.com, TV4U, Netflix, TVLand, ABC, CBS, NBC, FOX, The CW, TheWB.com, TBS, ABC Family, and Crackle. This is huge with college students who don't have the family TV with them in their dorm. The list continues to change based on rights to the material. On TV.com alone there are about 550 different sitcoms both current and recently past available for viewing. This thrills us because we believe that so much knowledge can be acquired by viewing[9]. When we teach with this book, our philosophy is to teach by introducing all types of jokes, drilling them until their delivery is mastered, watch other students do the same and learn by observing their mastery or road to mastery and finally, viewing those same jokes within the context of the show that broadcast them. Beware of internet piracy though, we're adamantly against that!

WEB SERIES

Many original sitcom series are being developed as **webisodes**, multiple episodes of programming designed for watching initially on the internet. Michael Eisner's company, Vuguru's, philosophy is that "audiences love great stories & want to consume them in a multi-platform environment." They offer their advertisers a targeted audience with what they call "multiple levels of engagement." Starting on-line with AOL, their delightful single camera sitcom is shot in "small chapters." *Little Woman Big Cars*[10] stars Amy Yasbeck from *Wings* among many other notable actors. Actress/Producer Illeana Douglas has been making a branded web series sitcom *Easy to Assemble* since 2008. The Swedish furniture store, Ikea, agreed to be the focus and location of the episodes without giving Illeana any restrictions or specific requirements for product plugs.

Branding is a throwback to the original television shows. Some variety shows were *The Texaco Star Theater, The Colgate Comedy Hour,* and sitcom *The Burns and Allen Show* was "brought to you by Carnation Evaporated Milk." There the commercials were integrated into the show--a slightly different product placement was introduced to other shows. Often, the advertising agency was the production company for the programs. With branding, the product references provide all the money for the production. Illeana thinks that branding will continue to grow, but she is still hoping that her series will become a regular television show while the internet continues to grow.

The Directors Guild of America and the Screen Actors Guild/AFTRA have

---

9 Yes we're saying to watch TV...as much as you can!

10 These forms of exhibition will undoubtedly make us add them to Appendix Three with the next edition of this book. Right now, it contains only American Television Sitcoms.

provisions to allow their members to work in this new medium for future compensation. This mirrors the Guilds embracing the start of FOX, the syndicated market, and the new small networks in the last two decades. Their theory is that their members have the knowledge and skills to make these market work and they will continue to be employed at increasing salaries in time.

No one is really sure exactly when the internet can provide enough money to create the full quality of production that we are used to seeing similar to sitcoms on television. Although changing with time, there is a reluctance of computer users to stay long with videos. Right now, most sitcom webisodes are three to five minutes long.

OUR WEB EXPERIENCES

Co-author Phil Ramuno has experimented with creating his own no-budget sitcom about a Vampire Family living in the suburbs *The Vamps Next Door.* Writing a regular length sitcom script, he has broken it down to between four and seven shorter webisodes, while identifying each full script as a "season." As this is written, YouTube has sent Phil a check for $113 for revenue sharing from the ads placed next to his first "season" of webisodes. So, there is money to be made[11]. Co-author Mary Lou Belli has directed two different web series. The first one, *3Way*, was targeted to a specific audience: lesbians.

SheWired wrote on July 2009:

> After only one season, the delightfully hysterical lesbian web series *3Way* took its final bow in March, leaving a gaping void in the world of non-porn online lesbian entertainment. The always amusing series debuted on Feb. 4th of last year and quickly built a loyal fan following on the net. Sadly, however, apparently not enough of one to keep the show going past the first season. Due to a lack of funding, the show's creators finally had to call it quits and move on to other projects...Staring Maeve Quinlan, Cathy Shim, Jill Bennett and Maile Flanagan, *3Way* was a riotous bout of fun in every too short episode. The premise for the show was inspired by real life events in straight girl Maeve Quinlan's own life, blown up to epically comedic proportions.

That web series went on to win two Logo awards and the AfterEllen.com 2008 Visibility Award. Mary Lou just finished shooting her second web series, *Jenifer and Shangela*, starring Jenifer Lewis (*Fresh Prince of Bel-air, Girlfriends, Think Like a Man*) and DJ Pierce, AKA Shangela (*RuPaul's Drag Race*) was named Indiegogo's top 10 web series of 2012.

---

11 In this case, enough to reimburse the out of pocket lunch expense for the actors and crew on the first day of production.

MARY LOU WORKING ON SPEC

Full length sitcoms are even being produced on spec. Mary Lou directed eight back to back episodes of a series called *All Rise*. It reunited her with *3Way* Executive producer Nancylee Myatt and Cedric the Entertainer with whom she had worked with on *Eve*. The rest of the first rate cast included Hank Harris, Tania Gunadi, Erron Jay, and Vanessa M. Villegas. The recurring cast included the very funny Persia White (*Girlfriends*), Kevin Hart (*Think Like a Man*), and Eddie Griffin (*Malcolm and Eddie*). It was created by Arthur Harris (*Reed Between the Lines*)[12].

YouTube owner Google is now investing in companies to create programming that they will air. Netflix, Yahoo, Microsoft, Hulu and many others have grand plans to try to develop this medium as an eventual replacement for television. With many people viewing programs on computers, phones and internet tablets, the transition from traditional television is well under way. So far, comedy and sitcom in particular, is already a big part of it.

WORLD WIDE AMERICAN SITCOM

The other market that has developed is the exporting of American culture to foreign lands. Sitcom is a rich part of our culture. British sitcom also has been well established for many decades. From *Hancock's Half Hour* in the 1950s to the recent multi-can *Miranda* and single-cam *Rev.* they have their own rich history. In fact, many of our sitcoms were adaptations of theirs. *Steptoe and Son* there became *Sanford and Son* here. *Till Death Do Us Part* became *All in The Family*. *The Office* was done there before here. *Absolutely Fabulous* was copied here to just name some. So, Britain is a not a new market for us.

Canada, Australia, Turkey, India, New Zealand, Austalia Serbia, Denmark, Romania, Czech Republic, Spain, and Russia all have a history of creating at least one original sitcom for their countries. In the 1970s, Mexico produced *El Chavo del Ocho* and this was seen in many South American countries, as well. Even China, in the 1990s, had sitcoms that were roughly based on American examples.

Many countries in the world bought syndicated repeats of American sitcoms. In some countries, they were subtitled. In many, they were dubbed by local actors[13]. Especially after the dissolution of the Soviet Union in Eastern Europe, the American sitcoms of the 1980s, 1990s, and 2000s became quite popular. Some local sitcoms were still being made, but the audiences noticed that they were not in the "American" style that they enjoyed in reruns. It has been reported that American sitcoms have been seen in approximately 150 different countries.

Sony is owner of Columbia Pictures and Columbia Television. Columbia Television was responsible for many sitcoms from that era. So, Sony created a large

12 She mentions all these names because it brought a lot of talented and experienced people together to do new material that hadn't yet been sold...a new model for sitcoms!

13 The original American actors' dialogue can still be heard in the background.

business of syndicating these dubbed and subtitled Columbia sitcoms. When Russia wanted to create an ambitious historical telanovela entitled *Bednaya Nastya* (*Poor Anastasia*) in 2003, they turned to Sony International looking for some scripts that could be adapted.

Poor Anastasia became a giant hit in Russia. The Russians then syndicated it to more than twenty other countries including Ukraine, China, Israel, Serbia, Georgia, Greece, and Bulgaria. Russia had a new industry! A big part of this success was the American scripts. They then turned to looking to create sitcoms from American scripts.

> While the sitcom is generally perceived to be an American invention, we are discovering more and more that comedy is universal; that themes and humor travel across geographic boundaries. Well-told stories are able to transcend cultures and speak to audiences around the world. And while the specifics of a given story (a holiday, a sports team, etc.) may be tied to a particular place and time, in the majority of cases the underlying human experience driving the story's conflict is not. The key to adapting an American sitcom to another culture is in stripping it down to its barest essence, an examination of some aspect of the human condition, and then mining it for all of its comedic potential.
>
> Over Hollywood's 60-plus year history producing TV comedy, sitcom storytelling has been refined to a science. What looks so effortless to viewers is really carefully crafted and the result of decades of refinement and honing and sharpening. A trait that the most memorable and enduring comedies to emerge during those years share, is their relatability – the feeling one gets when watching, that "I know those people," or "that's me!" This combination of tried-and-true storytelling technique and recognizable characters is what makes American-style sitcoms among the most popular genres on TV today, making viewers watch -- and laugh in record numbers.
>
> Sitcoms provide the same function regardless of their country of origin – they are escapism -- half-hour mini-vacations, departures from whatever may be going on in the world or in our lives at a given moment, a diversion that is especially welcome in today's troubling times. They offer audiences a reprieve from reality, an excuse to laugh.
>
> My group at Sony Pictures Television has produced nearly 2,000 episodes of sitcom in over 20 countries over the past decade. And although we develop original series as well, much of our output has been localized sitcom remakes. Three of our most popular series around the world are local versions of *The Nanny, Married with Children,* and *Everybody Loves Raymond*. The three series are very different in tone, yet all three share one key element: their focus on regular people. These are not super-heroes. They're not going through some profound life-experience. They're

> not even necessarily that unique. But, because of that, they are all relatable, and immensely popular in widely different cultures.
>
> Audiences around the world know dysfunctional families, bickering siblings...intrusive neighbors...mothers-in-law. The human experience that all three shows mine for their humor allows them to speak across cultures. Put in other words, the elements that made these three sitcom hits and a select group of other TV comedies popular in America, make them popular in any country around the world, because people are people, and what separates us pales in comparison to all that we share in common.
>
> Jeff Lerner, Senior Vice President
> Development and Current Programs Sony Picture Television

PHIL WORKING IN MOSCOW

Phil Ramuno was part of that exporting of American sitcom style. Jeff hired him to go to Moscow and join several other experienced Americans starting several different sitcom projects. For him, it was *Married With Children.* For Phil's first three days, the Russian crew was welcoming and eager to learn. Since Phil and Mary Lou had just written *The Sitcom Career Book* and both had been teaching sitcom techniques for years, it seemed a natural fit. Then came reality. The crew was very experienced in creating television. But their style was to shoot a scene with almost no rehearsal and no planning of camera coverage. With each take, the camera coverage got better until about take thirteen or so. They were happy with the scene.

Phil was not happy. He said that the scene looked fine, but that the actors' performances peaked at take three or four and were not very good at all when the cameras finally got it. Phil insisted that the methods that you are reading in this book were the best way to get the project done well. A standoff in the control room ensued. Phil and his interpreter were on one side of the booth and the entire crew with the Lean-M production company's owner on the other. The promise of saving money by finishing the day earlier was the clincher.

Now, the following day was critical. To the crew's credit, they really gave our methods a chance even though some of them had to relearn decades of successful work habits. The practice day finished ninety minutes earlier than ever and "Phil's Way" won out.[14]

Another part of Phil's way was making sure that jokes got delivered in the cadence that suited the Russian ear for comedy. Now, since they had already been watching American sitcoms our Sitcom Rule **THINK YIDDISH. TALK BRITISH.** already applied. But what we really want to say is that this rule is not Yiddish specific. The bigger rule is that comedy has a cadence, no matter what the language and must be adhered to mine the funny. A comedian who has done

14 For months, Phil would get an occasional email from the production company saying that they were still happily doing it "Phil's Way."

stand-up comedy in Russia told Phil that the biggest difference in the Russian sense of humor from ours is that they don't laugh at fart jokes.[15] He tested that during rehearsal, when someone moved some equipment that made a loud noise. Phil held his stomach and said "Excuse me." The Russians laughed. Phil's great lesson was that "Story is story and funny is funny."

Tim Ryder worked with editors in countries that needed to add all the laughs when there was no audience. There is no such thing as a "laugh guy" with the machine outside of the U.S.

> Laughter is a human trait, not belonging to any one culture. Think about it. When we think something is funny our natural reaction is to laugh. We don't laugh in English, Spanish, Arabic, Korean or Tagalog. We just laugh, as humans. So I found it interesting that, in one particular instance while working with an international client that I was told that a particular culture laughs differently, that their culture hesitates first before laughing. Now, I can agree that what we laugh about may be different, but our reaction of laughing about something is the same. And our timing of that spontaneous reaction is the same. We laugh when we find something funny. Not necessarily some moments later after we find something funny. The following day a few of us were invited to a film premiere of one of the actors in the show we were consulting. My viewpoint was proven correct. The three hundred audience members mostly from their culture laughed instantly after the jokes were delivered on screen. It's a human thing.
>
> Tim Ryder, Co-Producer, *3rd Rock From The Sun*
> Associate Producer/Editor, *That '70s Show*
> Editor, *Anger Management*

All of our rules point to the fact that the funny part of the joke is the last thing in the sentence. This way it is not telegraphed and it is clean. The great challenge is that other languages have different sentence construction. This was part of the American consultants' challenge and the thoughts of others that share similar foreign sitcom experiences:

> Having worked for nearly four years abroad, adapting sitcoms for Russia and Eastern Europe, I discovered that *pure human comedy is universal.* Stories that are driven by and based in personal comedy conflict (as opposed to situational) will span language and culture. Mining the humor in pesky in-laws, stinginess, jealousy, ignorance, desire, insecurity, greed and dishonesty can make the whole world laugh. Regardless of the coun-

15 No, we are not going to make that bold print and include it in the sitcom vocabulary.

try of origin, if your scripts are rooted in human comedy they have a far better chance of longevity in syndication or international adaptation.

Rick Hawkins, the Emmy-winning Writer/Executive Producer, International Television Consultant, University Teaching Artist

Comedy gurus – and I count myself among them – will always tell you that when you're constructing a joke you should always put the funny word last. There's a scientific reason for this, or at least a pseudo-scientific reason, and that's always been good enough for me. See, when you tell a joke, you're actually giving the listener or reader a little puzzle to solve. You're giving them clues, if you will, to what's supposed to be funny here. At the same time, believe it or not, you're also creating and storing tension, tension that wants to be released and – if you do your job right – will be released in the form of the laugh when the puzzle of the joke is solved. By putting the funny word last, you allow the puzzle to be solved all at once, fully and emphatically, and that will trigger the biggest explosion of laughter.

Consider this joke: "I'm so dumb that I couldn't pass a blood test." The joke works (if you laughed, and I hope you did) because the key word, "test," the one that connects blood to intelligence, comes last. It is, literally, the last piece of the puzzle. It tells you why you're supposed to laugh and (again, one hopes) you do. What if it's phrased this way? "I'm so dumb that if I took a blood test, I couldn't pass." That joke will misfire because upon hearing the word "pass," the listener then has to go back and, in a sense, collect the word "test" in order to put the pieces of the puzzle together. Tension is dissipated and the joke fizzles.

Now as you can imagine, this rule – funny word last – can become problematic when you're translating jokes across language platforms. German, for instance, is notorious for putting their verbs at the ass-end of the sentence, sometimes *miles* removed from the meat of the line or the point of the joke. English, God bless it, is a highly flexible language (as mutts are wont to be). We can put the funny word wherever we damn well please. Or we can damn well put the funny word wherever we please. Or, damn, well, we can put the funny word wherever we please. You get the idea.

But how do you get out of the trap? By breaking down the rules of language. Whether yours is a highly formal language (like Romanian) or one with a hundred words for penis (like Bulgarian), it's up to you as the writer to morph that language to suit your needs. Situation comedy language is not the same as street language. It's snappier, more shorthand, and much freer to mess with the rules of grammar and usage. All that's required is your own willingness to break those rules. I can't help you with that, except to say that the rules are usually made for the benefit of the rule-makers, and if they don't benefit you, kick them to the curb.

Bear in mind, always, that when constructing jokes in any language – or translating across platforms – you don't have to get it right on the first try. In my universe, there's something called a "jokoid." It looks like a joke, sounds like a joke, smells, walks, talks, barks and quacks like a joke except for one thing: it's not funny. Usually it's not funny because I don't yet have the words in the proper order. Well, rearranging the words is called *editing*. It should be a natural and fun part of your creative process, and it will be, once you let go of the need to get things right on the first try. First you write, then you rewrite – mine it and refine it – and that's true of jokes, stories, scripts, novels, everything. Write it wrong, then write it right. I can't think of a healthier writing strategy than that.

John Vorhaus is the author of the classic comedy writing text, THE COMIC TOOLBOX, *and its companion,* THE LITTLE BOOK OF SITCOM, *which has been called, "The Elements of Style of situation comedy." He has created television shows in Nicaragua, Romania, Switzerland and Germany, and bears a special love for* Married...with Children, *which he wrote for back in the day and now teaches and trains writers for its foreign adaptations.*

Tim Ryder shared some more thoughts on working with foreign editors on their preference for naming cameras 1, 2 ,3 and 4 or A, B, C, and X[16]:

Of course, these camera designations don't make sense to foreign productions. If you're a television professional in a foreign country, in my observation, you're used to numbered camera designations: 1-2-3-4. Especially for those having extensive experience in news and/or talk shows. Changing to letters creates chaos, so much so, that production stops down for an hour or so until everyone gives up and you're lucky enough to get a shot off before lunch.

Happy Together (*Married With Children* Russia) became a number one hit for the Russian TNT network and the show completed all 250 scripts purchased from Sony. Now, Sony has helped them create new original episodes of *Married With Children* that were never seen in the United States. *Who's the Boss, The Nanny, Bewitched and Everyone Loves Raymond* have all succeeded in Russia.

16 On ambitious sitcoms like *How I Met Your Mother,* fantasy scenes and musical production numbers might also have a Y and Z camera to designate cranes and/or high-speed shots, etc.

Phil Rosenthal, who created *Everyone Loves Raymond* made a documentary film of his experience in Russia. *Married With Children* is the most popular foreign script sale for Sony. It has been produced in sixteen countries and counting.

Phil Ramuno has since worked on *Bewitched* in Russia and *Married With Children, Bulgaria*. Independently from Sony, he has also helped MediaPro in Romania on several series as well as, a Finnish pilot shot in Los Angeles, and three sitcoms in Vancouver, Montreal and Toronto, Canada.[17] The U.S. has refined the style of sitcom to a fine art that the rest of the world enjoys.

17 All, except Russia, without any interpreters.

Sitcom Vocabulary Quick Review

Read these sentences. If the director gave you these notes, would you instantly know what he meant? If not, go back and review the explanation in this chapter.

We are going to build the audience by using this as a **web series.**

Do you have the prop for your **gag***?*

We can only pay you **syndicated** *scale.*

That scene will be **block and shoot.**

Make sure you don't block that label. It's part of the **branding.**

This script is going to be used as four short **webisodes.**

Sitcom Insider

Directing a multi camera sitcom is a marriage between theater and television. Just like theater, sitcoms have rehearsal days, usually three, and because it is a TV show, there are shoot days, typically two. The duties and responsibilities of the sitcom DGA team is spelled out in the DGA contract. Directors are responsible for rehearsing and directing the actors as well as camera blocking, or shooting, the show. The best and most experienced sitcom Directors take pride in having a grasp of the art of rehearsing the actors as well as knowing how to communicate the camera coverage to the camera operators. It is up to the Director to facilitate and execute this marriage of theater and TV. Seasoned Directors embrace the craft of directing and take pride in rehearsing the actors and shooting the show. Both of these duties are rarely, if ever, relinquished to anyone else by A-List Directors

The Associate Director, like the 1st & 2nd Assistant Directors, serves as a supporting role to the Director. Associate Director duties include being a liaison between the Director and the four camera operators, notating and keeping track of all the shots in each scene, delivering the Director's camera notes to the camera operators after each take, help address and resolve camera blocking issues that the Director and the camera operators may encounter, and when needed, suggest camera coverage to the Director. The Associate Director is there to help the Director with the camera coverage.

Kevin Sullivan, Associate Director

Sitcom Insider

I was standing to the side of the set during a live filming of an episode when a talented, established exec-writer came quickly up to me and, referring to the seated audience watching a scene being recorded, exclaim "They're not supposed to laugh there! That's not the joke! They are supposed to laugh here!" He pushed his script in front of my face with his index finger racing back and forth over the two phrases that butted up against each other.

I turned to him and asked him a bit forcefully, "You want me to tell 250 people that they're wrong?"

"But that's not the joke!"

I smiled. "Don't worry; we'll fix it in post."

Can everything be fixed in post? Well, most executive producers think so, but that's not the case. Sometimes you have to just say that's the best we can do because we didn't have enough time, enough money, or enough quality. You can have two of these, but not all three. Ever.

Tim Ryder, editor

Sitcom Career Profile

RANDY N. BARBEE

1ST ASSISTANT DIRECTOR

Mary Lou met Randy on BET's The Game, *which was a hybrid show using a single camera schedule, doing a lot of locations, and then utilizing three cameras in the studio. He comes from the one-hour world and is always employed because his organizational and scheduling skills are exceptional. His dedication to a production knows no bounds and on top of this, he's a really nice guy!*

What shows have you worked on?

In Atlanta, I've done a lot of BET half-hour comedies: *The Game, 2nd Generation Wayans.* In New York, five seasons of *The Sopranos* -AD'ing, producing and directing HBO's internet *Sopranos* site, acting in 8 episodes in Seasons 4 and 5. Various DGA jobs on *New York Undercover* for 4 seasons and *Law & Order* for 2 seasons. *Twin Peaks* and lots of other commercial and theatrical work with David Lynch. 2nd AD--*Presumed Innocent, Parenthood, Cadillac Man, See You in the Morning, Jackknife, Lean on Me, Running on Empty, Orphans.*

What are your responsibilities?

I am responsible for breaking down production scripts for their various production elements and scheduling the work to be done in the most efficient manner (and efficiency pertains to both economic and time, as well as to efficiency in helping the director and actors best tell the story, because in the end, what we do is all about the director and the actors telling a story, a point often overlooked in hurry-up TV.) During the shoot, I run the set and coordinate the various departments so that everybody shows up at the right time, with the right people carrying the right piece of equipment, so that all our time is spent on rehearsing and shooting the scene, not waiting for a missing component to show up.

That is the official job description. My unofficial description: I communicate. I spread information, to EVERYBODY. What we do in TV today is all about time, and somebody has to have an overview. That's what I do. Therefore, my responsibility is, simply, everything. Not doing it myself, but in knowing how it's going to work and that it will work.

Did you have specific training in this field?

I have a Bachelors degree in theatre, and a Masters in theatre management I interned at Williamstown, which led directly to me getting an Equity card. I got into the Directors Guild Assistant Director Training Program in New York, a highly competitive program which accepts 6 or 8 applicants from thousands. So those two years as a Trainee gave me--if not the skills to be an AD, then at least the foundation that was to be a springboard for me to eventually work as a 1st AD.

How did you get your first job?

The DGA Training program provided a connection and a conduit, to the working world. I developed two close associations in particular with 2nd AD's who I impressed, and when I graduated they took me on their next job as their 2nd 2nd, then when they became 1st AD's, who hired me as their Key 2nd, etc., etc.

What advice would you give someone who wants to do what you do?

Never stop knocking on doors. You don't have to be completely obnoxious as you look for work. But it's critical that the people who hire production know that you're out there. Everybody's got to start somewhere. Jump in. Everybody's road is different. When you get that job, show up strong. Positive. Never stop thinking; never stop anticipating. And remember ... be really really nice to people on your way up. You're going to meet them again on your way back down.

What do you like best about your job?

Variety. Because of what we do, no day is ever the same. It's always challenging, often infuriating, but generally, unless you're shooting too long a stretch in the studio, it's never boring. It's the only business I know that you show up a half-hour before call, shoot 6 or 7 hours till lunch, which is often eaten standing up or walking, then go back and shoot another 6 or 7 hours, and then walking out the door 14 or 15 hours after you first showed up, you think, "Thank God it was a short day."

1ST ADS
UNION: DGA (DIRECTORS GUILD OF AMERICA)
TYPICAL WEEKLY SALARY: $3900-5000
HOURS PER WEEK: UNTIL THE WORK IS DONE.

Appendix 1 SITCOM VOCABULARY

above the line:
the "creative" team of producers, writers, directors, actors, casting directors and others who also usually get residuals.

act break:
the dividing point in the story usually punctuated by a twist in the plot that makes the audience want to come back after the second commercial break.

AD:
the director's assistants. Evolved differently in film and live television (which became videotaped television). Film shows have an Assistant Director, Second Assistant and sometimes a 2nd Second AD. Taped shows have an Associate Director, Stage Manager and Second Stage Manager. The new DGA contract will change the title of Technical Coordinators to Associate Directors.

air check:
recording a show off the air for purposes of archiving it or checking its content

air show:
the live performance of show in front of cameras and audience while film or tape is recording.

background artists:
extras. Members of the SAG-AFTRA.

below the line:
the crew and production staff. Some are paid only for the weeks they work. Others are "carried" and receive payment for the weeks that a show is not in production and on hiatus. Above the line staff includes the writers, producers and the director. Above and below the line are either under contract to the studio, sign a production company deal-memo or get paid by the day.

block and shoot:
multi-camera style shooting with no audience. It is very common now; not just an occasional pre-shoot.

blow:
a final joke at the end of a scene, usually a big joke. See *button.*

boarded:
scheduled. Refers to day to day shooting schedule for single camera shows. It is chronicled by each eighth of a page of a script.

boom:
the stand for the microphone.

booth:
the video control room or hub.

branding:
a marketing technique associating a name, logo, slogan, with a product, show, or characters on that show

breakdown:
the tool by which agents submit their clients for a possible audition. A breakdown, at its best, is a description of the character and what makes that character tic. At it's least; it's a summation of how a character serves the plot. It gives the actor insight into what the writers had in mind.

business:
any physical action: any movement or gesture. It may support dialogue or exist on its own.

button:
joke at the end of a scene, usually a small joke. Emphasis given to the end of any joke. See *blow.*

blow:
a final joke at the end of a scene, usually a big joke. See *button.*

callback:
A reference to a previously mentioned material or piece of business. Repeating a big joke. A second audition for an actor.

call time:
the time an actor or crew member is expected to be on stage ready to work.

carrying:
having scripts in hands.

cold open:
short scene which precedes the first act. It appears before the opening credits to entice or tease the audience into not changing the channel and watching the entire episode. The networks try to get the viewing audience to watch their channel without switching after each program ends. They sometimes make the teaser so "cold" or unanticipated that it may start immediately as the other show ends, not even a station break to separate them.

collate:
putting the script in order with the new pages

counter:
to adjust your position after another actor moves.

coverage:
all the camera shots. If a show has many characters, the producers may want you to "cover" all the actors with close-ups.

craft service:
one or two people who provide snacks and (sometimes meals) for the crew working on stage.

cross shooting:
shooting coverage with two or more cameras from opposite directions simultaneously.

cueing:
saying the words aloud for one character with a partner saying the lines for all the other characters.

cue bite:
to take out the pauses between the lines.

dissolve:
an edit that simultaneously eliminates one image while creating the next.

deadpan:
a face that shows no emotion; poker face. The human face has been referred to as a "pan" since the 19th century possibly because the face is broad and shallow like a frypan.

dichotomy:
literary tool employed to evoke humor. It divides an idea into separate classes thereby bringing out the funny.

director's cut:
the first completed assembly of the show. The DGA contract stipulates that directors get to edit their show first...or at least give notes on the first assembly.

dollies:
a sophisticated wagon for the camera. It is usually pushed but can also be pulled. It can operate on the floor or on tracks. The film camera operator rides on the wagon.

double take:
a sight gag involving rapidly turning the head twice.

doubling:
having multiples of props, wardrobe, or actors.

dovetailing:
see cue bit

downstage:
the part of the stage closer to the audience. It is so named because when stages (not audiences) were raked (tilted), as the actors walked away from the audience, they literally were traveling up the lower part of the stage.

down to time:
the time that network is allowing for this program including opening titles and end credits.

dramedy:
show that has both comedy and drama.

dress show:
first audience show. This name came from live television's final dress rehearsal. This show is taped/filmed and serves as the first of at least two performance choices for the editor.

dressed:
decorated.

dry blocking:
a part of rehearsal in which the crew watches the actors perform the scene just to see where the actors go and listen to what they say.

dump:
a camera term referring to following an actor as he moves and switching coverage to the actor who the first actor passes.

echo:
an exact callback. Repetition of same word or business.

end credits:
The end of the show where the names of the crew are listed.

ESU:
engineering set up.

feed:
see set-up. To cue actors on a specific line. Usually proceeded by an actor calling for a line by saying, "Line!"

film style shooting:
the kind of shooting done on hour episodic television; a way of describing the visual recording of a television show where multiple cameras are used but the coverage is not shot to shot but good all the time because every camera move is motivated and usable in editing.

first assembly:
the director's cut.

first pass:
the first of multiple times that a scene is shot when the coverage from pass to pass changes; allows for many different pieces of coverage to be shot each time.

50/50:
the mirror-like physical relationship between two actors. It facilitates each actor being equally visible to the audience or cameras.

first team:
the actors who are in the scene. They are replaced by stand-ins called the second team.

fourth wall:
a theatre term referring to the imaginary wall through which the audience is watching. Breaking the fourth wall in theatre is when a character speaks directly to the audience. Breaking the fourth wall in television is when the actor looks directly into the camera lens and appears to be talking directly to the viewers.

gaffer:
a person on the electrcis crew incharge of hanging and focussing the lighting instruments.

gag:
a joke or piece of physical business

getting read:
the show runner reading spec script.

give it away:
to prematurely reveal to the audience. To telegraph what or where the joke will be.

green bed :
floor or walkway hanging above the lighting grid.

handle:
one or more incidental words that lead in a sentence. It gives dialogue a conversational tone.

hanging:
attaching lamps to the grid for use in lighting a show.

hiccup:
a reset of 30 seconds or less. A short pause in the scene usually taken so cameras, sets, or props can change, move or reset. The cameras continue to roll and the delay is edited out later.
The film or tape continues to roll during a hiccup.

hi-def:
high definition TV.

hold:
waiting for the audience to finish laughing.

irony:
a literary device in which the meaning of the words used is the opposite of their usual sense.

iso coverage:
cameras that are not on-line as the active camera of the switched feed are also being recorded or "isolated" for use during postproduction.

J.T.C:
joke to come.

jumped laughs:
continuing with dialogue when the audience wants to laugh. Causes a problem by shortening the laugh and causes the audience not to hear dialogue that follows.

land:
the ability of a joke to get a laugh or score.

laying pipe:
providing the exposition.

line feed:
the edit made live during a taping.

L.T.C.:
abbreviation for "line to come".

live cutting:
an edit that is simultaneously broadcast.

load in:
moving scenery on to the sound stage at the beginning of the week.

marks:
locations the actors have to stand on in each shot, usually defined by tape.

master:
a shot that holds all the actors in the frame; it is usually shot first.

match action:
to repeat exact physical action of what has been done before in order to maintain continuity from one take to another. Used during overlap or reset, or repeated takes or coverage.

mislead:
to intentionally take the audience in one direction with information or an idea so that you can surprise them by going in the other direction. The information given before a turn.

monitors:
TV screens that show either the live feed or the isos.

off air moves:
camera moves in film-style shooting that will not be unusable because the camera is switching to another shot without motivation.

off air moves:
camera moves in film-style shooting that will be unusable because the camera is switching to another shot with motivation.

off book:
when an actor no longer needs to carry a script in his hands because he has memorized the words. This makes it easier for him to act, handle props, and move about the stage more freely.

on the floor:
describes the position of the director (or other) on the shooting the floor of the sound stage as opposed to in the booth.

opening titles:
the opening of the show, sometimes accompanied by the theme song. It always give the name of the show, the names of the actors and often the name of the show creators.

operative word:
the word to be stressed; the important word to understand the plot or the joke.

overlap:
to repeat action or dialogue

over the top:
a description for a performance that is too large or exagerated.

page 1 rewrite:
a complete reworking of the script beginning with the first page.

patter:
amusing lines delivered rapidly by a performer(s).

pay it off:
deliver the punchline.

pedestal dolly:
Requires less manpower than film dolly.

picking up the cues:
see cue bite.

pickups:
retakes after the audience goes home. Partial sections of scene re-shot after whole scene has been completed.

pilot:
the first script of a series; the actual first show of a series.

pipe:
the exposition in a script.

pitch:
telling your original idea to a network, in the hopes that they will like the idea enough to order a script. Suggesting individual jokes as part of an ongoing re-writing process.

playback:
an already recorded portion of the show. Because of the time code imprinted on tape, and the script supervisor's records, it is easy to locate an exact part of the already recorded scene.

practical:
a light or appliance that functions and is used by an actor in a scene.

prep:
period of time before principal photography begins also known as pre-production period.

post:
period of time after principal photography ends also known as post-production period.

producer's cut:
2nd version of show (after Director's Cut) on which the producers have given notes.

punch:
to review the joke and make it better.

punchline:
the funny part of the joke. It will not be funny without the set-up.

pulled:
removed; what a grip does to a wall in order that a camera can shoot where the wall used to be.

quad split:
simple four-way output of each of the cameras.

reaction shots:
a shot where a character doesn't speak but reacts; enhances the scene to cut to these kind of shots because it extends the laugh by showing the audience what the character is thinking.

replace:
to come up with an entirely new joke.

resets:
changing camera positions or scenery. It may be a long enough pause to require the film or tape to stop.

residuals:
payments negotiated by a union for re-use of a TV show.

retake:
doing a scene over.

(the) room:
writer's room

room tone:
the sounds that go on in an empty room with no one moving. It may appear silent to the naked ear, but actually there is ambient sound. During pickups it is common to record 45 seconds of room tone in a swing set used only on that episode. It is pre-laid for scenes with no background actors.

second:
DGA position of Second AD or Second Stage Manager.

second banana:
the second comedic character of importance; a term from Burlesque.

second pass:
the second of multiple times that a scene is shot when the coverage from pass to pass changes; allows for many different pieces of coverage to be shot each time.

second team:
the stand-ins.

setup:
the statement or premise that has to be understood for a joke to get a laugh. The front half of the joke.

set-line:
the edge of the set. This line is called the proscenium line in the theatre.

(the) shoot:
the days when principal photography occurs; the days when filming occurs.

shooting off:
composing a camera shot beyond where there is a set.

show runner:
the head writer. His official title is Executive Producer.

shtick:
an extreme piece of physical business such as a pratfall. The old Yiddish term for piece or routine. It described the physical comedy or little dances of vaudeville.

sides:
a few pages of the script; Used at an audition, these pages are an actor's guide to the story and character. Used on the set while shooting, it is the pages being shot that day.

sight gag:
a joke whose laugh is predicated upon a visual.

slate:
to identify yourself at the beginning of an audition tape.

slow burn:
sight gag involving slow turn of the head

speed-thru:
an exercise in which actors recite their lines or dialogue at a quicker speed than normal (sometimes devoid of meaning).

spit take:
a sight gag involving spitting.

staffing:
getting a season as a writer on a series.

standing sets:
sets that are used every week.

steadicam:
a handheld device for moving the camera; the operator wears a harness and the camera is attached to a floating head.

subtext:
what an actor is thinking while he says the line: Sub meaning "under" and text meaning "wording. It is his silent or hidden message. Subtext is an important tool for an actor not only when understating something but whenever a character is thinking something different from or more complex than what his actual words (or lack of words) allows him to say aloud.

suits:
network or studio executives named because of the odd uniform they wear.

sweetening:
adding laughs or to the entire process of audio postproduction.

swing sets:
sets that are new to a particular episode. On some very busy shows, the crew actually "swings" them into a space between two regular sets.

syndicated:
a method of distributing TV shows in alternative market; usually done with shows that have already reached 100 episodes with primetime airing in major network; other times, TV shows are made cheaper for sale directly to this secondary market.

table draft:
the version of the script that actually gets read the first time the cast is assembled. This reading takes place around a table rather than on a set.

tag:
short final scene before or during the end credits.

take:
each re-do of a scene or portion of a scene. It is assigned a take number for keeping things straight during editing

tally light:
a light (usually red) on the camera that comes on when that camera is on-line.

tape style shooting:
the kind of shooting done on half hour episodic television; a way of describing the visual recording of a television show where multiple cameras are used and the coverage is shot to shot so the camera may be moving when it is not on-line and unusable in editing all other times.

teaser:
a short scene that precedes the first act. This scene introduces the theme of the episode.

telegraph:
to give away what is about to come. Tipping the joke.

the room:
the writer's room

throw it away:
to not emphasize information. A direction given to make information more casual so as not to telegraph the joke that is coming.

tipping the joke:
to telegraph information that is coming

topper:
a punchline on top of another punchline.

turn:
the point between the set up and punch line or mislead and punch line where the information or emotion switches unexpectedly into another direction. Often accompanied by a physical turn.

turn around:
to shoot in the opposite direction after all the coverage is done in the initial direction.

tweaking:
adjusting flags and barn-doors on the lights.

24P:
a recording method progressively scanning a film-like 24 complete frames each second. Standard video uses electricity's 60 cycles to scan each frame twice and then interpolate them to make 30 video frames for each second of action.

twist:
an unexpected plot point. A surprise.

understatement:
a joke employing irony. It deliberately states the truth inaccurately or too weakly in order to make the audience laugh.

UPM:
Unit Production Manager, Directors Guild members since 1964.

usable:
able to be used in edit.

video village:
the bank of monitors and podiums set up on the stage floor as the technical hub.

walla:
nondescript conversations when mixed in the sound track.

warm-up:
a stand-up comic hired to be the official host for the audience.

web series:
multiple short episodes made for distributing on the internet.

webisodes:
short individual episodes made for distributing on the internet as part of a web series.

wrapped:
the finish of the day, episode, or series for an individual or the entire company.

wrinkle:
the complication during Act Two.

Appendix 2 LIST OF U.S. NETWORK SITCOMS

Year is of first airing. Listed networks aired first run episodes. Some unrelated sitcoms have the same title (even on the same network) as little as two years apart. Several predominately drama "dramedies" are not included.

1947 *Mary Kay and Johnny* (DUMONT/NBC/CBS) 15-min., then 30, then 15 daily

1948 *The Morey Amsterdam Show* sitcom with variety (CBS/Dumont)

1949 *Mama* (CBS) a.k.a. *I Remember Mama*
Mixed Doubles (NBC)
That Wonderful Guy (ABC)
The Aldrich Family (NBC)
The Family Genius (DUMONT)
The Goldbergs (CBS/NBC/DUMONT/SYND)
The Hartmans (NBC) a.k.a. *The Hartmans at Home*
The Life of Riley (NBC) starred Jackie Gleason, William Bendix version 1953
The Ruggles (ABC)
The Wren's Nest (ABC) three 15-min. sitcoms a week
Wesley (CBS)

1950 *Beulah* (ABC) first sitcom to star an African American
Hank McClune first show using a laugh track with no audience present, local Los Angeles show the year before.
Menasha the Magnificent (NBC)
The George Burns and Gracie Allen Show (CBS) a.k.a. *The Burns and Allen Show*
The Jack Benny Program" (CBS) sitcom with variety
The Stu Erwin Show (ABC) a.k.a. *Life With Stu Erwin, The New Stu Erwin Show, The Trouble With Father*
Young and Gay (CBS) a.k.a. *The Girls*

1951 *A Date with Judy* (ABC)
Actors Hotel (ABC) summer series
I Love Lucy (CBS)
The Amos 'n' Andy Show (CBS)
The Egg and I (CBS) 15 minute daily sitcom
Two Girls Named Smith (ABC) aired 12 noon Saturdays
Young Mr. Bobbin (NBC)

1952 *Boss Lady* (NBC)
Claudia: The Story of a Marriage (NBC)
Doc Corkle (NBC)
Heaven for Betsy (CBS) two 15-minute sitcoms a week
I Married Joan (NBC)
It's a Business (DUMONT)
Leave it to Larry (CBS)
Life with Luigi (CBS)
Meet Millie (CBS)
Mr. Peepers (NBC)
My Friend Irma (CBS)
My Hero (NBC)
My Little Margie (CBSNBC)
Our Miss Brooks (CBS)
The Abbott and Costello Show (SYND)
The Adventures of Ozzie and Harriet (ABC)
Those Endearing Young Charms (NBC)

1953 *Bonino* (NBC)
Colonel Humphrey Flack (DUMONT) a.k.a. *The Fabulous Fraud, The Adventures of Colonel Flack, The Imposter*
Ethel and Albert (NBC/CBS/ABC) last regular live sitcom ending in 1956
It's a Business (DUMONT)
Jamie (ABC) dramedy before that term existed
Life With Elizabeth (SYND)
Life with Father (CBS)
Make Room for Daddy (ABC/CBS) later *The Danny Thomas Show*

Marge and Jeff (DUMONT) 15 minutes daily
Meet Mr. McNutley (CBS) a.k.a. *The Ray Milland Show* a.k.a. *Meet Mr. McNulty*
My Favorite Husband (CBS)
My Son Jeep (NBC)
Private Secretary (CBS)
The Alan Young Show (CBS) started earlier as a variety show
The Jean Carroll Show (ABC) a.k.a. *Take it From Me*
The Pride of the Family (ABC)
The Red Buttons Show (NBC) started earlier as a variety show
Topper (CBS)
Where's Raymond? (ABC) a.k.a. *The Ray Bolger Show*
Wonderful John Acton (NBC)

1954 *Dear Phoebe* (NBC)
December Bride (CBS)
Duffy's Tavern (SYND)
Father Knows Best (CBS)
Honestly, Celeste! (CBS)
It's a Great Life (NBC)
Meet Corliss Archer (SYND)
Mickey Rooney Show (NBC) a.k.a. *Hey Mulligan*
That's My Boy (CBS)
The Duke (NBC) summer series
The Halls of Ivy (CBS)
The World of Mr. Sweeney (NBC) 15 minutes, started as part of a variety show
Willy (CBS)

1955 *Homer Bell* (SYND) sitcom-western
It's Always Jan (CBS)
Joe and Mabel (CBS)
Norby (NBC)
Professional Father (CBS)
So This Is Hollywood (NBC)
The Bob Cummings Show (NBC/CBS) a.k.a. *Love That Bob*
The Eddie Cantor Comedy Theater (SYND) anthology, sitcom some weeks
The Great Gildersleeve (SYND)
The Honeymooners (CBS) started in 1950 as part of a *Cavalcade of Stars* variety show
The People's Choice (NBC)
The Soldiers (NBC)
Those Whiting Girls (NBC)
You'll Never Get Rich (CBS) later *The Phil Silvers Show* a.k.a. *Sgt. Bilko, Bilko*

1956 *Hey, Jeannie* (CBS)
Oh! Susanna (CBS/ABC)
Stanley (NBC)
The Adventures of Hiram Holiday (NBC)
The Brothers (CBS)
The Charles Farrell Show (CBS)

1957 *A Date with the Angels* (ABC)
Bachelor Father (CBS/NBC/ABC)
Blondie (NBC)
Leave it to Beaver (CBS/ABC)
Mr. Adams and Eve (CBS)
Sally (NBC)
The Adventures of Tugboat Annie (SYND) Canadian-American
The Eve Arden Show (CBS)
The Lucy-Desi Comedy Hour (CBS) 60-min sitcom, originally part of *Westinghouse Desilu Playhouse*
The Marge and Goer Champion Show (CBS)
The Real McCoys (ABC/CBS)

1958 *How to Marry a Millionaire* (SYND)
Love That Jill (ABC)
The Ann Southern Show (CBS)
The Donna Reed Show (ABC)
The Ed Wynn Show (NBC)
The George Burns Show
This is Alice (SYND)

1959 *Dennis the Menace* (CBS)
Fibber McGee and Molly (NBC)
Hennesey (CBS)
Peck's Bad Girl (CBS)
The Betty Hutton Show (CBS) a.k.a. *Goldie*
The Dennis O'Keefe Show (CBS)
The Many Loves of Doby Gillis (CBS)
This Is Alice
Too Young to Go Steady (NBC) 8 episodes, all live

1960 *Angel* (CBS)
Bringing up Buddy (CBS)
Guestward, Ho! (NBC)
Happy (NBC)
Harrigan and Son (ABC)
My Sister Eileen (CBS)
My Three Sons (ABC/CBS)

Pete and Gladys (CBS)
Peter Loves Mary (NBC)
The Andy Griffith Show (CBS)
The Flintstones (ABC/NBC) animated
The Jim Backus Show (SYND) a.k.a. *Hot Off the Wire*
The Tab Hunter Show (NBC)
The Tom Ewell Show (CBS)

1961 *Calvin and the Colonel* (ABC) animated
Car 54, Where Are You? (NBC)
Father of the Bride (CBS)
Hazel (NBC/CBS)
Holiday Lodge (CBS) summer series
Ichabod and Me (CBS)
Margie (ABC)
Mister Ed (Synd)
Mrs. G Goes to College (CBS)
One Happy Family (NBC)
The Alvin Show (CBS) animated
The Bob Cummings Show (CBS)
The Dick Van Dyke Show (CBS)
The Hathaways (ABC)
The Joey Bishop Show (NBC/CBS) later *The New Joey Bishop Show*
Top Cat (ABC) animated
Westinghouse Playhouse (NBC) a.k.a. *The Nanette Fabray Show, Yes, Yes Nanette*
Window on Main Street (CBS)

1962 *Don't Call Me Charlie* (NBC)
Ensign O'Toole (NBC)
Fair Exchange (CBS)
Going My Way (ABC)
I'm Dickens, He's Fenster (ABC)
McHale's Navy (ABC)
McKeever and the Colonel (NBC)
Mr. Smith Goes to Washington (ABC)
Oh, Those Bells! (CBS)
Our Man Higgins (ABC)
Room For One More (ABC)
The Beverly Hillbillies (CBS)
The Jetsons (ABC/CBS/NBC/SYND) animated
The Lucy Show (CBS)

1963 *Broadside* (ABC)
Glynis (CBS)
Grindl (NBC)
Harry's Girls (NBC)
My Favorite Martian (CBS)
Petticoat Junction (CBS)
The Bill Dana Show (NBC)
The Farmer's Daughter (ABC)
The New Phil Silvers Show (CBS)
The Patty Duke Show (ABC)

1964 *Bewitched* (ABC)
Broadside (ABC)
Gilligan's Island (CBS)
Gomer Pyle, U.S.M.C. (CBS)
Harris Against the World (NBC) part of *90 Bristol Court* trilogy
Karen (NBC) part of *90 Bristol Court* trilogy
Many Happy Returns (CBS)
Mickey (ABC)
My Living Doll (CBS)
No Time for Sergeants (ABC)
The Addams Family (ABC)
The Baileys of Balboa (CBS)
The Bing Crosby Show (ABC)
The Cara Williams Show (CBS)
The Munsters (CBS)
The Tycoon (ABC)
Tom, Dick and Mary (NBC) part of *90 Bristol Court* trilogy
Vallentine's Day (ABC)
Wendy and Me (ABC)

1965 *Camp Runamuck* (NBC)
F Troop (ABC)
Get Smart (NBC/CBS)
Gidget (ABC)
Green Acres (CBS)
Hank (NBC)
Hogan's Heroes (CBS)
I Dream of Jeannie (NBC)
Mona McCluskey (NBC)
Mr. Roberts (NBC)
My Mother the Car (NBC)
O.K. Crackerby! (ABC)
Please Don't Eat the Daisies (NBC)
Tammy (ABC)
The John Forsythe Show (NBC)
The Smothers Brothers Show (CBS) sitcom, not their variety show
The Wackiest Ship in the Army (NBC) one hour sitcom

1966 *Family Affair* (CBS)
Hey Landlord (NBC)
It's About Time (CBS)

Love on a Rooftop (ABC)
Occasional Wife (NBC)
Pistols N' Petticoats (CBS)
Run, Buddy, Run (CBS)
That Girl (ABC)
The Abbott and Costello Show (SYND) animated
The Double Life of Henry Phyfe (ABC)
The Hero (NBC)
The Jean Arthur Show (CBS)
The Monkees (NBC)
The Pruitts of Southhampton (ABC)
The Rounders (ABC)
The Tammy Grimes Show (ABC)

1967 *Accidental Family* (NBC)
Captain Nice (NBC)
Good Morning World (CBS)
He & She (CBS)
Mr. Terrific (CBS)
Rango (ABC) sitcom-western
The Flying Nun (ABC)
The Mothers-In-Law (NBC)
The Second Hundred Years (ABC)

1968 *Blondie* (CBS)
Here Come the Brides (ABC)
Here's Lucy (CBS)
Julia (NBC)
Mayberry R.F.D. (CBS)
That's Life (ABC) sitcom-musical
The Doris Day Show (CBS)
The Ghost and Mrs. Muir (NBC/ABC)
The Good Guys (CBS)
The Ugliest Girl in Town (ABC)

1969 *Love, American Style* (ABC) anthology, including some failed sitcom pilots
Mr. Deeds Goes to Town (ABC)
My World and Welcome To It (NBC)
Room 222 (ABC)
The Bill Cosby Show (NBC)
The Brady Bunch (ABC)
The Courtship of Eddies Father (CBS)
The Debbie Reynolds Show (NBC)
The Governor and J.J. (CBS)
The Queen and I (CBS)
To Rome with Love (CBS)

1970 *Arnie* (CBS)
Barefoot in the Park (ABC)
Make Room for Granddaddy (ABC)
Nancy (NBC)
Nanny and the Professor (ABC)
The Mary Tyler Moore Show (CBS)
The Odd Couple (ABC)
The Partridge Family (ABC)
The Tim Conway Show (CBS)

1971 *All in the Family* (CBS) later *Archie Bunker's Place*
Doctor in the House (SYND) British
From a Bird's Eye View (NBC)
Funny Face (CBS)
Getting Together (ABC)
Headmaster (CBS) dramedy, later *The New Andy Griffith Show*
Shirley's World (ABC) filmed, all on location
The Chicago Teddy Bears (CBS)
The Good Life (NBC)
The Jimmy Stewart Show (NBC)
The New Dick Van Dyke Show (CBS)
The Partners (NBC)

1972 *Bridget Loves Bernie* (CBS)
*M*A*S*H** (CBS)
Maude (CBS)
Me and the Chimp (CBS)
Sanford and Son (NBC)
Temperatures Rising (ABC) later *The New Temperatures Rising*
The Bob Newhart Show (CBS)
The Corner Bar (ABC)
The Don Rickles Show (CBS)
The Little People (NBC) later *The Brian Keith Show*
The Paul Lynde Show (ABC)
The Sandy Duncan Show (CBS)
The Super (ABC) summer series
Wait 'til Your Father Gets Home (SYND) animated

1973 *A Touch of Grace* (ABC)
Adam's Rib (ABC)
Anna and the King (CBS)
Bob & Carol & Ted & Alice (ABC)
Callucci's Department (CBS)
Diana (NBC)
Dusty's Trail (SYND)
Here We Go Again (ABC)
Lotsa Luck (NBC)
My Favorite Martians (CBS) animated
Needles and Pins (NBC)

Ozzie's Girls (SYND)
Roll Out! (CBS)
The Addams Family (NBC/ABC) animated
The Girl with Something Extra (NBC)
Thicker Than Water (ABC)

1974 *Barney Miller* (ABC)
Chico and The Man (NBC)
Friends and Lovers (CBS) a.k.a. *Paul Sand in Friends and Lovers*
Good Times (CBS) first spinoff of a spinoff
Happy Days (ABC)
Paper Moon (ABC)
Partridge Family: 2200 A.D. (CBS) animated
Rhoda (CBS)
That's My Mama (ABC)
The Texas Wheelers (ABC)

1975 *Barney Miller* (ABC)
Big Eddie (CBS)
Doc (CBS)
Far Out Space Nuts (CBS)
Fay (NBC)
Grady (NBC)
Hot L Baltimore (ABC)
Joe and Sons (CBS)
Karen (ABC)
On The Rocks (ABC)
One Day at a Time (CBS)
Phyllis (CBS)
Sunshine (NBC)
The Bob Crane Show (NBC)
The Cop and the Kid (NBC)
The Ghost Busters (CBS)
The Jeffersons (CBS)
The Montefuscos (NBC)
We'll Get By (CBS)
Welcome Back, Kotter (ABC)
When Things Were Rotten (ABC)

1976 *Alice* (CBS)
All That Glitters (SYND)
All's Fair (CBS)
Ball Four (CBS)
Big John, Little John (NBC)
C.P.O. Sharkey (NBC)
Good Heavens (ABC)
Holmes and Yoyo (ABC)
Ivan the Terrible (CBS) summer series
Laverne and Shirley (ABC)
Mary Hartman, Mary Hartman (SYND)
Mr. T and Tina (ABC)
Pop (CBS)
Popi (CBS)
Sirota's Court (NBC)
The Dumplings (NBC)
The King of Kensington (SYND) Canandian-American
The McLean Stevenson Show (NBC)
The Nancy Walker Show (ABC)
The Practice (NBC)
The Tony Randall Show (ABC)
Viva Valdez (ABC)
What's Happening!! (ABC/SYND)

1977 *A Year at the Top* (CBS)
Blansky's Beauties (ABC)
Busting Loose (CBS)
Carter Country (ABC)
Fernwood Tonight (SYND)
Fish (ABC)
Loves Me, Loves Me Not (CBS)
On Our Own (CBS)
Operation Petticoat (ABC)
Quark (NBC)
Sanford Arms (NBC)
Soap (ABC)
Szysznyk (CBS)
Tabitha (ABC)
The Betty White Show (CBS)
The Harvey Korman Show (NBC)
The Kallikaks (NBC)
The San Pedro Beach Bums (ABC)
Three's Company (ABC)
We've Got Each Other (CBS)

1978 *A.E.S. Hudson Street* (ABC)
America 2Night (SYND)
Another Day (CBS)
Apple Pie (ABC)
Baby, I'm Back (CBS)
Diff'rent Strokes (NBC/ABC)
Free Country (ABC)
Grandpa Goes to Washington (NBC)
Husbands, Wives & Lovers (CBS) 60-min. sitcom
In the Beginning (CBS)
Joe and Valerie (NBC)
Mork and Mindy (ABC)
Please Stand By (SYND)
Roller Girls (NBC)

Taxi (ABC/NBC)
The Hee Haw Honeys (SYND)
The Ted Knight Show (CBS)
The Waverly Wonders (NBC)
Who's Watching the Kids (NBC)
WKRP in Cincinnati (CBS)

1979 *13 Queens Blvd.* (ABC)
A New Kind of Family (ABC)
Angie (ABC)
Benson (ABC)
Billy (CBS)
Brothers and Sisters (NBC)
Co-Ed Fever (CBS)
Delta House (ABC)
Detective School (ABC)
Dorothy (CBS)
Flatbush (CBS)
Hanging In (CBS)
Hello Larry (NBC)
House Calls (CBS)
Joe's World (NBC)
Makin' It (ABC)
Miss Winslow & Son (CBS)
Out of the Blue (ABC)
Stockard Channing in Just Friends (CBS) later *Just Friends*
Struck by Lightning (CBS)
The Associates (ABC)
The Bad News Bears (CBS)
The Facts of Life (NBC)
The Last Resort (CBS)
The Ropers (ABC)
Turnabout (NBC)
Working Stiffs (CBS)

1980 *Aloha Paradise* (ABC)
Bosom Buddies (ABC)
Flo (CBS)
Good Time Harry (NBC)
Goodtime Girls (ABC)
I'm a Big Girl Now (ABC)
It's a Living (ABC/SYND) a.k.a. *Making a Living*
Ladies' Man (CBS)
Me and Maxx (NBC)
Nobody's Perfect (ABC)
One in a Million (ABC)
Phyl and Mikhy (CBS)
Sanford (NBC)
Semi-Tough (ABC)
The Life and Times of Eddie Roberts (SYND) a.k.a. *L.A.T.E.R.*
The Six O'Clock Follies (NBC)
The Stockard Channing Show (CBS)
Too Close for Comfort (ABC/SYND) later *The Ted Knight Show*
When the Whistle Blows (NBC)

1981 *Best of the West* (ABC) sitcom-western
Checking In (CBS)
Gimme a Break! (NBC)
Harper Valley PTA (NBC) a.k.a. *Harper Valley*
Laverne & Shirley (ABC) animated
Lewis & Clark (NBC)
Love, Sidney (NBC)
Maggie (ABC)
Mr. Merlin (CBS)
Open All Night (ABC)
Park Place (CBS)
Private Benjamin (CBS)
The Brady Brides (ABC)
The Two of US (CBS)

1982 *9 to 5* (ABC/SYND)
Cheers (NBC)
Family Ties (NBC)
Filthy Rich (CBS)
Gloria (CBS)
It Takes Two (ABC)
Joanie Loves Chachi (ABC)
Making the Grade (CBS)
Newhart (CBS)
No Soap, Radio (ABC)
One of the Boys (NBC)
Police Squad! (ABC)
Report to Murphy (CBS)
Silver Spoons (NBC/SYND)
Square Pegs (CBS)
Star of the Family (ABC)
Teachers Only (NBC)
The New Odd Couple (ABC)

1983 *Ace Crawford, Private Eye* (CBS)
AfterMASH (CBS)
Amanda's (ABC)
At Ease (ABC)
Baby Makes Five (ABC)
Buffalo Bill (NBC)
Condo (ABC)
Foot in the Door (CBS)
Goodnight Beantown (CBS)
Gun Shy (CBS) sitcom-western

It's Not Easy (ABC)
Jennifer Slept Here (NBC)
Just Our Luck (ABC)
Mama's Family (NBC/SYND)
Mr. Smith (NBC)
Oh Madeline (ABC)
Reggie (ABC)
Small & Frye (CBS)
We Got It Made (NBC/SYND)
Webster (ABC/SYND)

1984 *a.k.a. Pablo* (ABC)
Brothers (SHOWTIME)
Charles in Charge (CBS/SYND)
Domestic Life (CBS)
Double Trouble (NBC)
Dreams (CBS)
E/R (CBS)
Empire (CBS)
It's Your Move (NBC)
Kate & Allie (CBS)
Maggie Briggs (CBS)
Mama Malone (CBS)
Night Court (NBC)
Punky Brewster (NBC/SYND)
Shaping Up (ABC)
Spencer (NBC) later *Under One Roof*
The Cosby Show (NBC)
The Duck Factory (NBC)
The Four Seasons (CBS)
The New Leave it to Beaver (DISNEY/TBS) a.k.a. *Still the Beaver*
Three's A Crowd (ABC)
Who's the Boss? (ABC)

1985 *227* (NBC)
Charlie & Co. (CBS)
Foley Square (CBS)
George Burns Comedy Week (CBS) sitcom anthology
Growing Pains (ABC)
Hail to the Chief (ABC)
It's Punky Brewster (NBC) animated
Mary (CBS)
Mr. Belvedere (ABC)
Off the Rack (ABC)
Rocky Road (TBS)
Sara (NBC)
Small Wonder (SYND)
Stir Crazy (CBS)
The Golden Girls (NBC)
The Lucy Arnaz Show (CBS)
You Again? (NBC)

1986 *ALF* (NBC)
All Is Forgiven (NBC)
Amen (NBC)
Better Days (CBS)
Bridges To Cross (CBS)
Dads (ABC)
Designing Women (CBS)
Easy Street (NBC)
Fast Times (CBS)
Fathers and Sons (NBC)
Gung Ho (ABC)
Hangin' In (SYND) Canadian
He's the Mayor (ABC)
Head of the Class (ABC)
It's Gary Shandling's Show (SHOWTIME)
Joe Bash (ABC)
Leo & Liz in Beverly Hills (CBS)
Life with Lucy (ABC)
Me & Mrs. C (NBC)
Mr. Sunshine (ABC)
My Sister Sam (CBS)
One Big Family (SYND)
Perfect Strangers (ABC)
Sledge Hammer! (ABC)
The Cavenaughs (CBS)
The Ellen Burstyn Show (ABC)
The New Gidget (SYND)
The Redd Foxx Show (ABC)
Throb (SYND)
Together We Stand (CBS) later *Nothing Is Easy*
Tough Cookies (CBS)
Valerie (NBC/CBS) later *Valerie's Family*, then *The Hogan Family*
What a Country! (SYND)
You Again (NBC)

1987 *A Different World* (NBC)
Beans Baxter (FOX)
Bustin' Loose (SYND)
Dennis the Menace (SYND) animated
Down and Out in Beverly Hills (FOX)
Duet (FOX)
Everything's Relative (CBS)
Frank's Place (CBS)
Full House (ABC)
Hard Knocks (SHOWTIME)
Hooperman (ABC)
I Married Dora (ABC)

Karen's Song (FOX)
Mama's Boy (NBC)
Marblehead Manor (SYND)
Married...with Children (FOX)
Mr. President (FOX)
My Two Dads (NBC)
Out of This World (SYND)
Pursuit of Happiness (ABC)
Roomies (NBC)
Second Chance (FOX) later *Boys Will Be Boys*
She's the Sheriff (SYND)
Sweet Surrender (NBC)
The 'Slap' Maxwell Story (ABC) a.k.a. *Slap*
The Charmings (ABC)
The Munsters Today (SYND)
The New Monkees (SYND)
The Popcorn Kid (CBS)
The Tortellis (NBC)
Trying Times (PBS) anthology
Women in Prison (FOX)
You Can't Take it With You (SYND)

1988 *Annie McGuire* (CBS)
Baby Boom (NBC)
Beverly Hills Buntz (NBC) sitcom-dramedy
Coming of Age (CBS)
Day By Day (NBC)
Dear John... (NBC)
Dirty Dancing (NBC)
Eisenhower & Lutz (CBS)
Empty Nest (NBC)
Family Man (ABC)
First Impressions (CBS)
It's Gary Shandling's Show (SHOW-TIME/FOX)
Just In Time (ABC)
Just the Ten of Us (ABC)
Murphy Brown (CBS)
My Secret Identity (SYND) Canadian
Raising Miranda (CBS)
Roseanne (ABC)
Starting From Scratch (SYND)
The Munsters Today (SYND)
The Thorns (ABC)
The Van Dyke Show (CBS)
The Wonder Years (ABC)
The Wonder Years (ABC) sitcom-drama
Trial and Error (CBS)

1989 *13 East* (NBC)
Ann Jillian (NBC)
Anything But Love (ABC)
Chicken Soup (ABC)
Coach (ABC)
Doctor Doctor (CBS)
Family Matters (ABC/CBS)
FM (NBC)
Free Spirit (ABC)
Have Faith (ABC)
Heartland (CBS)
Homeroom (ABC)
Knight & Daye (NBC) summer series
Live-In (CBS)
Living Dolls (ABC)
Major Dad (CBS)
Nearly Departed (NBC)
Nick & Hillary (NBC)
One of the Boys (NBC)
Open House (FOX)
Saved by the Bell (NBC)
Seinfeld (NBC)
Sister Kate (NBC)
The Famous Teddy Z (CBS)
The Nutt House (NBC)
The People Next Door (CBS)
The Robert Guillaume Show (ABC)
The Simpsons (FOX) animated, started on a sketch show

1990 *A Family for Joe* (NBC)
American Dreamer (NBC)
Babes (FOX)
Bagdad Café (CBS)
Bobby's World (FOX) animated
City (CBS)
Down Home (NBC)
Dream On (HBO/FOX)
Evening Shade (CBS)
Evening Shade (CBS)
Family Man (CBS)
Ferris Bueller (NBC)
Get a Life (FOX)
Going Places (ABC)
Good Grief (FOX)
Grand (NBC)
Harry and the Hendersons (SYND)
His & Hers (CBS)
Lenny (CBS)
Little Rosie (ABC) animated
Married People (ABC)
Married People (ABC)

Molloy (FOX)
New Attitude (NBC)
Normal Life (CBS)
Parenthood (NBC)
Parker Lewis Can't Lose (FOX)
Singer & Sons (NBC)
Sugar and Spice (CBS)
Sydney (CBS)
The Family Man (CBS)
The Fanelli Boys (NBC)
The Fresh Prince of Bel-Air (NBC)
The Marshall Chronicles (ABC)
True Colors (FOX)
Uncle Buck (CBS)
What a Dummy (SYND)
Wings (NBC)
Wish You We're Here (CBS)
Working Girl NBC)
Working It Out (NBC)
You Take the Kids (CBS)

1991 *Baby Talk* (ABC)
Blossom (NBC)
Brooklyn Bridge (CBS)
Charlie Hoover (FOX)
Clarissa Explains It All (NICK)
Davis Rules (ABC/CBS)
Dinosaurs (ABC)
Drexell's Class (FOX)
Eerie, Indiana (NBC)
Flesh 'N Blood (NBC)
Good & Evil (ABC)
Good Sports (CBS)
Herman's Head (FOX)
Hi Honey, I'm Home (ABC/NICK)
Home Improvement (ABC)
Man of the People (NBC)
Nurses (NBC)
Pacific Station (NBC)
Princesses (CBS)
Roc (FOX)
Sibs (ABC)
Stat (ABC)
Step By Step (ABC/CBS)
Sunday Dinner (CBS)
Teech (CBS)
The Man in the Family (ABC)
The New WKRP in Cincinnatti (SYND)
The Royal Family (CBS)
The Torkelsons (NBC)
Top of the Heap (FOX)
Walter & Emily (NBC)

1992 *Arresting Behavior* (ABC)
Billy (ABC)
Bob (CBS)
California Dreams (NBC)
Camp Wilder (ABC)
Delta (ABC)
Down the Shore (FOX)
Fish Police (CBS) animated
Flying Blind (FOX)
Frannie's Turn (CBS)
Golden Palace (CBS)
Grapevine (CBS)
Great Scott! (FOX)
Hanging With Mr. Cooper (ABC)
Hearts Afire (CBS)
Here and Now (NBC)
Home Fires (NBC)
Julie (ABC)
Laurie Hill (ABC)
Love and War (CBS)
Mad About You (NBC)
Martin (FOX)
On the Air (ABC)
Out All Night (NBC)
Rachel Gunn, R.N. (FOX)
Rhythm & Blues (NBC)
Room for Two (ABC)
Scorch (CBS)
Shaky Ground (FOX)
Stand by Your Man (FOX)
The Addams Family (ABC) animated
The Amazing Live Sea Monkeys (ABC)
The Golden Palace (CBS)
The Jackie Thomas Show (ABC)
The Larry Sanders Show (HBO)
The Powers That Be (NBC)
Top of the Heap (FOX)
Vinnie & Bobby (FOX)
Woops! (FOX)

1993 *Almost Home* (NBC)
Bakersfield P.D. (FOX)
Big Wave Dave's (CBS)
Black Tie Affair (NBC)
Boy Meets World (ABC)
Café Americain (NBC)
Cutters (CBS)
Daddy Dearest (FOX)
Dave's World (CBS)
Dudley (CBS)
Family Album (CBS)
Frasier (NBC)

George (ABC)
Getting By (ABC/NBC)
Good Advice (CBS)
Grace Under Fire (ABC)
Home Free (ABC)
It Had to Be You (CBS)
Joe's Life (ABC)
Living Single (FOX)
Phenom (ABC)
Running the Halls (NBC)
Saved by the Bell: The College Years (NBC)
Saved by the Bell: The New Class (NBC)
Tall Hopes (CBS)
The Boys (CBS)
The Building (CBS)
The John Larroquette Show (NBC)
The Mommies (NBC)
The Nanny (CBS)
The Second Half (NBC)
The Sinbad Show (FOX)
The Trouble with Larry (CBS)
Thea (ABC)
Where I Live (ABC)

1994 *704 Hauser* (CBS)
Absolutely Fabulous (COMEDY CENTRAL) British
All-American Girl (ABC)
Blue Skies (ABC)
Daddy's Girls (CBS)
Duckman (USA) animated
Friends (NBC)
Hardball (FOX)
Madman of the People (NBC)
Me and the Boys (ABC)
Monty (FOX)
Muddling Through (CBS)
On Our Own (ABC)
Sister, Sister (ABC/WB)
Someone Like Me (NBC)
Something Wilder (NBC)
The Boys Are Back (CBS)
The Critic (ABC/FOX) animated
The Five Mrs. Buchanans (CBS)
The George Carlin Show (FOX)
The Good Life (NBC)
The Martin Short Show (NBC)
These Friends of Mine (ABC) later *Ellen*
Thunder Alley (ABC)
Tom (CBS)
Wild Oats (FOX)

1995 *A Whole New Ballgame* (ABC)
Almost Perfect (CBS)
Bless This House (CBS)
Bringing Up Jack (ABC)
Brotherly Love (NBC/WB)
Can't Hurry Love (CBS)
Caroline in the City (NBC)
Cleghorne! (WB)
Cybill (CBS)
Double Rush (CBS)
Dr. Katz (COMEDY CENTRAL) animated
Dweebs (CBS)
First Time Out (WB)
Get Smart (FOX)
Hang Time (NBC)
High Society (CBS)
Hope and Gloria (NBC)
Hudson Street (ABC)
If Not For You (CBS)
In the House (NBC/UPN)
Kirk (WB)
Maybe This Time (ABC)
Minor Adjustment (NBC)
Misery Loves Company (FOX)
Muscle (WB)
My Wildest Dreams (FOX)
Ned and Stacy (FOX)
NewsRadio (NBC)
Partners (FOX)
Pig Sty (UPN)
Platypus Man (UPN)
Pride & Joy (NBC)
Simon (WB)
The Bonnie Hunt Show (CBS) a.k.a. *Bonnie*
The Crew (FOX)
The Drew Carey Show (ABC)
The George Wendt Show (CBS)
The Home Court (NBC)
The Jeff Foxworthy Show (ABC)
The Naked Truth (ABC)
The Office (CBS)
The Parent'hood (WB)
The Preston Episodes (FOX)
The Pursuit of Happiness (NBC)
The Single Guy (NBC)
The Wayans Bros. (WB)
Too Something (FOX) later *New York Date*
Unhappily Ever After (WB)
Women of the House (CBS)

1996 *3RD Rock From the Sun* (NBC)

Aliens in the Family (ABC)
American Pie (?) one episode, before the later movies
Arliss (HBO) logo rendered as *Arli$$*
Boston Common (NBC)
Buddies (ABC)
Champs (ABC)
Clueless (ABC)
Common Law (ABC)
Cosby (CBS)
Crumbs (ABC)
Everybody Loves Raymond (CBS)
Good Company (CBS)
Goode Behavior (UPN)
Homeboys in Outer Space (UPN)
Ink (CBS)
Kenan & Kel (NICK)
Life With Roger (WB)
Life's Work (ABC)
Local Heroes (FOX)
Love and Marriage (FOX)
Lush Life (FOX)
Malcolm and Eddie (UPN)
Men Behaving Badly (NBC)
Moesha (UPN)
Mr. Rhodes (NBC)
My Guys (CBS)
Nick Freno: Licensed Teacher (WB)
Party Girl (FOX)
Pearl (CBS)
Public Morals (CBS)
Sabrina, The Teenage Witch (ABC)
Second Time Around (UPN)
Secret Service Guy (FOX)
Something So Right (NBC/ABC)
Sparks (UPN)
Spin City ABC
Suddenly Susan (NBC)
The Faculty (ABC)
The High Life (HBO)
The Jamie Foxx Show (WB)
The Last Frontier (FOX)
The Louie Show (CBS)
The Show (FOX)
The Steve Harvey Show (WB)
Townies (ABC)

1997 *Alright, Already* (WB)
Arsenio (ABC)
Austin Stories (MTV)
Between Brothers (FOX/UPN)
Built to Last (NBC)
Chicago Sons (NBC)
City Guys (NBC)
Claude's Crib (USA)
Daria (MTV) animated
Dharma & Greg (ABC)
George & Leo (CBS)
God, the Devil and Bob (NBC/ADULT SWIM) animated
Good News (UPN) a.k.a. *The Good News*
Head Over Heels (UPN)
Hiller and Diller (ABC)
Hitz (UPN)
Jenny (NBC)
Just Shoot Me! (NBC)
King of the Hill (FOX) animated
Life...and Stuff (CBS)
Lost on Earth (USA)
Meego (CBS)
Over The Top (ABC)
Pauly (FOX)
Smart Guy (WB)
Soul Man (ABC)
South Park (COMEDY CENTRAL) animated
Teen Angel (ABC)
Temporarily Yours (CBS)
The Gregory Hines Show (CBS)
The Tom Show (WB)
Union Square (NBC)
USA High (USA)
Veronica's Closet (NBC)
Working (NBC)
You Wish (ABC)

1998 *Ask Harriet* (FOX)
Becker (CBS)
Brother's Keeper (ABC)
Conrad Bloom (NBC)
Costello (FOX)
Cousin Skeeter (NICK)
DiResta (UPN)
Encore! Encore! (NBC)
Fired Up (NBC)
For Your Love (NBC/WB)
For Your Love (WB)
Getting Personal (FOX)
Guys Like Us (UPN)
Holding the Baby (FOX)
House Rules (NBC)
Jesse (NBC)
Kelly Kelly (WB)
Lateline (NBC)

Living in Captivity (FOX)
Maggie (LIFETIME)
Maggie Winters (CBS)
Malibu, CA (SYND)
Oh Baby (LIFETIME)
One World (NBC)
Reunited (UPN)
Rude Awakening (SHOWTIME)
Sports Night (ABC)
Style & Substance (CBS)
That 70's Show (FOX)
That's Life (ABC)
The Army Show (WB)
The Brian Benben Show (SHOWTIME)
The Closer (CBS)
The Hughleys (ABC/UPN)
The King of Queens (CBS)
The New Addams Family (FOX FAMILY) Canadian-American
The Secret Diary of Desmond Pfeiffer (UPN)
The Secret Life of Men (ABC)
Two of a Kind (ABC)
Will & Grace (NBC)
You're the One (WB)

1999 *100 Deeds for Eddie McDowd* (NICK)
Action (FOX)
Angela Anaconda (FOX FAMILY/ABC FAMILY)
Cluless (ABC/UPN)
Dilbert (UPN)
Downtown (MTV) animated
Everything's Relative (NBC)
Family Guy (FOX) animated
Family Rules (UPN)
Futurama (FOX) animated
Grown Ups (UPN)
Home Movies (UPN/ADULT SWIM) animated
It's Like, You Know (ABC)
Kate Joplin(WB)
Ladies Man (CBS)
Love & Money (CBS)
Movie Stars (WB)
Odd Man Out (ABC)
Oh Grow Up (ABC)
Payne (CBS)
Shasta McNasty (UPN) a/k/a/ *Shasta*
Stark Raving Mad (NBC)
Thanks (CBS)
The Chimp Channel (TBS)
The Downtowners (WB) a.k.a. *Mission Hill* animated
The Mike O'Malley Show (NBC)
The Norm Show (ABC) a.k.a. *Norm*
The Parkers (UPN)
The PJ's (FOX/WB) animated
Then Came You (ABC)
Two Guys, a Girl and a Pizza Place (ABC) later *Two Guys and a Girl*
Work with Me (CBS)
Zoe, Duncan, Jack and Jane (WB)

2000 *Battery Park* (NBC)
Bette (CBS)
Brutally Normal (WB)
Clerks (ABC) animated
Cursed (NBC) later *The Weber Show*
Daddio (NBC)
DAG (NBC)
Even Stephens (DISNEY)
Girlfriends (UPN/CW)
God, the Devil and Bob (NBC) animated
Harvey Birdman, Attorney at Law a.k.a. *Harvey Birdman* (CARTOON NETWORK) animated
M.Y.O.B. (NBC)
Madigan Men (ABC)
Malcolm in the Middle (FOX)
Manhattan, AZ (USA)
MTV's Now What? (MTV) Canadian-American
Nikki (WB)
Normal, Ohio (FOX)
Opposite Sex (FOX)
People Who Fear People (ABC)
Sammy (NBC) animated
Son of the Beach (FX)
Strip Mall (COMEDY CENTRAL)
Talk to Me (ABC)
The Brak Show (ADULT SWIM) animated
The Brothers Garcia (NICK)
The Geena Davis Show (ABC)
The Michael Richards Show (NBC)
The Trouble with Normal (ABC)
The War Next Door (USA)
Then Came You (ABC)
Titus (FOX)
Tucker (NBC)
Welcome to New York (CBS)
Yes, Dear (CBS)

2001 *According to Jim* (ABC)

All About Us (NBC)
Bob Patterson (ABC)
Danny (CBS)
Emeril (NBC)
Gary & Mike (UPN) animated
Go Fish (NBC)
Grounded for Life (FOX/WB)
Inside Schwartz (NBC)
Kristin (NBC)
Lizzie McGuire (DISNEY)
Maybe it's Me (WB)
Men, Women & Dogs (WB)
My Wife and Kids (ABC)
Off Centre (WB)
One on One (UPN)
Raising Dad (WB)
Reba (WB/CW)
Scrubs (NBC/ABC)
Some of My Best Friends (CBS) a.k.a. *Macho Man, Me and Frankie Z*
State of Grace (ABC FAMILY)
Taina (NICK)
That's Life (CBS)
That's My Bush! (COMEDY CENTRAL)
The Bernie Mack Show (FOX)
The Chris Isaak Show (SHOWTIME)
The Ellen Show (CBS)
The Fighting Fitzgeralds (NBC)
The Tick (FOX)
Three Sisters (NBC)
Undeclared (FOX)
What About Joan (ABC)

2002 2002 *8 Simple Rules for Dating My Teenage Daughter* (ABC)
Andy Richter Controls the Universe (FOX)
Baby Bob (CBS)
Bram and Alice (CBS)
Clone High a.k.a. *Clone High U.S.A.* (MTV) Canadian-American animated
Family Affair (WB)
George Lopez (ABC) a.k.a. *The George Lopez Show*
Good Morning, Miami (NBC)
Greetings From Tucson (WB)
Greg the Bunny (FOX)
Half & Half (UPN)
Hidden Hills (NBC)
Imagine That (NBC)
In-Laws (NBC)
Leap of Faith (NBC)
Less Than Perfect (ABC)
Life With Bonnie (ABC)
Still Standing (CBS)
That 80's Show (FOX)
The Random Years (UPN)
Watching Ellie (NBC)
Wednesday 9:30 (8:30 Central) (ABC)
What I Like About You (WB)

2003 *A Minute with Stan Hooper* (FOX)
A.U.S.A. (NBC)
Abby (UPN)
All About the Andersons (WB)
All of Us (UPN/CW)
Arrested Development (FOX/NETFLIX)
Charlie Lawrence (CBS)
Coupling (NBC)
Eve (UPN)
Free for All (SHOWTIME) animated
Happy Family (NBC)
Hope & Faith (ABC)
I'm with Her (ABC)
It's All Relative (ABC)
Like Family (WB)
Lost at Home (ABC)
Luis (FOX)
Married to the Kellys (ABC)
My Big Fat Greek Life (CBS)
Oliver Beene (FOX)
On the Spot (WB) improv-sitcom
Regular Joe (ABC)
Rock Me Baby (UPN)
Run of the House (WB)
That's So Raven (DISNEY)
The Mullets (UPN)
The O'Keefes (WB)
The Ortegas (FOX)
The Pitts (FOX)
The Tracy Morgan Show (NBC)
Two and a Half Men (CBS)
Wanda at Large (FOX)
Whoopi (NBC)

2004 *Center of the Universe* (CBS)
Come to Papa (NBC)
Complete Savages (ABC)
Cracking Up (FOX)
Darcy's Wild Life (NBC)
Drake & Josh (NICK)
Drawn Together (Comedy Central) animated
Father of the Pride (NBC) animated
Fatherhood (NICK AT NITE) animated

Good Girls Don't (OXYGEN)
Joey (NBC)
Listen Up! (CBS)
Method & Red (FOX)a.k.a. *Meth and Red*
Ned's Declassified School Survival Guide (NICK) a.k.a. *Ned's Declassified*
Phil of the Future (DISNEY)
Quintuplets (FOX)
Rodney (ABC)
Significant Others (BRAVO)
The Big House (ABC)
The Cramp Twins (CARTOON NETWORK) animated, originally British
The Help (WB)
The Stones (CBS)
Tom Goes to the Mayor (CARTOON NETWORK) animated
Unfabulous (NICK)

2005 *American Dad!* (FOX) animated
Barbershop (SHOWTIME)
Committed (NBC)
Cuts (UPN)
Everybody Hates Chris (UPN/CW)
Extras (HBO) originally BBC
Fat Actress (SHOWTIME)
Freddie (ABC)
How I Met Your Mother (CBS)
It's Always Sunny in Philadelphia (FX)
Jake in Progress (ABC)
Kitchen Confidential (FOX)
Life on a Stick (FOX) a.k.a. *Related by Family*
Life with Derek (DISNEY)
Living With Fran (WB)
Love, Inc. (UPN)
My Name Is Earl (NBC)
Out of Practice (CBS)
Second Time Around (UPN)
Stacked (FOX)
Starved (FX)
The Bad Girl's Guide (UPN)
The Comeback (HBO)
The Office (NBC)
The Suite Life of Zack & Cody (DISNEY)
The War at Home (FOX)
Twins (WB)
Zoey 101 (NICK)

2006 *10 Items or Less* (TBS) part improv
30 Rock (NBC)
All of Us (UPN/CW)
Assy McGee (ADULT SWIM) animated
Bakersfield, P. D. (FOX)
Big Day (ABC) originally *A Day in the Life*
Class of 3000 (CARTOON NETWORK) animated
Courting Alex (CBS)
Crumbs (ABC)
Emily's Reasons Why Not (ABC)
Four Kings (NBC)
Freak Show (COMEDY CENTRAL) animated
Free Ride (FOX)
Girlfriends (UPN/CW)
Hannah Montana (Disney)
Happy Hour (FOX) also Canada
Help Me Help You (ABC)
Kappa Mikey (NICK TOONS) animated
Lucky Louie (HBO)
Modern Men (WB)
Mr. Meaty (NICK) animated Canadian-American
My Boys (TBS)
Reba (WB then CW)
So NoTORIous (ABC)
Sons and Daughters (ABC)
Suburban Shootout (OXYGEN) British-American
Teachers (NBC)
The Class (CBS)
The Game (CW/BET)
The Loop (FOX)
The New Adventures of Old Christine (CBS)
'Til Death (FOX)
Twenty Good Years (NBC)
Tyler Perry's House of Payne (SYND/TBS)

2007 *About a Girl* (TEEN NICK)
Aliens in America (CW)
Andy Barker, P.I . (NBC)
Back At The Barnyard (NICK) animated
Back to You (FOX)
Carpoolers (ABC)
Cavemen (ABC)
Cory in the House (DISNEY)
Flight of the Conchords (COMEDY CENTRAL)
I Hate My 30's (VH-1)

iCarly (NICK)
In Case of Emergency (ABC)
Just Jordan (NICK)
Notes from the Underbelly (ABC)
Rick & Steve: The Happiest Gay Couple in All the World (LOGO) animated
Rules of Engagement (CBS)
Samantha Who? (ABC)
The Big Bang Theory (CBS)
The Bill Engvall Show (TBS)
The Knights of Prosperity (ABC) a.k.a. *Let's Rob*
The Naked Brothers Band (NICK)
The Sarah Silverman Program (COMEDY CENTRAL)
The Winner (FOX)
Wizards of Waverly Place (DISNEY)

2008 *Click and Clack's As the Wrench Turns* (PBS) animated
Do Not Disturb (FOX) a.k.a. *The Inn*
Factory (SPIKE)
Gary Unmarried (CBS)
Jonas L.A. a.k.a *JONAS* (DISNEY)
Kath & Kim (NBC)
Miss Guided (ABC)
Rita Rocks (LIFETIME)
Somebodies (BET)
Sordid Lives (LOGO)
Testees (FX) Canadian-American
The Captain (CBS) a.k.a. *Welcome to the Captain*
The Life & Times of Tim (HBO) animated
The Return of Jezebel James (FOX)
The Suite Life on Deck (DISNEY)
True Jackson, VP (NICK)
Under One Roof (MY NETWORK TV)
Unhitched (FOX) a.k.a. *The Rules for Starting Over*
Worst Week (CBS)

2009 *10 Things I Hate About You* (ABC FAMILY)
Accidentally on Purpose (CBS)
Archer (FX) animated
Better Off Ted (ABC)
Big Time Rush (NICK)
Brothers (FOX)
Community (NBC)
Cougar Town (ABC/TBS)
Glen Martin DDS (NICK) animated
Hank (ABC) originally *Awesome Hank and PRYORS*
I'm in the Band (DISNEY XD)
In the Motherhood (ABC)
Modern Family (ABC)
My Name Is Earl (NBC)
Outer Space Astronauts (SYFY)
Parks and Recreation (NBC)
Party Down (STARZ)
Roommates (ABC FAMILY)
Ruby and the Rockits (ABC FAMILY)
Sherri (LIFETIME)
Sit Down, Shut Up (FOX) animated
Sonny with a Chance (DISNEY)
Surviving Suburbia (ABC)
The Assistants (THE N)
The Cleveland Show (FOX) animated
The Goode Family (ABC) animated
The League (FX)
The Middle (ABC)
The Troop (NICK)
Tyler Perry's Meet the Browns (TBS) a.k.a. *Meet the Browns*
Zeke and Luther (DISNEY XD)

2010 *$#*! My Dad Says* (CBS) pronounced "Bleep My Dad Says"
100 Questions a.k.a. *100 Questions for Charlotte Payne* (NBC)
18 to Life (CW) originally Canada
Are We There Yet? (TBS)
Better with You (ABC)
Big Lake (COMEDY CENTRAL)
Fish Hooks (DISNEY) animated
Good Luck Charlie (DISNEY)
Hot in Cleveland (TV LAND)
Louie (FX)
Love That Girl! (TV ONE)
Melissa & Joey (ABC FAMILY)
Mike & Molly (CBS)
Outsourced (NBC)
Pair of Kings (DISNEY XD)
Raising Hope (FOX)
Romantically Challenged (ABC)
Running Wilde (FOX)
Shake It Up a.k.a. Shake It Up! (DISNEY)
Sons of Tucson (FOX)
The Hard Times of RJ Berger (MTV)
The Increasingly Poor Decisions of Todd Margaret (IFC)
Ugly Americans (COMEDY CENTRAL) animated
Victorious (NICK) stylized as *VICTORiOUS*

2011 *2 Broke Girls* (CBS)
A.N.T. Farm (Disney)
All About the Andersons (WB)
Allen Gregory (FOX) animated
Austin & Ally (DISNEY)
Bob's Burgers (FOX) animated
Breaking In (FOX)
Bucket & Skinner's Epic Adventures (NICK)
Death Valley (MTV)
Episodes (SHOWTIME)
Free Agents (NBC)
Friends with Benefits (NBC)
Happily Divorced (TV LAND)
Happy Endings (ABC)
How to Be a Gentleman (CBS)
I Hate My Teenage Daughter (FOX)
Jessie (DISNEY)
Kickin' It (DISNEY XD)
Last Man Standing (ABC)
Let's Stay Together (BET)
Mad Love (CBS) a.k.a. *True Love*
Man Up! (ABC)
Mr. Sunshine (ABC)
Mr. Young (DISNEY XD) originally Canada
New Girl (FOX)
Perfect Couples (NBC)
Portlandia (IFC)
Reed Between the Lines (BET)
Retired at 35 (TV LAND)
State of Georgia (ABC FAMILY)
Suburgatory (ABC)
Supah Ninjas (NICK)
The Exes (TV LAND)
The Looney Tunes Show (CARTOON NETWORK) animated
Traffic Light (FOX)
Tyler Perry's For Better or Worse (TBS)
Up All Night (NBC)
Whitney (NBC)
Wilfred (FX)
Workaholics (COMEDY CENTRAL)
Working Class (CMT)

2012 *1600 Penn* (NBC)
Anger Management (FX)
Animal Practice (NBC)
Are You There, Chelsea? (NBC)
Baby Daddy (ABC FAMILY)
Ben and Kate (FOX)
Best Friends Forever (NBC)
Brickleberry (COMEDY CENTRAL)
Don't Trust the B---- in Apartment 23 (ABC) a.k.a. *Apartment 23, Don't Trust the Bitch in Apartment 23*
Family Time (BOUNCE)
Go On (NBC)
Guys with Kids (NBC)
How to Rock (NICK)
Lab Rats (DISNEY XD)
Malibu Country (ABC)
Marvin Marvin (NICK)
Men at Work (TBS)
Napoleon Dynamite (FOX) animated
Partners (CBS)
The Rickey Smiley Show (TVONE)
Rob (CBS)
See Dad Run (NICK)
Sullivan & Son (TBS)
The First Family (SYND)
The Inbetweeners (MTV)
The Mindy Project (FOX)
The Neighbors (ABC)
The New Normal (NBC)
The Soul Man (TV LAND)
Work It (ABC)

2013 *Back in the Game* (ABC)
Friend Me (CBS)
How to Live with Your Parents (For the Rest of Your Life) (ABC)
Kroll Show (COMEDY CENTRAL)
Legit (FX)
Next Caller (NBC)
Out There (IFC) animated dramedy
The Rickey Smiley Show (TV ONE)
Save Me (NBC)
Second Generation Wayans (BET)
The Family Tools (ABC)
The Goodwin Games (FOX)
We Are Men (CBS)
Wendell & Vinnie (NICK)

Appendix 3 SITCOM EXERCISES

APPENDIX TO CHAPTER 2 SITCOM EXERCISE

STYLE AND SUBSTANCE - PILOT

(B)

INT. CHELSEAS'S OFFICE - LATER THAT MORNING (D-1)

(CHELSEA, JANE, TERRY)

CHELSEA IS LISTENING TO TERRY, HER YOUNG MALE SECRETARY, RUN DOWN A LIST OF PHONE MESSAGES. CHELSEA MAKES HIM NERVOUS.

TERRY

Francine Messinger called and said thanks for the padlocks.

CHELSEA

That's Nancy Kissinger, and she's thanking me for the gravlax. ✓✓✓

TERRY

Right. Franklin Carter called...

CHELSEA

Frank Langella. ✓✓✓

TERRY

Okay. Needs advice on planting an urban garden.

CHELSEA

An herb garden.✓✓✓ Breathe, Terry.

TERRY

Okay. Ken Klein called...

CHELSEA

Kevin Kline?✓✓✓

TERRY

No.

CHELSEA

Calvin Klein?✓✓✓

TERRY SHAKES HIS HEAD NO.

CHELSEA (CONT'D)

Kelly Klein. Carol Kane. Carol King.✓✓✓ (A BEAT) Beverly Sills?

TERRY

Yes. You're good at this.✓✓✓

CHELSEA

Thank you. Terry. Much better today.✓✓✓

TERRY

I thought so too.✓✓✓

<u>TERRY EXITS</u> AS <u>JANE ENTERS</u>.

JANE

Hi, Chelsea. Listen I don't want to be a bugaboo, but have you had a chance to sign that budget agreement yet?

CHELSEA STARES AT HER FOR A SECOND.

JANE (CONT'D)

Jane Sokol. From Ferber Communications?

CHELSEA

Jane, please. I know who you are. What a darling suit.

JANE

Thanks. I really need you to sign that agreement. Being put in charge of your office is the first major assignment the company's given me, so I want to keep Mr. Ferber happy happy. So sign sign.✓✓✓

CHELSEA

I'll look at it right away.

JANE NOTICES A PURSE ON THE DESK.

JANE

We have the same purse.

CHELSEA

Really?

JANE

Yes. It's exactly the same purse.

CHELSEA

How about that?

JANE

I mean...it's the same purse. (A BEAT) That's my purse, isn't it?✓✓✓

CHELSEA

Why don't we talk about something else? (PICKING SOMETHING UP FROM THE DESK) Oh, look. A recipe for flan.✓✓✓

JANE

Chelsea. You have my purse.

CHELSEA

Don't get upset, Jane. You're new here, I want to get to know you. You know the old saying. The fastest way to get to know another woman is to look in her purse.

JANE

Here's another old saying. I want my purse back.✓✓✓

CHELSEA

You have something to hide?

JANE

No.

CHELSEA
I'd let you look in my purse.

JANE
I doubt that.

CHELSEA
I would.

JANE
Right.

CHELSEA
Go ahead.

JANE
Where is it?

CHELSEA
At home.✓✓✓ But if it were here, I'd let you look at it.

JANE
Chelsea, this is a major invasion of my privacy.

CHELSEA HOLDS OUT A SMALL JAR OF JAM TO JANE.

CHELSEA
Jane, I'd like you to have this. It's a jar of my lovely homemade preserves. I hope you like rhubarb.✓✓✓

JANE
Do you honestly believe that giving me a little jar of jam will make this okay?

CHELSEA
I have a bigger jar.✓✓✓

JANE
That is so not my point.

CHELSEA
Oh, I get it. There's a jam hater in our midst, is there?✓✓✓

JANE

Oh, please. I love jam.

CHELSEA

I wish I could believe that.

JANE

I am crazy about jam.

CHELSEA

You do not seem jam friendly to me.✓✓✓

JANE

(AFTER A BEAT) Okay. Okay. You want to look in my purse? You go right ahead. This is unbelievable.

CHELSEA

Oh, pooh. You really know how to take the fun out of things.

CHELSEA STARTS DIGGING AROUND IN THE PURSE.

CHELSEA (CONT'D)

Somebody clips coupons.✓✓✓

CHELSEA TAKES A COUPON OUT AND GRIMACES.

CHELSEA (CONT'D)

Macaroni and cheese? From a box?✓✓✓

JANE

It's filling and inexpensive.

CHELSEA

I can't argue, Jane, but if those were the only criteria for nourishment, there'd be a lot more recipes for dirt.✓✓✓ (DIGGING) Lip gloss, rouge...I see tweezers. Eyebrows on the march, Jane?✓✓✓

JANE

Are we done yet?

CHELSEA
Oh, Jane. Jane, Jane, Jane...

CHELSEA REMOVES A PACKAGE OF HOSTESS SNOBALLS FROM THE PURSE.

CHELSEA (CONT'D)
Hostess Snoballs? Why, Jane?✓✓✓

JANE
I like them. They're fun.

CHELSEA
Have you heard the expression, "You are what you eat?" Add bangs and a business suit, this is you, Jane.✓✓✓

JANE
I'll be going now...

JANE GATHERS UP HER PURSE AND STARTS TO EXIT. CHELSEA HOLDS UP A SMALL PHOTOGRAPH.

CHELSEA
Who's this?

JANE
Give me that, please.

CHELSEA
Brother?

JANE
None of your business.

CHELSEA
Friends?

JANE
I'm not telling you.

CHELSEA
Fiance?

JANE

(A BEAT) No.

CHELSEA

You paused.✓✓✓

JANE

Darn!

CHELSEA

What's his name?

JANE

Why would I tell you?

CHELSEA

Because I really think you want to talk about it. Mint?✓✓✓

CHELSEA HOLDS OUT A SMALL CONTAINER OF MINTS.

JANE

(GRABBING THEM) Those are mine.✓✓✓ Chelsea, I appreciate your trying to be friendly, but I'm not going to discuss my personal life with you.

CHELSEA

He looks like a Paul.

JANE

I'm here to do a job. It's a job I take seriously.

CHELSEA

Doug? Dennis?

JANE

There's a line between business and personal...

CHELSEA

Tony? Mike?

JANE

I'm a professional, and I'm going to maintain a professional...

CHELSEA
Chuck?

JANE
(END OF ROPE) Steve! Steve! The man's name is Steve!✓✓✓ Are you happy now?

CHELSEA
I knew you wanted to talk about it.✓✓✓

JANE
I don't! This is the office. The office is where we talk about office things. My ex-fiance is not an office thing.

CHELSEA
Your ex-fiance?

JANE
Darn!✓✓✓

CHELSEA
What happened? He hit you, didn't he? (TO THE PHOTO) You bastard.✓✓✓

JANE
This is really inappropriate, How would you like it if I just waltzed in here and started asking you about your divorce? Which by the way, I would never do. I know it must've been difficult and I hope you're okay.

CHELSEA
(THROWN) I'm sorry?

JANE
I said I hope you're okay.

CHELSEA
(COVERING) Well, yes...of course I am. My husband wasn't giving me what I needed, he was a lox, I kicked him out. Let's get back to you.✓✓✓

JANE
Look, I need that agreement signed and on my desk by the end of the day.

CHELSEA

I'll look it over right now. Jane, if I upset you, I'm sorry. It was wrong to take your purse.

JANE

Okay. I'll be in my office if you need me.

JANE EXITS AND CLOSES THE DOOR BEHIND HER. CHELSEA TAKES OUT THE SNOBALLS AND TAKES A BITE OF ONE. JANE ENTERS.

JANE (CONT'D)

Where are they?

A BEAT, THEN CHELSEA MAKES A MUFFLED RESPONSE.

CHELSEA

Where's what?✓✓✓

CHELSEA HANDS THE REMAINING SNOBALL BACK TO JANE.

FADE OUT.[1]

APPENDIX TO CHAPTER 3 SITCOM EXERCISE

LUIS
"PILOT"

INT. DONUT SHOP - DAY

(LUIS, GREG, MARLY)

GREG KISSES MARLY. HE NOTICES LUIS WATCHING AND BREAKS IT OFF.

GREG

Oh, I guess I shouldn't kiss your daughter in front of you, huh?

LUIS

You can kiss my daughter in front of me. You just can't kiss my daughter in front of me without a job.

GREG

What else can I do in front of you if I get a job? Grab her ass?

1 Used by permission of Touchstone Television. All Rights Reserved.

LUIS

A good job, yes.[2]

GREG

What can I do for eighty-five grand and a dental plan?

LUIS

You make eighty-five grand a year, you can grab my ass.

GREG

(RE: GREG'S SMALL HANDS AND LUIS'S LARGE ASS) I don't think that's possible.

LUIS TAKES A BEAT THEN LUNGES AT HIM.

GREG (CONT'D)

You know, Luis, most artists don't achieve success until after they're dead.

LUIS

How 'bout I make you successful right now? (THEN, RE: GREG'S DONUT) Did you pay for that?

GREG

Of, course.

LUIS

(MENACING) Did you?

GREG

Yes!

LUIS

(MENACING) Did you?

GREG

Marly, can I borrow a dollar? (THEN) I'm kidding. Of course I paid for it. I mean, come on. (LOUD WHISPERS) Marly. Dollar bill. Quickly!

LUIS

I don't get it. She's a smart girl. What does she see in you?

2 This is the second punchline for the same set-up. It is a perfect example of a topper!

GREG

Maybe a guy who loves her, who's sensitive, talented, and from time to time (OFF LUIS) not afraid to show fear. (LOUD WHISPER, TO MARLY) Dollar... bill. Now. If you love me!

MARLY BRINGS HIM A DOLLAR.

GREG (CONT'D)

Here you go.

LUIS

I don't understand you. I mean, how can you let a woman pay your bills?

GREG

It'd be a hell of a lot easier if you didn't bring it up all the time. (THEN, RE: DOLLAR) Do I got some change skating my way, how does that work?

CUT TO:

APPENDIX TO CHAPTER 4 SITCOM EXERCISES

HOME IMPROVEMENT

"PILOT"

ACT TWO

SCENE 2

EXT. BACKYARD-DUSK (DAY 2)

SPFX: BARBEQUE SMOKE FROM WILSON'S YARD

(WE SEE WILSON BARBEQUING. TIM SEARCHES FOR THE DISHWASHER PARTS)

TIM

What a mess.

WILSON

Hi, ya, Tim!

PHYSICAL COMEDY-CAN'T SEE HIS FACE

TIM

Hi Wilson. Mmm. Smell good. What are you cooking? Baby back ribs?

WILSON

Squirrel.

TWIST-K SOUND

TIM

Squirrel. What's that taste like?

WILSON

Sort of like chipmunk.

K SOUND

By the way, a couple of those bolts landed in the birdbath.

K SOUND

TIM

I was a little surprised by the torque on that compressor.

CHARACTER TRAIT - INEPT WITH TOOLS

WILSON

I tell you, Tim, this is what it's all about. Catch of the day cooking, sun setting, men standing around the campfire, telling stories.

PLAY ON WORDS-RUN OF 3 WITH ALLITERATION OF K SOUNDS AND S SOUNDS

TIM

Can I tell you one?

WILSON

Campfire's lit, good neighbor.

CALL BACK

TIM

Jill didn't get the job she wanted. I tell her not to feel bad and she gets angry at me.

WILSON

Hmm.

NOT APPARENT FROM THE WRITING, BUT ACTOR MADE THIS INTO AN INTERESTING CHARACTER TRAIT

TIM
And then I tell her what to do, she gets all bent out of shape and storms out of the rooom.

WILSON
Sounds like you were having an asymmetrical conversation.

TIM
Asymmetrical. How do you spell that?

WILSON
Let's just say one-sided.

PLAY ON WORDS

(TIM DOES A KNOWING GRUNT)

WILSON (CONT'D)
You see Tim,

CHARACTER TRAIT-PHILOSPHER

by nature, men are problem solvers. But Jill didn't want you to solve her problem.

TIM
She didn't?

WILSON
No. She just wanted you to listen while she shared her feelings.

TIM
Just stand there and listen? That's like doing nothing?

CHARCTER TRAIT - NAÏVE ABOUT WOMEN

WILSON
Sometimes the best thing you can do is nothing.

(TIM DOES AN UNDERSTANDING GRUNT)

TIM

I get it. Jill got mad at me because I didn't listen to her.

MISLEAD

WILSON

No, she got mad at you because you blew up the damn dishwasher.

TURN - ALLITERATION [3]

CUT TO:[4]

STYLE AND SUBSTANCE

"PILOT"

ACT ONE

(A)

FADE IN:

INT. OUTER LOBBY - MORNING (D-1)

(JANE)

CAMERA STARTS IN CLOSE ON A BEAUTIFUL FLORAL ARRANGEMENT ON A TABLE IN THE OUTER LOBBY (THE SHOW TITLE WILL BE SEEN HERE). CAMERA PANS UP AND WE SEE THE SIGN ON THE WALL: "CHELSEA STEVENS, A DIVISION OF FERBER COMMUNICATIONS." WE FIND JANE TALKING ON HER CELLULAR PHONE.

JANE

Everything's under control, Mr. Ferber. You sent me to run things here, that's what I'm doing. No, Chelsea hasn't signed the budget agreement yet. Yes, I did promise I'd have that signed by the end of my first week. Yes, that would be tomorrow. Yes, I'm aware I'm saying yes a lot. Yes.

RUN OF THREE

Mr. Ferber, I've just had a little trouble pinning Chelsea down, but I will pin her. Consider her pinned. Yes.

3 From the pilot episode of *Home Improvement* created by Matt Williams, David McFadzean, and Carmen Finestra. Used by permission of Touchstone Television. All Rights Reserved.

4 Used by permission of Touchstone Television. All Rights Reserved.

CALLBACK

Thank you sir.

JANE CLICKS OFF, GROWLS AND EXITS INTO THE OFFICES.

INT. PRODUCTION OFFICES - CONTINUOUS (D-1)

(CHELSEA, JANE, TRUDY, MR. JOHN, TERRY, OFFICE EXTRAS)

JANE ENTERS AND CROSSES OVER TO WHERE TRUDY IS MAKING HERSELF A CUP OF COFFEE.

JANE
Hi, Trudy. Have you seen Chelsea?

TRUDY
Not yet. She hasn't signed your budget thing, huh?

JANE
I'm getting desperate.

TRUDY
Jane, let me give you some advice. When you deal with Chelsea, you always, always have to remember one important thing.

MISLEAD

JANE
What's that?

TRUDY
She's a freak.

TURN-K SOUND

JANE
She's not a freak.

TRUDY
Oh, yes, she is. Last Christmas, she made a ginger-bread house? It was built to code.

ABSURD-K SOUND

There was a guest gingerbread house in the back.

ABSURD-K SOUND

JANE

Okay, she's a little obsessive, but she's built a very successful business. The magazine, the television show...

TRUDY

It's a great big freakdom.

PLAY ON WORDS-CALLBACK

JANE

Then why are you here?

TRUDY

Because I'm the best food stylist in the world and Chelsea knows it.

TRUDY OPENS HER PORTFOLIO AND FLIPS THROUGH IT.

TRUDY (CONT'D)

My award-winning chocolate sundae.

JANE

That ice cream looks delicious.

MISLEAD

TRUDY

Thank you. It's lard.

TURN

I can recreate any dish for photographic purposes. I use whatever it takes. That chocolate sauce?

JANE

It looks good.

MISLEAD

TRUDY

Quaker State motor oil.

TURN

That's thirty weight, if memory serves.

TOPPER

(TURNING THE PAGE) This is my fettuccine alfredo.

JANE

The noodles look real.

TRUDY

Oh, they are.

MISLEAD

JANE

How about the sauce?

TRUDY

Sears Weatherbeater house paint.

TURN

And that's one coat, Jane.

TOPPER-K SOUND

MR. JOHN CROSSES OVER. HE'S A DAPPER MAN IN HIS FIFTIES.

TRUDY (CONT'D)

Perhaps we should ask Mr. John.

MR. JOHN

Ask me what?

TRUDY

Do you think Chelsea's a freak?

MR. JOHN

No, I don't. I've been designing for Chelsea Stevens for ten wonderful years, and I believe her to be the apotheosis of taste and style.

MISLEAD

TRUDY

She's not in yet.

MR. JOHN

She's a freak.

TURN-CALLBACK

(TO TRUDY) Let's tell her about the gingerbread house.

TRUDY

I already did.

MR. JOHN

(TO JANE) It had plumbing.

TOPPER

Guy and I still talk about it.

JANE

Guy?

MR. JOHN

My life partner. I'm sorry if my frankness shocks you, Jane, but I'm proud of my relationship and I don't hide the fact.

JANE

I'm fine.

MR. JOHN

Well. I know you've come from the Midwest...so if I do say anything that makes you uncomfortable, I hope you'll speak up.

MISLEAD

JANE

It's not a problem. I am an adult.

MR. JOHN

Thank you, Jane. It's like I was saying to Guy in the shower this morning as we were lathering up...

TURN

JANE

Oh, dear.

MR. JOHN

Too much?

UNDERSTATEMENT

CHELSEA STEVENS, THE JUGGERNAUT OF STYLE AND TASTE, ENTERS FROM THE OUTER LOBBY. SHE CARRIES A SMALL WICKER BASKET COVERED WITH A RED-CHECKERED NAPKIN.

CHELSEA

Good morning, everyone!

STAFFERS ADLIB GREETINGS.

CHELSEA (CONT'D)

This morning before breakfast while I was restocking my trout pond and shearing my lamb,

ABSURD

I realized I wanted to tell you all how much I appreciate the hard work you do. But then later, while I was airing out my quilts and making prosciutto jerky,

ABSURD-K SOUND

I reminded myself that we can always work harder. I guess what I'm trying to say is...

MISLEAD

be more like me.

TURN

And one more thing. In the magazine, on the show...no more kiwi. Kiwi is over. If I could talk to a kiwi,

K SOUNDS

do you know what I'd say? I'd say "Get out, get a shave, you're through."

RUN OF 3-PERSONIFICATION

No kiwi. Let's all say it.

ALL

No kiwi.

ABSURD-K SOUND

CHELSEA

Thank you. And the big news. My divorce becomes final today, so I think we all knows what that means.

MISLEAD

A BEAT, THEN SHE PUTS THE BASKET ON THE TABLE.

CHELSEA (CONT'D)

That's right. I made scones!

TURN-K SOUND

CHELSEA DISAPPEARS INTO HER OFFICE.

MR. JOHN

She seems down today.

UNDERSTATEMENT

DISSOLVE TO:[5]

5 Used by permission of Touchstone Television. All Rights Reserved.

INDEX

Appendix 4 **SET PLAN**

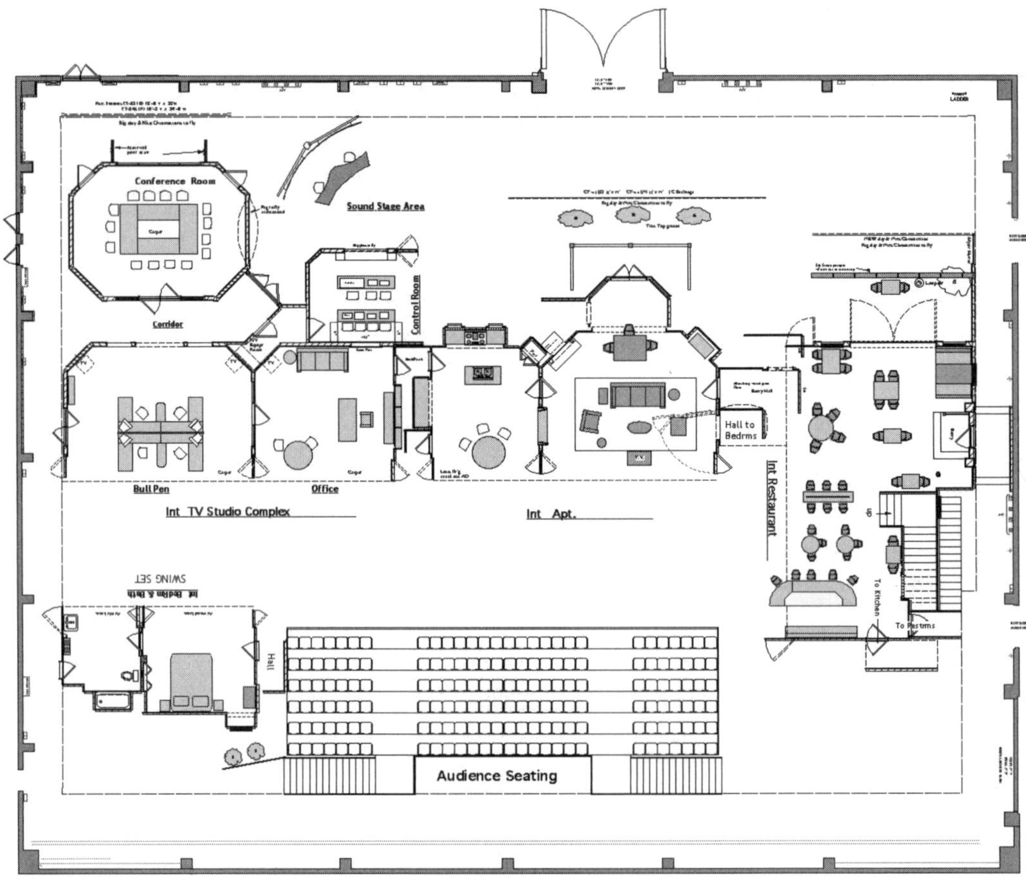

ABOUT THE AUTHORS

Phil Ramuno is an award-winning director, producer, writer, photographer, and teacher based in Los Angeles. He has directed eight pilots and hundreds of episodes of American network and syndicated situation comedies, variety and reality/ talk shows. This includes *Grace Under Fire, Charles in Charge, 9 to 5* and *The Ted Knight Show.*

Phil supervised a comedy series in Sofia, Bulgaria for Sony International and a prime-time police action series in Romania for MediaPro Pictures. His international credits include four other series in Romania, two in Moscow and three others in Canada. For the stage, Phil has directed the Ovation-nominated *Flirting with Morty* the world premiere of *Sundays in L.A.* and *Sugar Happens.* His short film *Bringing Up BayBay* was a feted at the Mill Valley Film Festival.

He is an adjunct professor at The University of Southern California prestigious graduate film school and has also taught at both his alma mater Emerson College and Endicott College in Boston. Phil also regularly teaches comedy at the Screen Actors Guild-AFTRA Conservatory, the Kennedy Center American College Theater Festival and the Los Angeles Inner City Filmmakers youth program. He has co-run workshops for actors with disabilities and casts them regularly for roles on television, stage and web series. Phil received a Media Access Award from the California Governor's Committee.

He and his wife, Jacqueline Zebal Ramuno, live in Los Angles. They have two children, Jessica and Jeffrey.

Mary Lou Belli is an Emmy Award winner producer, writer, and director. On BET, she currently directs *Second Generation Wayans, Reed Between the Lines* and *The Game,* the spinoff to *Girlfriends* which she directed for 7 consecutive seasons. With over 150 episodes to her credit, Mary Lou directed *Monk, Wizards of Waverly Place, Living with Fran* starring Fran Drescher, *Misconceptions* starring Jane Leeves, and *Eve* starring hip hop artist Eve, as well as *The Hughleys, Charles in Charge, Major Dad,* and *Sister, Sister.* Mary Lou received BET nominations for directing *Girlfriends and One on One* as well as a Prism Award for *Girlfriends. The Game* won the Image Award for best television comedy series.

She directed the pilot of the Web series *3Way,* winner of 2 Logo awards and The AfterEllen.com 2008 Visibility Awards for Best Lesbian/bi Web Series. Her other web series include *Jenifer and Shangela* starring Jenifer Lewis. She just finished shooting a web series starring Marquita Terry and Kristen Miller as well as sizzle reel for Funny or Die. She will next direct Hart of Dixie on the CW.

She is the co-author of two other books: *Acting for Young Actors* and *Directors Tell the Story.* She teaches at USC's School of Cinematic Arts. She has served as a judge a at the CSU Media Arts Fest, the Miss America Outstanding Teen Pageant, California Independent Film Festival, and the Newport Beach Film Festival, as well as the Sapporo Short Festival in Japan. She has lectured at the Chautauqua Institute, Northwestern University, NYU, and been a panelist for Women In Film, the DGA, SAG, and AFTRA.

Mary Lou lives in Los Angles with her husband, Charles Dougherty. They have two children, Maggie and Tim.